Administering the Company

Accounting Function

Second Edition

Administering the Company

Accounting Function

SECOND EDITION

Jerome V. Bennett

Prentice-Hall, Inc.   Englewood Cliffs, N.J.

Prentice-Hall International, Inc., *London*
Prentice-Hall of Australia, Pty. Ltd., *Sydney*
Prentice-Hall of Canada, Ltd., *Toronto*
Prentice-Hall of India Private Ltd., *New Delhi*
Prentice-Hall of Japan, Inc., *Tokyo*
Prentice-Hall of Southeast Asia Pte. Ltd., *Singapore*
Whitehall Books, Ltd., *Wellington, New Zealand*

© 1981 by

Prentice-Hall

Englewood Cliffs, N.J.

This publication is designed to provide accurate and authoritative
information in regard to the subject matter covered. It is sold with
the understanding that the publisher is not engaged in rendering
legal, accounting or other professional service. If legal advice
or other expert assistance is required, the services of a competent
professional person should be sought.
> —*From the Declaration of Principles jointly
> adopted by a Committee of the American
> Bar Association and a Committee of Publishers
> and Associations.*

Library of Congress Cataloging in Publication Data

Bennett, Jerome V.
    Administering the company accounting function.

    Includes index.
    1. Controllership.   2.   Corporations–
Accounting.   I.   Title.
HG4026.B395   1981   658.1'51   80-25947
ISBN 0-13-004804-6

Printed in the United States of America

To Anne

About
the
Author

Jerome V. Bennett, Ph.D., M.B.A., C.M.A., is Chairman of the Accounting Department of the E. Claiborne Robins School of Business, University of Richmond, Virginia. Prior to joining the University, he had accumulated over twenty years of experience in industry and government. He organized and managed the Division of Computer Systems Management for the State of South Carolina. In industry, he was Controller with Uniroyal, Inc.; Riegel Paper Corp.; and Tamper, Inc. Dr. Bennett has also served as Consultant to Philip Morris, USA; Anchor-Continental, Inc.; and the Cash Management Project/President's Reorganization Project, among others.

Dr. Bennett is a member of the American Accounting Association, National Association of Accountants, the Institute of Internal Auditors and the Virginia Society of CPA's. He holds the Certificate in Management Accounting from the Institute for Management Accounting. He is also a Registered Professional Engineer and holds the Certificate in Data Processing from the ICCP.

In this revised edition, Dr. Bennett has incorporated the professional discipline of the engineer with the practical accounting experience of industry. It was as an industrial controller that he developed and put into practice the control philosophy which forms the foundation of this book.

He holds a Bachelor of Textile Engineering degree from the Georgia Institute of Technology, a Master of Business Administration from the University of North Carolina-Chapel Hill and a Ph.D. from the University of South Carolina.

Preface to the Second Edition

In the ensuing years since publication of the First Edition, the realm of accounting has seen vast change. Changes have come from all directions—from within (Financial Accounting Standards Board, American Institute of Certified Public Accountants, National Association of Accountants), from regulatory bodies (Securities and Exchange Commission, Cost Accounting Standards Board) and from the public via the Congress. Technology has put the computer within the reach of every accountant. Because of the Foreign Corrupt Practices Act, internal auditing has become a matter of urgent concern, even to the board of directors level. New certifications of professional accounting competence have become widely accepted, such as the Certificate in Management Accounting (CMA).

In this Second Edition, each of the sources of change is extensively referenced and resultant changes are included, in depth. There is a critical need for a current, comprehensive, practical guide to administration of the control function.

All of the information in this book is based on the experiences of the author and other controllers of high corporate and governmental rank. The role of the controller is defined in clear-cut terms. Major emphasis is given to proven techniques of control reporting and proven devices for effective display of management-oriented exception information.

Divided into four Parts, the book is structured in recognition of the major aspects of the job of the controller.

Part One—Organization defines the job of the controller, his relationships with other managers and his own managerial role.

Part Two—General Accounting Duties includes the financial accounting and support tasks of the controller.

Part Three—Managerial and Cost Accounting Duties fully describes the role of the controller in support of managerial decision making.

Part Four—Computerized Accounting Information Systems is structured to give full recognition to the vast impact of the computer on the job of the controller.

This book is not written to be casually read once and then shelved in the library. It is intended to be referred to again and again as fresh solutions to problems, new and old, are sought. It is a book which should be used, put to work—a book which will help get the job done.

Jerome V. Bennett

ACKNOWLEDGMENTS

In compiling the chapters of the First Edition, I realized—perhaps for the first time—just how much each of us is the product of his environment. In the world of business, our peers and our immediate superiors constitute a major portion of that environment; to a great degree, we are molded, educated, and developed by them. In that first volume, I expressed appreciation to Dwight Wheeler and Alan Schenck for just such a role. In addition, I want to acknowledge the impact on my growth and development to Lindsay Wylie, Pat Smith, and Ron Copeland.

The balance of one's environment is composed of family and friends. To my daughter, Christelle, and to my mother and father—thanks for your love and affection. To my wife, Anne—my appreciation for inspiration, support, intellectual stimulation and love. Those who have participated in the preparation of the manuscript were and remain true friends as well as co-workers; for their hard work on drafts and manuscript, sincere thanks are due to Sandra Hodnett, Cyndy Medlock, and Helen Wren and for graphics to Steve Reese.

CONTENTS

Part One ORGANIZATION

Part Two GENERAL ACCOUNTING DUTIES

14

15

EXHIBIT LIST

Part One

ORGANIZATION

1

Accounting Control

One of the most difficult jobs in current corporate hierarchy is the administration of the company accounting function. The person who is charged with this responsibility wears two hats, which, in effect, often results in conflict within himself.

On the one hand, this man is a line manager of a large, expensive and diverse function processing the many accounting systems required by the dictates of good management and by state and government regulations. On the other hand, he is a staff assistant to the president, acting as an internal consultant in the areas of cost control, profit planning, and information processing.

The difficulty is compounded in the larger company with decentralized management. The division accounting manager not only has to cope with the line and staff conflict, as presented above, but he is also faced with being a staff assistant simultaneously to two different people: the division manager and the corporate accounting manager.

Terminology being what it is in American business, there is no single job title that can be used across the board for this accounting manager. However, in the majority of cases, according to surveys by the National Industrial Conference Board and by the American Management Association, the title "controller" is the common and widely used title for this individual. Therefore, throughout this book, the word "controller" will be used to indicate the top corporate accounting executive and the top division accounting executive. Where it is necessary to differentiate one or the other, the titles "corporate controller" and "division controller" will be used; otherwise, the word "controller" alone will be used. This is consistent with the broad responsibility of the division controller who currently has duties equal to those of a corporate controller of a smaller company.

To more specifically state what is meant to be reported on herein in the overall responsibility area of the controller, the following statement of the Financial Executive's Institute on the concept of modern controllership is given as a concise and complete statement of the functions to be administered:

1. "Planning for Control. To establish, coordinate, and administrate as an *integral* part of management, an adequate plan for the control of operations. Such a plan would provide, to the extent required in the business, profit planning, programs for capital investing and for financing, sales forecasts, expense budgets, and cost standards, together with the necessary procedures to effectuate the plan." The following chapters of this book are specifically related to the fulfillment of the above: Chapter 1, Accounting Control; Chapter 7, Cost Accounting; Chapter 9, Profit Planning; Chapter 10, Short Range Planning; Chapter 12, Capital Appropriations.

2. "Reporting and Interpreting. To compare performance of operating plans and standards, and to report and interpret the results of operations to all levels of management and to the owners of the business." Toward the fulfillment of this objective, see the following chapters: Chapter 2, Control Reporting; Chapter 4, General Accounting; Chapter 8, Cost Reduction; Chapter 3, Cost Control Within the Control Function; Chapter 11, Cost-Volume-Profit Analysis.

3. "Evaluating and Consulting. To consult with all segments of management responsible for policy or action concerning any phase of the operation of the business as it relates to the attainment of objectives and the effectiveness of policies, organization structure and procedures." Relating specifically to this statement are: Chapter 1, Accounting Control; Chapter 9, Profit Planning; Chapter 10, Short Range Goals; Part Four, Computers.

4. "Tax Administration. To establish and administer tax policies and procedures." This is briefly covered in Chapter 4 under General Accounting.

5. "Government Reporting. To supervise or coordinate the preparation of reports to government agencies." This is covered under Chapter 2, Control Reporting.

6. "Protection of Assets. To assure protection for the assets of the business through internal control, internal auditing, and assuring proper insurance coverage." This is covered in Chapter 4 on General Accounting, Chapter 12 on Capital Appropriations and Chapter 6 on Accounting Services.

7. "Economic Appraisal. To continuously appraise economic and social forces and government influences, and to interpret their effect upon the business." Chapter 9 on Profit Planning and Chapter 10 on Short Range Plans relate to this statement.

This book is directed not to the controller who wants to do all of the work personally, but to the controller who wants to learn more about administration and good management, about delegation of more time-consuming specific responsibilities to the people working for him, about freeing his own time for the broader duties of the controller. To do this requires that the controller must provide himself with an adequate staff. Typically, the controller is the last man to add to his standard work force, but if he is to be the controller and not the bookkeeper, he must have an adequate staff to whom to delegate the routine responsibilities.

CONTROLLER: PROFESSIONAL AND MANAGER

The controller has a two-fold function to perform within the organizational structure. On the one hand, he is the line manager of his department. On the other, he is a staff assistant to the president. He is expected to perform cost analysis, interpretation, and advisory functions which assist the president in the fulfillment of his specific objective and assignment as overall manager of operations.

But the controller must be more than a staff assistant *to* management. He must be a vital part *of* management.

In analysis of division problems, the controller brings to bear talents and background not available from the other members of the management team. First, and most obvious, the controller has a unique familiarity with cost and profit statements as to content and as to significance for the future. Because profit is the underlying motivating factor on all organizational operations, the controller's knowledge of the profit structure is uniquely important to the management function. In addition to this particular talent, the controller is capable of performing as a professional manager in the analysis of general problems facing the division, just as his sales and manufacturing counterparts do.

As a line manager the controller must produce the primary numbers which identify what is going on throughout the organization. He must record and publish these numbers to the people who need them for interpretation and control with accuracy and efficiency. He is responsible for the reporting of sales orders received, for the reporting of production information as orders are started through the manufacturing process and for the reporting of sales information as orders are shipped to the customer. He is responsible for paying the bills and recording costs, item by item and by department. He prepares the expense budget and cost rates which are used in analytical phases and which are fundamental to control activities. His responsibility includes fixed asset accountability, product inventories and other working capital.

Having prepared the basic numbers as indicated above, the controller is next responsible for their interpretation in whatever form and fashion the other members of the management team desire for the optimum operating control of their assigned functions. This includes cost variance reporting, profit forecasting, profit planning, and the conduct of special cost and feasibility studies.

ORGANIZATIONAL CONSIDERATIONS

The neophyte controller is aware of how little he knows about what constitutes effective organization. He reads that in other companies the same size as his there is a bewildering variety of solutions to organization problems. He hears and reads inconclusive debates on the comparative merits of the existing organization structures and of proposed new ones. He knows that good organization is something more than charts and manuals, that what really counts is what people do and how they work together. Yet he knows that formal organization is necessary to good administration in a large, complex enterprise. Careful planning is, therefore, required to bring the diverse accounting functions together in an effective pattern of operation.

The Controller's Department must be organized effectively to recognize that:

1. The Controller's Department contributes to profits through the reporting services it provides to management.
2. The department is a drain on profits because of the actual cost of its operations.
3. Organization structure interacts with the quality of the people operating an organization.

To be effective, the Controller's Department must provide informational services of high quality at a minimum cost and must facilitate the long-range development of competent accounting executives. Because the Controller's Department is basically a service organization, any decisions concerning its internal organization structure must simultaneously be concerned with the relative decentralization of the operating and other staff departments. Centralization or decentralization in the Controller's Department must be consistent with the levels in other departments to which information and analytical and consulting services are supplied. The relative degree of decentralization desirable depends primarily on the decentralization of profit responsibility to divisions and on the geographical location of production operations.

CENTRALIZATION VERSUS DECENTRALIZATION

An organization is centralized when the authority to make major decisions is reserved to high corporate management and decentralized when the discretion and authority to make them are delegated by top corporate management to lower levels of executive authority, typically to division managers.

The argument whether to centralize profit responsibility or to decentralize profit responsibility to division management removed from the home office has been a favorite topic for author and for lecturer for many years. Many of the arguments for decentralization have recently been countered effectively with advances in data communications and data processing. While it is not my purpose to argue the pros and cons of this management decision, I will point out that a strong centralized organization often prevents a division controller from being what his title warrants; under such circumstances, a division *accountant* can function and certain staff specialists can operate, but by definition, a division *controller* cannot function as his job is defined in this book.

Decentralization of profit responsibility requires a strong-willed, well-qualified division controller to carry out adequately the assigned functions. Under these circumstances, corporate management looks to division management to maintain the condition of assigned equipment and markets and to insure the future through development of markets and products, all the while earning an adequate return on assigned investment. The division controller has a vital role to fulfill if the division is to perform that assignment.

FUNCTIONAL VERSUS LINE ORGANIZATION

Within the division, the controller has variations on two choices as to the type of organization to set up to take care of the full range of financial activities necessary to the division operations. He can either establish all financial operations on a strictly functional basis with specialist managers responsible for each functional activity within the division; or as an alternative to this, a line organization can be established in which a single individual at each operating location is responsible for all accounting activities.

All other things being equal, the functional organization leads to a much more effective use of manpower. It is axiomatic that an individual responsible for a single functional specialty can do a better job on that function than can an individual responsible for that and a dozen other activities simultaneously. The problem here is one of geography. If all operations are sufficiently close together so that one individual can effectively exercise his functional authority at all plant locations, then this is the recommended course of action. If the geography is such that the plants are located so far apart that the functional assignments are impractical, then obviously the choice must revert to a plant-by-plant line organization. There are degrees between the two, however, which can be pursued to attain some of the advantages of functional specialization even with adverse geographical considerations. For instance, all general accounting and statement preparation for the division can be done at a central division headquarters location. To accomplish this, each plant location must do a certain amount of preparation of information which is then forwarded each accounting period to division headquarters to be entered formally into the books of account and to be entered in division operating statements. Similarly, the accounting service functions such as payroll, order entry, billing, and accounts payable, can also be done on a centralized functional specialty basis even though the geography requires that production accounting, budgeting, control reporting, and standard costing be done on a geographically decentralized basis.

Regardless of the functional or line decision, it is recommended that personnel and units responsible for each of the three major kinds of functions be separated organizationally:

1. Bookkeeping and preparation and distribution of accounting reports.
2. Assistance to the operating departments and current analysis for scorecard and attention-directing purposes.
3. Participation in the use of accounting information for problem solving.

When accountants have heavy supervisory responsibilities for report preparation, the pressures of supervision and report deadlines lead to a relative neglect of analytical work. Where one supervisor is responsible for routine record keeping and special analytical services, the bookkeeping activities are maximized and the analytical services are minimized: deadlines for period accounting reports are more urgent. Therefore, when the functions are combined, the controller retains little discretionary direct control over the amount of effort actually devoted to each.

A centralized accounting organization is one in which all control functions are assigned to people at the central division offices and in which the advantages of functional specialization are realized by grouping like functions together, as shown in Exhibit 1.

A decentralized accounting organization is one in which control functions are assigned to each plant location with policy guidance from the controller at headquarters. This is recommended only when geographic considerations—distance between plants—make it impractical to try to centralize. Even with great distances, some centralization is feasible and is recommended; modern data processing makes this increasingly desirable. Exhibit 2 shows certain functions centralized.

It is of considerable importance that accounting information be located where the units which need the information can have immediate access to them. This means that information must be physically accessible from the plant rather than in some remote, far-distant division headquarters. In fixing the geographical location of record keeping activities, the most important question is who needs access to the detailed data, not who uses the *reports* generated from the data. For most reports, mail service is adequate. Data processing remote-access devices linked with on-line data banks can provide centralized processing with decentralized accessibility.

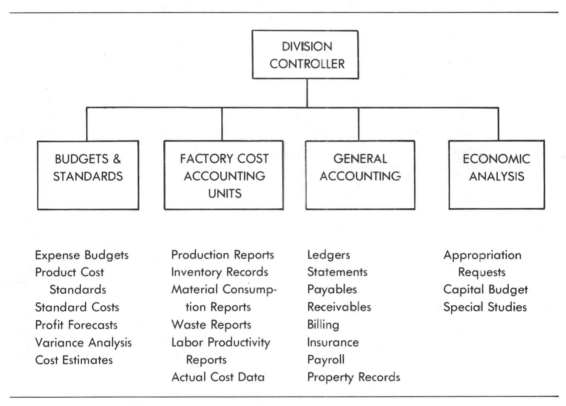

EXHIBIT 1

CENTRALIZED ORGANIZATION

DIVISION CONTROLLER

BUDGETS & STANDARDS	FACTORY COST ACCOUNTING UNITS	GENERAL ACCOUNTING	ECONOMIC ANALYSIS
Expense Budgets	Production Reports	Ledgers	Appropriation
Product Cost	Inventory Records	Statements	Requests
Standards	Material Consump-	Payables	Capital Budget
Standard Costs	tion Reports	Receivables	Special Studies
Profit Forecasts	Waste Reports	Billing	
Variance Analysis	Labor Productivity	Insurance	
Cost Estimates	Reports	Payroll	
	Actual Cost Data	Property Records	

Similarly, it is important that data be classified in the same way at all plant locations. Problems in insuring that this is done are frequently used as an argument against decentralization. This relatively minor problem can be solved by the issuance of written procedures and charts of accounts and the use of internal auditors to insure compliance.

A major problem to be resolved in the decentralization of the record keeping function is the accessibility of documents and the reliability of the source records. Both point in the direction of geographical decentralization. The only place where source data can be improved is where it originates and the only way to determine the validity of source data is to compare the data with the facts. There are definite cost advantages in centralizing to facilitate mechanization. The original time and production records, by definition, must be decentralized to the plant.

FUNCTIONS RESERVED TO THE CORPORATE CONTROLLER

It is the function of the corporate controller to insure that proper financial

EXHIBIT 2

DECENTRALIZED ORGANIZATION

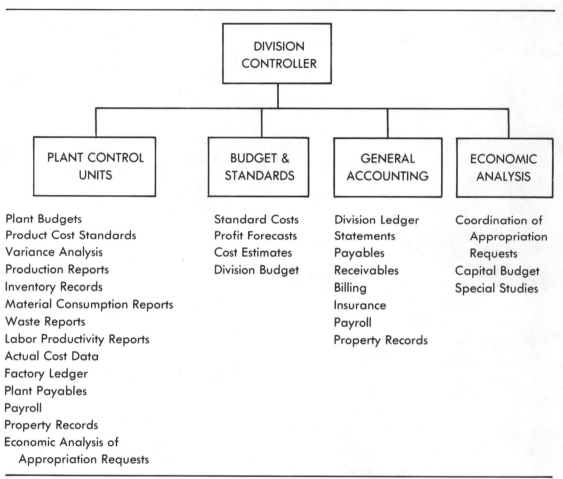

PLANT CONTROL UNITS	BUDGET & STANDARDS	GENERAL ACCOUNTING	ECONOMIC ANALYSIS
Plant Budgets	Standard Costs	Division Ledger	Coordination of
Product Cost Standards	Profit Forecasts	Statements	Appropriation
Variance Analysis	Cost Estimates	Payables	Requests
Production Reports	Division Budget	Receivables	Capital Budget
Inventory Records		Billing	Special Studies
Material Consumption Reports		Insurance	
Waste Reports		Payroll	
Labor Productivity Reports		Property Records	
Actual Cost Data			
Factory Ledger			
Plant Payables			
Payroll			
Property Records			
Economic Analysis of Appropriation Requests			

and accounting standards are maintained in all divisions and that financial reports reflect the results of operations factually and completely.

The corporate controller is responsible:

1. To insure that sound accounting methods are followed in all divisions and to insure the adequacy of division accounting systems and staff qualifications through publication of corporate policy statements.
2. To give competent advice to the division controller on all control and accounting matters.
3. To insure that the division controllers have adequate forecasting, budgeting, cost accounting, and inventory control systems, consistent with corporate policies.

4. To analyze operating results for corporate management.
5. To make special cost studies and financial analyses as requested by other corporate executives.
6. In the absence of an independent treasurer, the controller is responsible for credit policy, for financial planning, cash availability and cash flow control of the corporation, including all divisions.
7. To institute internal auditing programs necessary to insure that the above responsibilities are, in fact, being carried out.

RELATION OF CORPORATE TO DIVISION CONTROLLER

There are two arrangements for formal lines of authority. In one, the division controller is administratively and functionally under and reports to the corporate controller. In the other, he is functionally responsible to the corporate controller, but administratively responsible to and reports to the division manager.

Administrative authority refers to the day-to-day relation of a supervisor to his subordinates. This includes work assignments, operating problems, and settling questions involving relations among subordinates. Functional authority means the right to determine accounting policy, the chart of accounts, statement content and deadlines, bookkeeping procedures, and the like. In practice there is seldom confusion or disagreement as to the proper classification of matters to be settled by the administrative authority or the functional authority. Sometimes competing demands are made on accounting personnel to adhere to professional standards on the one hand and on the other to get along with factory management by not reporting unpleasant facts. With rare exceptions, conflicts of this sort are resolved in favor of the standards of the profession.

Centralized loyalties are fostered under both of these arrangements by the tendency of accounting personnel to look to the corporate controller's department for chances for promotion because, typically but unfortunately, there is little transfer of accounting managers to the manufacturing or sales departments.

With decentralized profit responsibility, it is generally undesirable to have the corporate controller exercise line authority over the division controller. To do so can inhibit the full exercise of the division controller's capabilities, and places a "corporate representative" in the midst of division management. These criticisms cannot be applied, however, to the retention by the division controller of a functional responsibility to the corporate controller while reporting administratively to the division manager. In this case, he *is* a part of division management with a vital, personal stake in the success of the division.

In most cases, then, it is desirable that the division controller report on a line basis to the division manager. This leads to unity of purpose and to a better operating attitude within the divisions. Greater understanding by the division controller of the objectives and requirements within the division results in a simultaneously greater rapport with division operating executives. The establishment of this rapport is essential to the full utilization of the talents and capabilities of a division financial staff. Simultaneously, it is necessary that the corporate controller have a dotted-line relationship to the division controllers. The corporate controller must maintain full responsibility throughout the entire corporation for the adequacy of financial operation. As such, the controller and his staff must have complete access to all division records, reports, systems controls, etc., for analysis, audit and verification of procedures. On the other hand, it is much to be preferred that the division controller exercise line control over all subordinate accounting personnel, including those at remote plants. There must be no diluting of the controller's authority to specify detailed accounting procedures and time-tables, to centralize functions if desirable, to staff for maximum efficiency consistent with cross-training and growth. Plant goals and programs are components of one cohesive whole as approved by the general manager; therefore, this line authority of division controller to plant controller will not inhibit full rapport with plant management.

INTERNAL AUDITING

In recent years there has been a greatly enhanced interest in internal accounting control systems and the means by which to assure that those systems are adequate. The Internal Audit activity has played a major role in that determination. An important question for the controller to ask is: "Does our Internal Audit operation meet our needs, given the present political and social environment?" This environment includes the Foreign Corrupt Practices Act with its requirement for reasonable assurance that certain specific objectives are met by a system of internal accounting control:

a. Transactions are executed in accordance with management's authorization.
b. Transactions are recorded as necessary to permit preparation of financial statements in accordance with Generally Accepted Accounting Principles.
c. Access to assets is permitted only in accordance with management's authorization.
d. Recorded assets are compared with existing assets at reasonable intervals and appropriate action is taken with respect to any differences.

Additional influences stem from the likelihood that the Securities and Exchange Commission will mandate some kind of management reporting on the sufficiency of internal accounting controls. It is also likely that the SEC will mandate comments by the outside auditors on the sufficiency of the internal controls.

Duties of Internal Audit

Given this level of interest in the sufficiency of internal controls, it will be incumbent on the controller to insure that Internal Audit is functioning at a level sufficient to meet its requirements.

In order that there may be no ambiguity about the role of internal audits in the firm, the purpose, responsibility, and authority of the department should be authoritatively stated by the Chief Executive Officer and documented in statements issued within the firm. There should be a policy statement describing the scope of activities which are assigned to the department; the policy statement should designate the authority necessary to perform the activities described in the policy statement. Complete and unrestricted access to all necessary records, to personnel, and to properties relevant to the process should be included in the authorization. A list of duties which should be assigned to Internal Audit are the following:

1. Evaluation of the system of internal control to determine its efficiency.
2. Evaluation of the operation of internal control to determine that it is working as it is supposed to work.
3. Evaluation of the updating process for the internal control system to insure that the system is changed as necessary to meet changing conditions.
4. Communication of and compliance with policy statements, including Codes of Conduct.
5. Making recommendations for improvements at any time that deficiencies are observed.
6. Evaluating specific programs as necessary, including the operational auditing.
7. Reporting to the audit committee as well as to management on a routine basis.

Focus of Internal Auditing

Internal auditing has been defined as a type of management control which operates by evaluating and reporting on the effectiveness of all other controls in the firm. Internal control has been defined as follows:

Internal control comprises the plan of organization and all of the coordinate methods and measures adopted within a business to safeguard its assets, to check the accuracy and reliability of its accounting data, to promote operational efficiency, and to encourage adherence to prescribed managerial policies.

There is often a distinction within internal control made between accounting controls and administrative controls. The outside auditors and the Foreign Corrupt Practices Act place great emphasis on accounting controls. These are the controls necessary to safeguard assets of the firm and to produce reliable financial information. However, the internal audit group has a broader responsibility than merely to assure the adequacy of internal accounting control. The internal audit group, therefore, should not merely concentrate on the accounting controls, but should, in addition, be interested in that which is labelled administrative controls. These controls basically have non-accounting objectives as their focus, including the issuance of goals and objectives and policies and the assurance of appropriate operational control systems for the firm. The Internal Auditors must be, by definition, interested in both accounting controls and administrative controls.

Operational Auditing

Historically, internal auditing has been deeply involved with and committed to operational auditing. This has come about because of an interest in improving the efficiency of the firm and achieving cost reductions. In many firms, this is the responsibility of an Industrial Engineering Department. It is not unreasonable to expect that there might be conflict and overlap between the normal assignments of industrial engineering and of operational auditors unless clear coordination between the two groups is established.

Management has looked to internal auditing for operational auditing activities. Internal auditors have accepted these assignments because operational auditing is of a greater level of excitement than financial auditing, and operational auditing produces measurable, tangible evidence of its worth through improved productivity and cost reductions. Internal auditors can perceive a direct relationship between their competency in operational auditing and their performance appraisals by their managers and supervisors.

Independence

A highly independent internal auditing operation is necessary if the internal auditors are to have access to all of the information they need, and if they are to feel free to comment as they should concerning the sufficiency of the internal accounting and administrative control. Auditors must be free from any organizational pressures that limit their objectivity. To the extent that Internal Audit reports administratively to a high level in the organization and to the extent that Internal Audit has free access to the audit committee, this independence is confirmed to all within the firm. The Director of Internal Audit must report administratively to a high-level executive who is knowledgeable about the auditing process, about the operation itself and those activities which will be audited, and who has sufficient authority to guarantee unrestricted audit coverage. It is easy to suggest that the Director of Internal Audit report to the Chief Executive Officer of the firm. However, the same argument can be made about many functions within the firm. It may well be that the chief executive may be sufficiently burdened with duties that he is unable to give Internal Audit the time and support that it must have for it to be effective. Historically, Internal Audit has been found within the financial organization, first as an arm of the Controller's Department, and then at a higher level, reporting to the Chief Financial Officer. If the Controller is responsible for the day-to-day activities of the accounting operation, there is a valid reason for not having Internal Audit reporting to the Controller. If that were the case, the internal auditors would be reporting on that for which the Controller is responsible. In such a situation, there are too many opportunities for inhibition of independence. However, if the Controller has delegated to someone within the organization those responsibilities for day-to-day activities and is instead the chief financial officer for the firm, reporting to the Chief Executive Officer, there should be no remaining valid criticism of having Internal Audit report to the Controller.

There must be a special relationship between Internal Audit and the Audit Committee of the Board of Directors. This Audit Committee, composed of all outside directors, will function as an independent agency within the board. The Audit Committee will have a very special interest in all matters relating to internal control, both accounting and administrative. The Audit Committee needs to be informed on a continuing and routine basis about the responsibilities, the scope, the performance, the findings, and the recommendations of the Internal Audit Department.

THE AUDIT COMMITTEE

Of the many changes which have affected the corporate board of directors in recent years, the rise in prominence of the Audit Committee is the change of most direct relevance to the Controller. In order, therefore, that the Controller be able to administer the accounting function, he must understand the background of and the status of the audit committee movement.

The advent of the Audit Committee came in part because of inadequate board of directors' involvement in certain financial matters. More specifically, the Audit Committee has been advocated and, indeed almost demanded, by the New York Stock Exchange, the Securities and Exchange Commission, many members of the accounting profession, and the Congress of the United States. It is a certainty that Audit Committees today are exercising much stronger and broader authority than in recent years. Audit Committees now require more information from and fuller cooperation of management. Audit Committees probe deeply if they have unanswered questions and otherwise proceed under the assumption that the Committee has absolute and full authority to do whatever is needed to cope with their responsibilities as they see the need to do so. The Foreign Corrupt Practices Act of 1977 has effectively mandated Audit Committee involvement in the internal control of the firm.

Committee Duties

The Securities and Exchange Commission has listed the following duties as appropriate and necessary for the adequate functioning of an Audit Committee. While the SEC has not mandated these duties, the Commission has acted in several legal actions as if the items are mandated. The items are as follows:

- Engagement or discharge or recommendations to the full Board on the engagement or discharge of the independent auditor;
- Direction and supervision of investigations into matters within the scope of its duties;
- Review with the independent auditors of the plan and results of the company's internal audit procedures;
- Approval of each professional service provided by the independent auditors prior to the performance of such services;
- Review of the independence of the independent auditors;
- Consideration of the range of audit and audit fees;
- Review of the adequacy of the company's system of internal accounting controls.

Clearly the controller will be intimately involved with the Audit Committee in its performance of the above listed duties.

Organizational Problems

In some quarters, it is argued that a strong Audit Committee might well begin to assume management's responsibilities or, at the least, interfere with management's independence and authority. In fact, however, management seldom takes that point of view. Management, instead, looks to the Audit Committee as an opportunity to insure more effective audits as well as an opportunity to strengthen the independence of the Internal Audit function. This gives top management additional assurance that accounting controls as designed and implemented by the Controller are effective and are being properly monitored and that financial statements are reliable and complete. The Committee might seem to be a threat to the Controller; instead, however, Controllers tend to look to the Audit Committee as a very strong champion of those accounting policies and procedures that are necessary which might otherwise be resisted by other members of the management team. It will come as a surprise to no one to recognize that the

Controller is sometimes subject to conflicting pressure: management often wants a more attractive financial statement, while Generally Accepted Accounting Principles impose an obligation on the Controller to report fairly and to disclose completely. The Audit Committee can be very useful to the Controller in gaining an appropriate resolution of these conflicts.

While much attention has been focused on the responsibilities and involvement of Audit Committees with the outside auditors, the oversight of the Internal Audit function was a prime committee responsibility for 80 percent of the firms responding to a National Industrial Conference Board survey made in 1978. It is not unusual to find the following in the board resolution establishing the responsibilities of the Audit Committee:

> To review and approve the Internal Audit program to be followed by the company and the adequacy of the related systems of internal controls and to ascertain that the accounting system is effective and responsive to management's needs through Audit Committee meetings and consultations with both internal auditors and the independent public accountant.

In performing the above function, the Audit Committee meets privately with the Controller, the Manager of Internal Audit, and other financial executives as appropriate and necessary. It is both appropriate and mandatory that the Controller fully disclose all matters to the Audit Committee. Any inappropriate pressures on the Controller or deficiencies in the system concealed deliberately by the Controller would inevitably result in the discharge of the Controller when such situations ultimately become known to the Audit Committee. This is a sensitive situation with which the Controller must be prepared to deal. General management must be made aware by the Audit Committee that this reporting requirement is being imposed on the financial officers of the firm.

Much has been written about the appropriate reporting relationships of internal auditors to audit committees versus to corporate managers. In point of fact, the internal auditor reports to the chief financial officer of the firm more frequently than to any other officer. If there is a Financial Vice-President, it is likely that this individual is the same one to whom the Controller reports. Hence, there is a peer relationship between the Controller and the Internal Auditor as well as a supervisory relationship in that the Internal Auditor will report to the Audit Committee on the adequacy of the work of the Controller. One must learn to be comfortable with such incongruities.

COST OF THE CONTROL FUNCTION

How much can be spent for the accounting and control function? This question can only be answered in terms of justification of the specific components of the broad function. Each must be measured against the yardsticks:

a. If it were not being done, would we start it?
b. What would it cost to do without?
c. Is it being done efficiently?

Many aspects of accounting simply must be done because of state and federal law or to keep the business operating. Included in this category are such functions as payroll, billing, accounts payable, and accounts receivable. In such cases, there is no equivocation in answering questions (a) and (b). These things have to be done. The only legitimate question in such cases is whether they can be done at less cost.

In the typical case, those functions account for a major fraction of the total cost of the control function. The balance is cost incurred for discretionary functions that are not required by law or are not routine operations. This is the area of simultaneous high discretionary cost and maximum opportunity for profit improvement. There is but one acceptable reason for spending money in this area: a high probability of a profit improvement that is at least twice as great as the cost to be incurred. Why a factor of two? Consider the following situation:

A company proposes to spend $100,000/year on a project to eliminate material waste currently costing $500,000/year. Sounds good! But, will all waste be eliminated? Not likely. At best, perhaps only as much as 50% will be permanently erased. There is risk present, even in assuming *any* reduction.

In the typical case, project costs will be underestimated and gains will be overestimated. In this example, assume costs will turn out to be 25% higher than estimated. Further, assume only 75% of savings originally projected will be realized. How good is the picture now?

	Cost	Gain
Estimate	$100,000	From total waste of $500,000 an improvement of 50% = $250,000
Actual	$125,000	75% ($250,000) =187,500 Net Gain $62,500

This is a net gain of 50% of the actual cost, on the surface a good return.

But the $125,000 is only the directly incurred cost of salaries and supplies. Not charged in are fringe benefits, general administration, services, personnel (including recruiting and training), time of production supervision also involved in the project—all the many costs affected to greater or lesser degrees by the mere presence of the newly created staff project. The *true* cost, obviously, becomes quite difficult to identify. Even worse, the gain is also often difficult to quantify with accuracy. All else being equal, the effect of the single change described above can be identified. But all else is never equal. The world doesn't stand still while we analyze variances! New employees come and old ones go. New equipment is installed to replace old. The new foreman's training program generates considerable enthusiasm for efficiency and cost reduction in the entire plant including the high waste department.

The controller cannot earn the respect of line and staff management if they know he does not practice the cost consciousness he preaches. Respect for his knowledge and ability is the keystone to successful controllership. Preceding and concurrent with an overall cost reduction program, the controller must have eliminated the waste in his own operation.

All of the techniques which the controller uses to control manufacturing costs can be applied to his own operation. Reference to the chapters on Accounting Control, Control Reporting, Cost Accounting, and Cost Reduction read within this particular context will yield useful ideas.

RESPONSIBILITY FOR INNOVATION

The controller must divide his time and his energies into these three parts for effective and complete administration of the control function:

1. Manager
2. Do-er
3. Innovator

1. Managerial responsibilities have already been mentioned and will be covered from many different angles in later chapters of this book. Therefore, no further comment will be made here except to say that the other two parts of the job *must* be given adequate attention if success is to be achieved.
2. Many projects will be of a kind which require that the controller, personally, perform himself, doing much of the detail work of data collection, calculation, and analysis. Discretion must be exercised to insure that a task really fits this do-it-yourself category, or the controller will find himself the only busy man in the office, having left little for anyone else to do. This may result in high-quality project reports, but management and innovation are left by the wayside when this happens.

   Usually, work the controller does himself requires sensitive value judgements or very confidential data. Or it may be a new job (innovation) being run through a break-in period. Or it may require a high degree of technical skill no subordinate is trained to exercise. The doing phase of the job should be constantly changing as the controller explores new areas, develops his staff in higher skills, and delegates newly perfected tasks.

3. Through innovation the controller improves for tomorrow what was adequate for today. Methods used now will not be competitive in the future. Just as products and plant must be continually upgraded, so must management control techniques be continuously upgraded. The controller should be a guiding force in developing new techniques, new reports, better controls for operating management.

This requires time. Good ideas seldom flow like Niagara when one decides to create. A definite amount of time, say 15 percent of the total work week should be allocated to innovating, creating, improving. In Chapter 3 are several suggestions for improving and controlling the utilization of time.

PRESENT AND FUTURE OF THE CONTROL FUNCTION AND PROFESSION

The controller's office is becoming increasingly important as the strategic and tactical intelligence center of the business, particularly as electronic computers and other data processing equipment are more available and generally located within the controller's organizational responsibility. The controller is gaining a new stature as the one man on the management team who may know more about the business than anyone, other than the president.

Not too many years past, the controller was looked upon as the chief accountant. Indeed, the change from the spelling of the word from "comptroller" to "controller" is in some mysterious way related to this same change in the corporate status of the controller.

A striking change in current organizational situations is that no longer is the controller an individual who has moved straight up through the accounting hierarchy from junior accountant to controller. In many cases, someone other than a technically trained accountant is at the controller's desk. Business administration graduates, in some respects not too far removed from accounting to be sure, are to be found in great numbers. Similarly, a large number of the current controller population has come up through the industrial engineering line of progression, moving from industrial engineering and its cost reduction and standards setting functions to budgeting, standard cost accounting, greater financial analysis assignments, and eventually to the top job itself.

Representative, too, of the current management stature of the controller is the fact that corporate organization provides for an assistant to the controller to be in direct, functional charge of the line accounting activities, including books of account and statement preparation. This leaves the controller free to devote his time and his energies to ranging throughout the length and breadth of the organization suggesting innovations, improvements, changes, and participating with other members of general management in planning for the future.

A recent survey by the Financial Executive's Institute gives concrete evidence of what the future holds for today's controller. Of its 5,200 members, only 46 percent had titles in which the word "controller" actually appeared, and 10 percent were inactive. In the remaining 44 percent were presidents, chairmen of the board, executive vice-presidents, finance committee chairmen, vice-presidents of other functions (10 percent of the 5,200, indicating that controllers can get out of strictly finance and into other operations responsibilities) and treasurers. This indicates that the controller who functions in the broader sense is a clearly identified candidate for positions of higher and broader executive responsibility.

It is equally clear, both from the writings in the field and from the author's own experience, that the extent to which these opportunities are developed by the individual controller depends to a great extent on that individual, his own interests, his own ambitions, and his own abilities. He can define his job in his mind in very narrow terms, and the job will, in fact, turn out to be that narrow. Or he can define the job broadly, as described, and he will find the job horizons continually moving away, becoming even greater, more challenging, and more rewarding.

2

Objective of
Control Reports

Accounting reporting and record keeping systems exist for one purpose: to report, in terms of cost and profitability, where the company has been, so that management can identify from these reports the sources and causes of good and bad performance, for future corrective action.

The operating manager, on a day-to-day basis, is well aware of what is going on in the manufacturing process under his supervision. All he has to do is walk out on the floor to see whether men are working, whether the product is moving, or whether inventories in process are building up. He can look in the finished inventory warehouse and find out whether inventory level is increasing or decreasing. He can look at today's machine production schedule and know whether there is an adequate backlog for his machines to operate now and in the relatively near future.

However, all of these are day-to-day, on-the-spot observations. It is extremely difficult for one man to observe operations and, from those observations, extrapolate trends. He needs feedback, as shown in Exhibit 3. The only sensible way for a manager to control his business is to be aware both of the day-to-day situation and of the trends that are developing in all aspects of his operation.

It is the responsibility of the controller to supply this trend information. It is the responsibility of the controller to collect, digest, and report information in a format easily understandable by the operating manager. The format of the report should be chosen to specifically highlight the trends that indicate low performance and high performance and to omit average or standard performance which is to be expected. There is no value in inundating the manager with a deluge of numbers which simply indicate that "everything is under control." Of much greater value is an understanding with the operating manager that a simple statement that all else is under control will accompany the few reports of specific deviations from standard.

It is the intent of this chapter to suggest techniques for maintaining the necessary records requisite to supplying control reports of the type described and to suggest more specifically the kind of reports which experience has shown to be most useful.

There are specific obligations that the controller has to the operating manager; there are also specific obligations that the operating manager has to the controller. Accounting texts abound with statements describing the obligation of the controller to the operating manager; these are fairly obvious from the job description of the controller. There is, however, very little written of the obligation of the operating manager to the controller. This is a subject which needs considerable development in terms of control concepts:

> The controller is expected to maintain a completely current status display on the performance of all operations. In order to be able to do this, the controller must be immediately and completely informed of all actual and anticipated changes in personnel, organization, and manufacturing equipment. He must know of plans to reassign products from one profit center to another. He must know major marketing plans that will have a significant effect on total sales and manufacturing cost, hence the budgets and standards for sales departments and manufacturing facilities.

EXHIBIT 3

FEEDBACK REPORTING CONCEPTS

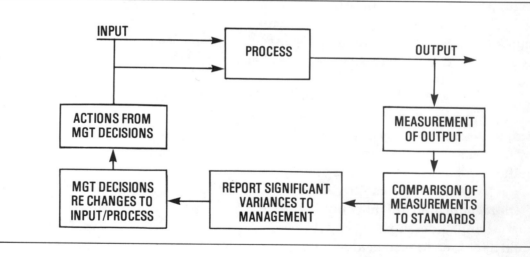

The frequency of reports is a matter requiring considerable judgement. There are pieces of information which need to be reported to operating management on a day-to-day basis. These are the kind of things that the manager can see but cannot quantify as he goes about the business of day-to-day management, such as orders received, major manufacturing or quality difficulties, and the like. On a weekly basis, the operating manager needs to have this information related to manufacturing control trends. On a monthly basis, a summary of operations and a manufacturing profit contribution statement for the period should be produced. All of these reports need to be a combination of the trend and of the exception reporting types. Trend reports of actual performance are vital to good operating management. Simultaneously, absolute comparisons with bench marks or standards are required. Derived data is reported to operating management as well as primary, actual measurements. Cost reports and variance analysis techniques will be considered in this chapter with illustrations of suggested formats of variance reporting; techniques of reporting the relationship of current performance to budget, to sales volume, to profit assignments, and to standard costs will be suggested. Questions relating to multi-plant cost comparisons, pricing, product profitability, marketing procedure, inventory policy, and labor negotiations ought to be the subject of special studies; they should not be built into control reporting systems. By definition, such problem solving situations are exceptions requiring detailed analysis.

OBLIGATION OF CONTROLLER TO OPERATING MANAGER

The operating manager's responsibility is to direct the production of company products to meet sales forecasts at lowest possible cost, consistent with proper quality, and to assist in forming company policy as to equipment and quality improvement. He has to work with the classic "men, materials, and machines" as the ingredients to be manipulated for successful operation. The operating manager must do the following to accomplish those objectives:

1. Plan
2. Organize
3. Implement
4. Control

Of these four areas, the two in which he and the controller work very closely are the areas of planning and control.

In planning, specifically profit planning, operating executives reduce to writing specific objectives for their own review and for the guidance of their subordinates. The controller has an important role in assuring that operating management has properly identified the objectives of its operation. With stated objectives, the organization, rather than drifting and reacting to emergency situations, works toward specific goals. The organization is oriented toward results. Results serve as a basis for organization appraisal and individual performance review. In specifically stating the objectives to be accomplished, whether a cost reduction, a quality improvement, a new product development, or a plant and equipment item, the dollar value of the objective must be stated for best results. This should be done by the Controller's Department in its function as the sole *official* source of financial data.

In control, the controller must provide to the operating manager the data and the analysis needed for cost and variance control. The operating man must know in specific and actionable terms in which areas he is doing well and in which he is not doing well. Only by clear, concise, and timely reporting of the facts of the situation can the operating manager be fully informed.

In addition to the traditional areas of manufacturing cost reporting of a product-oriented nature, there is an increasing and proper trend to more budget variance reporting of staff department activities. Manufacturing has long been the subject of variance reports. More recently, sales activities have come to accept this kind of organized variance reporting. Engineering and research and development have to date been the object of relatively little effort in this area, even though these are high cost staff departments which should be the object of just as thorough and precise cost review and control action.

All of the above are typical and well-known responsibilities of the controller to the operating manager. In all of these areas, however, the responsibilities form a two-way street. More than that, the underlying responsibility is for a team effort for effective cost control. When the combined efforts of manufacturing and control staffs are brought to bear on a problem, the total result is always greater than the sum of their individual efforts.

In spite of this, close cooperation between the two is not the normal case in most situations; while undesirable, this is not surprising. Fundamentally, the manufacturing man is suspicious of the controller. The controller's reports are inherently used to measure his performance while very little that he does relates to the measurement of the controller's performance. The common misconception too often held by the manufacturing function is that the financial people are pretty much necessary for score keeping, but the total contribution that financial management makes to manufacturing management is extremely limited and of little value. Where this feeling exists, it can permeate the entire corporation. It represents a strongly defensive attitude of some manufacturing people who view the controller as an individual who is not capable of working under day-to-day line responsibilities, who has reserved for himself the right to criticize at length but who will tolerate no criticism of his own reports and figures, who discusses at length problems of which he has no detailed personal knowledge, and who draws conclusions based on statistics without knowing the facts. Where this situation exists, the controller is not going to be accepted as a valuable contributor to the success of the operation. When this is found, the first task of the controller is to overcome such feelings by establishing rapport with operating management. He can do this only through becoming better known to operating management by establishing personal, direct, and short lines of communication with those members of operating management who hold important and responsible positions.

Respect for the control function does not derive from formal reporting relationships or from lines on organization charts but only through proven performance and demonstrated worth.

The controller can do two simple things to reduce friction and to promote closer cooperation:

1. In the words of one manufacturing executive, "If you observe an unexpected bad swing in variances, tell me before you tell my superior." This is the least that the controller can do to establish real rapport with the manufacturing men. No one, least of all the specific man responsible, likes to hear from his superior about an unfavorable situation before he, himself, has heard any of the facts or any of the background reasons for the situation.
2. Explain reports in terms and terminology familiar to production men. Do not use accounting jargon; use the same words that the manufacturing man is using. Remember, he digs into your reports once a week or once a month. Do not use words that have no significance to him between references to your reports.

The responsibility of the operating manager to the controller is similarly one that can be reduced to a few significant points. The operating manager who knows that the controller is interested in his opinions and his management needs and who knows that the controller will take action to accomplish his requests will work to establish a team spirit. He will tell the controller what he thinks he needs in the way of control information to carry out his objectives. He knows he can't leave it up to the controller to define his needs for reported and analyzed data. The operating manager has an obligation to inform the controller of impending changes in equipment, process, or product line. If changes are planned for the manufacturing operation, the controller must know about them in advance to be able to plan for the effect they may have on record keeping and on control information. Otherwise, he cannot provide reports at the proper time, at the proper place, and in the proper format. The controller must be taken into complete confidence in the creating and planning phases so that he has the needed lead time to integrate operating plans into his own control department organization structure.

THE CONTROLLER AS AN INTERNAL CONSULTANT

The controller who is well qualified in the broad functions of controllership and who has established a high degree of rapport with division operating management will be called upon many times to function as an internal consultant in a staff capacity to the division manager and other major division operating heads.

The controller is in an almost unique position, equal perhaps only to that of the general manager, of being able to roam over the entire division delving into all aspects of all division operations. In the process of doing this, he picks up a broad generalized knowledge of the activities of the division. This, coupled with his unique abilities in the areas of analytical thinking and financial analysis, matched with his earlier business experience, gives him a broad background pertinent to fulfilling the role of consultant.

In this capacity, the controller will be asked to advise and counsel on such matters as market planning, personnel selection and promotion, organizational alignment of operating functions, and managerial performance, particularly as it relates to profit and profit improvement.

In the area of organizational structure, the concept of responsibility accounting should be stressed by the controller; it is vital that organizational alignments be made on bases that are amenable to responsibility accounting. The division controller has both an opportunity and, indeed, a responsibility to insure that the concept of responsibility accounting is not lost sight of when organizational lines and organizational responsibilities are drawn. Operating management will look to the controller to generate reports which indicate sales, profit, and variance performance for each operating unit. The controller will be unable to do this if organizational lines and lines of authority are not clear-cut so that the correct information can be entered into the books in the first place.

In specific instances, the division controller may find it desirable to recommend, even to initiate, action relating to organizational problems in other than his own department. Unfortunately, many controllers seem to feel that they are limited to formal cost reporting concerning other departments and that they must avoid stepping beyond the bounds of their department so as not to become involved in the managerial organization and administration of other major departments. The major problem area here is, again, in establishing the right kind and degree of rapport that will permit such suggestions to be acceptable.

As an illustration of what can be achieved, in one case in the author's experience, a particular technical department was not operating at the proper level of efficiency and cost effectiveness. The man in charge of the department had superior qualifications in terms of the technical capabilities required of his office, but as an administrator and manager there were important things not being done consistently and routinely, particularly in his absence. The author recommended both to that department head and to his immediate superior that a full-time administrator be added to the department as a number one assistant to the technical man. The specific areas for which the administrator would be responsible were outlined in the presentation. It was obvious to all that this recommendation implied inadequate performance and a need for improvement and that a major organization change was necessary if improvements were to be realized. At no time, however, was any of this said solely in the form of specific, critical statements; it was said, rather, in the form of positive statements describing in some detail the areas in which the proposed administrator would function, as listed below:

1. Budget and cost control within the technical department.
2. To be present full time in the department to serve as a coordinating force currently not present.
3. Equitable application of the salary administration policy.
4. Supervision of technician training programs.
5. Management of project cost trends.
6. Approval of purchase requisitions.
7. Preparation and control of periodic written project reports.
8. Clerical systems improvements within the department.
9. Investigate and make recommendations concerning organizational changes such as the separation of service work from development work.

It was suggested that specific background knowledge which this person should have would include a knowledge of budgets, cost accounting, expense control procedures, and salary administration philosophy. He should be a gregarious rather than a retiring type who could establish a rapport with and earn the respect of the people who would be asked to recognize his authority. The recommendation—in spite of the implied criticism beyond accounting boundaries—was accepted in good will, and was implemented within two months.

Any controller should be free to do as much.

RESPONSIBILITY ACCOUNTING

Control reports must reflect the results of operations of homogeneous departments with clearly defined limits and managerial structure. Responsibility accounting is the name that has been given to the process of recording and reporting performance with no ambiguity of responsibility.

The chart of accounts must be designed to accomplish this. If the order department servicing four plants is Joe Williams' responsibility, the controller must report the total cost Mr. Williams expends and controls. Only in this way can costs be controlled at the point of expenditure. Budgets can be established for each such responsibility center and period variance reports can be issued showing whether the manager has his costs under control. Exhibit 4 is an example of such a monthly control report.

Budget data, constant for the year, is shown on the left-hand side. Actual costs are shown, by category, each period. The total variance for the period is given at the bottom of each column. Because staff departments often have annual lump sum expenditures as well as level, weekly expenditures, cumulative variances for the year have relevance. A line is provided for this figure.

In Exhibit 4, Mr. Williams has a budget of $137,208/year or $12,945/five weeks. In the first period, a five-week period, he spent $13,254. He is $309 over budget. Glancing down the five-week budget column, comparing this with the first period, you can see that salaries are underspent $1181 and supplies are over budget $1335. Williams should already be aware of the salary situation since this could come about only because of low overtime or deletions from the work force. Supplies will probably require further analysis by the controller's staff.

Having established a total cost, the general accountant can now distribute this total cost to user profit centers on some equitable basis.

Allocations of cost conflicts with the responsibility concept. As the basis of allocation gets farther from direct use and closer to a generalized basis such as value added or total sales, the greater the conflict. If profit must be reported for the center, costs must be allocated. There is merit, however, in considering not reporting profit on a fully allocated basis but in reporting profit contribution by profit center, leaving general and administration expenses to be reported in total only with the sum of the several profit contributions. This focuses attention where it belongs:

1. On profit contribution by plant. Product is manufactured and sold from the plant. Direct labor, material, and plant overhead are direct costs of those sales. The balance is that plant's contribution to division profit.
2. On the total cost of general and administration expenses. When allocated across the division, there is no emphasis on the magnitude of this cost. When subtracted in total from total contribution, the message is clear.

Exhibits 5 and 6 illustrate the difference. In Exhibit 5, it is impossible to evaluate the plant performance without careful scrutiny of the report. By doing some side calculations, you can discover that Plant A's performance is not nearly as good as Plant C's.

In Exhibit 6, this is clear immediately. Furthermore, it is strikingly clear that G & A costs were $441,000 in the period. The cost is 91% as great as plant term costs, an indication where future cost reduction efforts might be concentrated.

EXHIBIT 4

TREND VARIANCE REPORT

| PERIOD VARIANCE REPORT | COPIES TO: DEPT. HEAD | FROM: GENERAL ACCOUNTING | DEPT. Order/Billing |

ITEM	BUDGET			ACTUAL EXPENSE PER PERIOD													GRAND TOTAL ACTUAL	TOTAL VARIANCE
	$/YEAR	5 WK PERIOD	4 WK PERIOD	#1 (5 WEEKS)	#2	#3	#4 (5 WEEKS)	#5	#6	#7 (5 WEEKS)	#8	#9	#10 (5 WEEKS)	#11	#12	#13 ADJ.		
SALARIES	96208	9076	7261	7995	6393	6396	8276	6688	7118	8909	7104							
LABOR OVERHEAD	6844	550	442	550	442	442	550	461	461	516	461							
OPERATING MATERIAL	1130	107	85	1	11	1	1	10	—	230	8							
FORMS & SUPPLIES	10419	984	787	2419	890	698	1533	1552	683	752	436							
RENT & DEPRECIATION	23587	2226	1781	2226	1781	1781	2401	1921	1921	2401	1921							
ALL OTHER EXPENSE	—	—	—	164	353	163	50	—	27	—	411							
GRAND TOTAL	137208	12945	10356	13264	9670	9370	12810	10632	10210	12863	10377							
VARIANCE THIS PERIOD (OVER) UNDER BUDGET				(309)	686	986	135	(276)	146	82	(21)							
CUMULATIVE VARIANCE (OVER) UNDER BUDGET				(309)	377	1363	1478	1222	1368	1450	1429							

EXHIBIT 5

FULLY ALLOCATED COST P & L

	Division Total	Plant A	Plant B	Plant C	Plant D	Services	Selling	Admin.
Customer	2890	390	300	1200	1000			
Less: Customer Returns and Allowances	165	5	—	10	150			
Inter Division	350	300	50	—	—			
Total Net Sales	**3405**	**695**	**350**	**1210**	**1150**			
Salaries	401	15	15	30	40	10	130	161
Wages	314	39	35	70	150	20	—	—
Labor Overhead	32	4	4	7	15	2	—	—
Operating Materials	118	10	10	20	30	48	—	—
Rents and Royalties	35	5	—	—	10	—	20	—
All Other Expense	95	10	10	10	15	—	30	20
Power, Coal, Oil and Gas	60	10	10	20	20	—	—	—
Depreciation — Straight Line	255	20	25	130	80	—	—	—
Insurance and Taxes	35	2	3	20	10	—	—	—
Distributed Services, Selling & Admin.	—	80	36	165	160	(80)	(180)	(181)
Total Operating Expense	**1345**	**195**	**148**	**472**	**530**			
Raw Materials Consumed	1959	467	152	740	600			
Beginning Inventory	2100	100	300	700	1000			
Total	5404	762	600	1912	2130			
Less: Ending Inventory	2100	100	300	700	1000			
Total Cost of Sales	**3304**	**662**	**300**	**1212**	**1130**			
Income from Operations	101	33	50	(2)	20			

EXHIBIT 6

PROFIT CONTRIBUTION P & L

Item	Division Total	(Memo)	Services	Selling	Admin.	Plant A	Plant B	Plant C	Plant D
Customer									
Less: Customer Returns and Allowances									
Inter Division									
Total Net Sales	3405	3405				695	350	1210	1150
Salaries	401		10	130	161	15	15	30	40
Wages	314		20			39	35	70	150
Labor Overhead	32		2			4	4	7	15
Raw Materials Consumed	1959		48			467	152	740	600
Beginning Inventory	2100			20		100	300	700	1000
Total	2100			30	20	625	506	1547	1805
Less: Ending Inventory	2100					100	300	700	1000
Total Direct Cost	xxx	2383				525	206	847	805
Profit Contribution	xxx	1022				170	144	363	345
Operating Materials	118					10	10	20	30
Rents and Royalties	35					5	—	—	10
All Other Expense	95					10	10	10	15
Power, Coal, Oil and Gas	60					10	10	20	20
Depreciation — Straight Line	255					20	25	130	80
Insurance and Taxes	35					2	3	20	10
Total Plant Term Cost	xxx	480				57	58	200	165
Plant Income from Operations	xxx	542				113	86	163	180
Less: Services, Selling & Admin. (Memo)	xxx	441	(80)	(180)	(181)	80	36	165	160
Income from Operations	101	101				33	50	(2)	20

51

In summary, responsibility accounting is a technique for emphasizing a management concept in accounting reports, for identifying results with the manager responsible for producing those results. Only through the application of this concept can the controller provide meaningful control reports for executives below the division manager level.

COST VARIANCE REPORTS

Operating executives dislike having voluminous reports sent to them once a month when their actual need is for specific information piecemeal all during the month. Further, voluminous reports can create the impression of waste simply because of the great amount of time obviously required to produce the report.

Accounting information should be requested and will be used when any one of the following four conditions is satisfied:

1. If the executive is convinced the information helps him do his job, he uses it.
    a. He may be convinced because of the presentation that the data is useful in improving his own operations.
    b. He may use the data in spite of the way it is presented to him because of his better-than-average ability to comprehend and reorient the data.
2. If the operating executive realizes that success in his job is measured by an evaluation made in terms of the accounting records, he uses the information. He may, unfortunately, spend valuable time trying to reclassify costs for a more favorable picture because of this same reason.
3. The executive may use the information because he knows his superior is going to ask him about that same information.
4. Information is used if the controller and his assistants help the operating manager fully to understand his reports.

The right way to motivate the operating executive to the most effective use of the data is to bring about its use through #2, #3, or #4. Ultimately, #1a. will develop as a consequence of #2, #3 and #4.

A once-a-period formal meeting at which each operating manager personally reports on his department can bring about a greater interest in control reports than any other single action. Presentations should be addressed to the general manager who responds with probing questions about the oral report and the written report, copies of which he also has.

Exhibit 7 is a directive used in one company by the author to formalize the meeting plan, with notable success.

EXHIBIT 7

DIRECTIVE FOR FORMAL COST MEETING

TO: Area Managers   cc: General Manager
         Department Heads

FROM: J. V. Bennett

PERIOD COST AND OBJECTIVES MEETING

The format of the Period Cost and Objectives Meeting was discussed by the General Manager and the Area Managers on Tuesday, May 8th. The following specific format was accepted for future Period Cost and Objectives Meetings and should be followed without exception.

In order to determine the proper format, the objective of the meeting had first to be stated, as follows:

> To communicate cost information upward to Division Top Management and sideways to other Department Heads. This communication is to be done by oral reports in an organized and systematic way on (1) the cause of and corrections for variances as incurred during the prior period, and (2) progress on Cost Reduction Objectives.

The format of the meeting is to be as described in the following paragraphs:

I. *Division Controller*

Report on profit dollars for the Division as a whole and for each of the profit centers. Use cumulative graphs showing actual profit versus assignment.

II. *Area Managers*

a) Period Variances. Report on total variances of the prior period using a bar graph as shown in the Exhibit attached hereto. The chart should be a trend chart for use during the full year. The base reference figures should be the average variance for the last half of last year.

Select specific variances for the oral report on the basis of Pareto's Law. Cover the three or four major items.

b) Cost Reduction. Report progress on cost reduction objectives. Refer to objectives by number, as listed in the original set of objectives for the year.

Mention only those objectives on which there is progress. This report should be verbal. Use no handouts. Assume that the listeners have the last written set of Quarterly Objectives with them.

EXHIBIT 7

DIRECTIVE FOR FORMAL COST MEETING (Cont.)

III. *Staff Department Heads*

    a) Report variances from budget. Use a bar chart to show, for each period, variances from budget.

    b) Report orally on Cost Reduction Objectives only. Use no handout.

IV. *Technical Director*

    a) Report on variances from budget and on Cost Reduction Objectives, as under III above.

    b) In addition, orally report on progress on "A" priority projects. Include only those projects which have been completed, or on which there are major bottlenecks. Use no handout.

V. *Time Schedule*

The following time schedule will be adhered to strictly:

Sequence	Presentation	Discussion
Controller	5 Minutes	
Manager Plant A	15 Minutes	5 Minutes
Manager Plant B	7 Minutes	5 Minutes
Manager Plant C	15 Minutes	5 Minutes
Technical Director	10 Minutes	5 Minutes
Staff Department Heads (2)	5 Minutes (each)	

This should result in a meeting of approximately one hour and a half.

SIGNIFICANCE OF COST VARIANCES

Exception reports are designed around the idea that only significant variances—the exceptions—will be reported. Nonsignificant items will be filtered out of the reporting system so as not to waste managers' time. The intent is desirable but the implementation requires an operational definition of "significance."

Variances have significance only in relation to management decisions. But there is, and always will be, random variation in costs. Standards are attainable over time, not all the time. Random variances are not significant variances.

The simplest rule to follow is to investigate a variance if it is greater than some fixed percentage of the standard. One might adopt the "materiality" rule of

Exhibit A (See II in Exhibit 7)

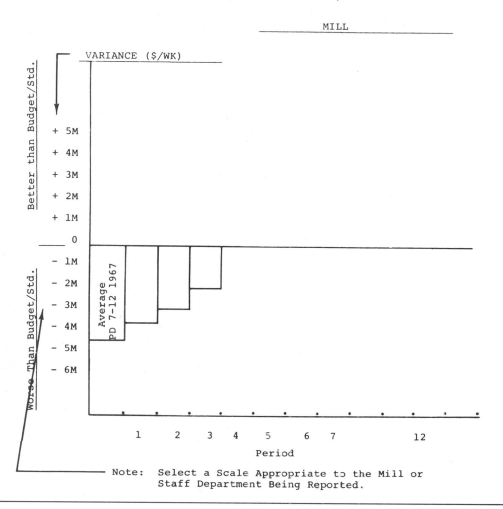

accounting and investigate if the variance exceeds, say, 10 percent of the standard cost. This would imply that it is likely that any variance that is less than 10 percent is due to random factors, in which case an investigation of the process would not yield benefits. In contrast, variances in excess of 10 percent would be nonrandom, and an investigation would lead to an elimination of future variances.

This rule implies that if a variance is less than 10 percent, the probability that the process is still in control is equal to 1.0 and the probability that the process is out of control is zero. If the variance is greater than 10 percent, the probability that the process is in control is zero.

Statistical quality control chart concepts can be applied to this significance matter. SQC is based on confidence limits (probabilities) of random variation around a standard. The random variability can be measured by the "variance," the expected value of the sum of the square deviations from the mean. The variance of the distribution of sample means is equal to the true variance divided by the sample size. Since the true variance will not be known, an estimate of the variances can be calculated as follows:

$$s^2 = \frac{\Sigma(x - \overline{x})^2}{n - 1}$$

where $\overline{x}$ is the average cost per unit, x is a specific unit cost from which $\overline{x}$ is calculated and n is the sample size.

Assuming a normal distribution around the standard cost, control limits can be set in terms of standard deviations (S) to define significance in terms of the probability of that random variance would occur where a cost variance is observed:

        Standard ± 1.0S includes 68% of random variation
           "   ±1.96S   "   95% "   "   "
           "   ±2 S   "   97% "   "   "
           "   ±3 S   "   99.7% "   "   "

There is only a 5 percent probability that a random variance will fall as far from standard as ±1.96S; hence, a variance beyond that point could be labeled significant, that is nonrandom.

To illustrate, assume a standard cost of $1.00. Assume that observations of actual costs average $1.40 per unit for a sample of a recent lot of units. Assume that we have estimated a statistical variance of the averages as $.04. What is the probability that we would observe a cost variance of $.40 or more? Specifically, if the sample averages have a statistical variance of $.04, the standard deviation (the square root of the variance) is S = $.20. Hence, the standard cost variance of $.40 is 2.0 standard deviations above the mean. The probability of observing a value 2.0 or more standard deviations above the mean of a normal distribution is less than 5 percent. This would allow a controller to conclude that the $.40 cost variance *is* truly significant.

PRIMARY VERSUS DERIVED DATA

Actual results of physical measurements on the floor are the most useful control data for the operating manager. He lives in the physical world where things happen. Most of the events he causes to happen can be counted or measured. If he is doing well, some counts will be high—total production—and some will be low—pounds of raw material wasted.

The controller who wants his reports used will include those physical measurements. If it is useful to dollarize them, he will do this, as well. But he will not subordinate direct measurements to the dollarized or otherwise derived numbers.

Negative variances will be reported in actual, not derived, numbers. If the foreman is to improve his performance, he must get out more units of production at a lower cost in a given unit of time, not "increase his efficiency." He can't "do" anything about efficiency. Efficiency is a derived number which indicates the degree to which actual manufacturing costs conformed to the standard number for the same time period. The only way he can raise efficiency is to produce more or to reduce costs. So, express the variance in those units.

Representative actual terms and often used derived units are listed below. Strive to use more actual units and less derived data. This may have another beneficial result—shorter reports. There are many more possible derivations than physical measurements!

Physical	*Derived*
Production/day (pounds, units, yards)	Machine efficiency, Quality rejects, Sales value of rejects, Standard versus actual cost/unit.
Down (loss) time	Machine efficiency, Value of excess time, Downtime efficiency.
Material cost per unit of production	Yield, Waste as percent of input, Quality rejects, Sales value of rejects, Standard versus actual cost/unit, Phantom shrinkage, Material substitution, Inventory losses, Sales value of salvaged materials.
Man hours paid	Conversion efficiency, Labor efficiency, Direct and indirect labor, Standard versus actual cost, Labor cost per unit of production, Wage rate variance, Overtime excess cost, Hours worked versus standard.
Shipments/day	Total sales value, Standard profit of shipments.

FREQUENCY OF REPORTING

Some discrimination of data to be reported at daily, weekly, and period frequencies must be established. The decision should be based on the significance and usefulness for control of the knowledge after delivery to operating management.

Each period, overall summaries of operations and cost versus budget reports are useful. Each week, summary sales and production data are useful. On a daily basis reports of major problems of the past twenty-four hours can be valuable.

A division along the following lines would be a useful point of departure around which to build your own system:

a. *Daily.* Total production. Machine downtime, if high; report unusual or major causes. Waste or rejects, if large, by category. Unusual quality problems.

b. *Weekly*. Summarize week's production. Total orders booked. Finished production. Effect on manufacturing backlog. Shipments. Effect on inventory. Mix of shipments, measured by profit contribution ratio. Average selling price. Manufacturing efficiency, overall. Trend format.

c. *Period*. P & L statement for profit centers. Manufacturing standard cost variances. Staff cost variances. Variance from forecast, assignment. Variance analysis reports, devoted to reasons, as identified through cost records. Trend format.

WORK FORCE CONTROL REPORTS

In today's economy the most costly ingredient, after direct labor and raw materials, and the least well controlled is salary cost.

Hourly costs have been studied, measured, standardized in dozens of industrial engineering techniques since Frederick W. Taylor started it in the 1880's; nothing further will be said here on that score, except that the controller should use industrial engineering data in his control reports on hourly labor costs.

One technique useful to emphasize additions as soon as they are made is the use of a monthly report, naming all additions, terminations, and transfers, and showing in trend format the effect on the number of employees. This also builds a detailed history of the work force. Only through a detailed log such as this provides can one trace back through successive years to analyze growth patterns and reasons, now long forgotten, for growth in years past.

A summary letter, Exhibit 8, names all changes for the month. Attached to the letter in Exhibit 9 is the trend data logging changes for the year. A pre-selected base and budget comparisons are shown in the letter and on the trend chart.

TREND COMPARISONS

Reference to trend reports have been made several times. Because a high or low variance in one single period is not cause for drastic action, we must know whether a particular situation is a freak or whether there is a definite tendency in the observed direction. Trend reports fill a definite need by showing several consecutive sets of actual cost data as well as standard or historical comparisions.

Exhibit 10 shows a typical period trend report of manufacturing variances. In successive columns, data from each period is entered. For ease in making comparisons, the figures are expressed as "average dollars per week"—total dollars for the period divided by the number of weeks in the period. Selected variance detail is given for items considered of major importance.

EXHIBIT 8

CHANGES IN WORK FORCE

TO: Area Managers   cc. General Manager
          Department Heads

FROM: J. V. Bennett

SALARIED WORK FORCE

The 12th Period changes are summarized in the attachments to this memorandum. Totals are as follows:

	Base 5/x3	12/x3	19x4 Budget	11/x4	12/x4
Sales	60	62	62	62	62
Non-Exempt	100	100	105	104	100
Manufacturing Exempt	63	64	62	64	62
Staff Exempt	87	90	95	95	96
Total	310	316	324	325	320

Details of the changes this period are as follows:

Sales: No change.

Non-Exempt:

Code 964	Hazel Smith retired, not replaced	—1
967	William Smith terminated	—1
967	Sue Smith terminated	—1
972	Frank Smith terminated	—1
	Difference	—4

Manufacturing Exempt:

Code 100	George Brown retired, not replaced	—1
405	James Brown retired, not replaced	—1
	Difference	—2

Service & Staff Exempt:

Code 521	William Jones hired	+1
	Difference	+1

EXHIBIT 9

TREND OF CHANGES IN WORK FORCE

			MANUFACTURING DEPARTMENTS NUMBER EXEMPT EMPLOYEES (Published by Division Controller)												DATE
RESP. CODE	DEPARTMENT	BASE NO. EMP 5/X3	BUD-GET 19x4	PERIOD											
				1	2	3	4	5	6	7	8	9	10	11	12
001	RECEIVING	3	4	4	4	4	4	4	4	4	4	4	4	4	3
002	TANK FARM	3	4	4	4	4	4	4	4	4	4	4	4	4	4
003	MELT AREA	3	2	2	2	2	3	3	3	3	3	3	3	3	3
004	CHEMICAL MIX	1	2	2	2	2	2	2	2	2	2	2	2	2	2
005	CALANDRIA	1	1	1	1	1	1	1	1	1	1	1	1	1	1
006	POLYMERIZER		1	1	1	1	1	1	1	1	1	1	1	1	1
010	SLURRY MIX	2	2	2	2	2	2	2	2	2	2	2	2	2
011	SPINNING ROOM	7	5	5	5	5	5	6	6	6	6	6	6	6	6
012	PACK MAKEUP	1	1	1	1	1	1	1	1	1	1	1	1	1	1
020	ELECTRICIAN	1	1	1	1	1	1	1	1	1	1	1	1	1	1
021	MECHANIC	1	1	1	1	1	1	1	1	1	1	1	1	1	1
022	INSTRUMENT	3	3	3	3	3	3	3	3	3	3	3	3	3	3
023	RECOVERY	-0-	0	0	0	0	0	0	0	0	0	0	0	0	0
024	TOW TESTING	1	1	1	1	1	1	1	1	1	1	1	1	1	1
025	SPINNERET REPAIR	1	1	1	1	1	1	1	1	1	1	1	1	1	1
030	YARN GENERAL	2	2	2	2	2	2	2	2	2	2	2	2	2	2
040	STAPLE GENERAL	1	3	3	3	3	3	3	3	3	3	3	3	3	3
031	DRAW-WIND	4	2	2	2	2	2	2	2	2	2	2	2	2	2
032	DRAW-TWIST	-0-	6	6	5	5	5	5	5	5	5	5	6	6	6
041	STAPLE CUTTING	5	0	0	0	0	0	0	0	0	0	0	0	0	0
042	BALING	-0-	0	0	0	0	0	0	0	0	0	0	0	0	0
033	YARN INSPECTION	5	6	6	5	5	6	6	6	6	6	6	6	6	5
034	HUMIDITY CONTROL	-0-	0	0	0	0	0	0	0	0	0	0	0	0	0
035	YARN PACKING	4	3	3	3	3	3	3	3	3	3	3	3	3	3
050	TRAFFIC	1	2	2	2	2	2	2	2	2	2	2	2	2	2
051	SHIPPING	6	5	7	7	7	7	7	6	6	6	6	6	6	6
060	YARD GANG	5	5	5	1	1	1	1	1	1	1	1	1	1	1

EXHIBIT 10

SALES AND MANUFACTURING SUMMARY

		SALES & MANUFACTURING SUMMARY		Mill *PLANT A*			
		☐ Weekly ☒ Period		*9th* Period 19*XX*			

OPERATING STATISTICS

ITEM		7th Period	8th Period	9th Period	10th Period	11th Period	12th Period	First Half Yr.
Days Run	A	5.1	5.3	5.0				5.7
Days Down-Lack of Bus.	B	1.9	1.7	2.0				1.3
Orders Booked	C	63	50	73				79
Finished	D	59	65	72				79
Shipped	E	52	62	64				79

PROFIT PROJECTION

		7th Period	8th Period	9th Period	10th Period	11th Period	12th Period	First Half Yr.
Net Sales Value	F	27.1	39.2	58.7				58.2
Sales Value/Ton	G	522	634	918				740
Mfg. Ret. & allow. (Memo)	H	(2.2)	(0.2)	(0.3)				(0.7)
Sales Ret. & allow. (Memo)	I	—	—	—				—
Standard Material	J	(13.8)	(20.1)	(30.4)				(28.8)
Standard Direct Cost	K	(2.7)	(4.2)	(5.7)				(6.3)
Standard P.C.	L	10.6	14.9	22.6				23.1
Std. P.C. as % of Net Sales	M	39.1%	38.0%	38.5%				39.7%
Material Variance	N	(3.2)	0.4	1.6				(0.1)
Direct Cost Variance	O	(1.4)	0.9	1.0				0.5
Actual P.C.	P	6.0	16.6	25.2				23.5
Term Cost — Budgeted	Q	(12.7)	(13.5)	(15.0)				(16.6)
Adjustments	R	(1.7)	(3.8)	(1.2)				(0.6)
	S							
IFO	T	(8.4)	(1.1)	9.0				6.2

VARIANCE DETAIL

			7th Period	8th Period	9th Period	10th Period	11th Period	12th Period	First Half Yr.
MAT'L USAGE	Waste Substitution	1	824	(137)	224				326
	P.M. Waste	2	(318)	(72)	1158				1121
	Shrinkage	3	(2340)	138	574				(781)
	Other	4	554	409	(1319				2
		5							
	Total	6							
QUALITY	Fin. Waste	7	(1280)	338	637				668
	Rejects	8	9	(367)	—				(105)
	Gain on Class 3-Mat.	9	(264)	(418)	(1198)				(151)
		10	682	238	769				159
		11							
		12							
	Total	13							
EFF.	Prime Machine Eff'y	14	427	(547)	(429)				(97)
	Finishing Efficiency	15	(890)	480	719				257
		16	(41)	(10)	(23)				33
	Total	17	(931)	470	606				290

Important factors in the 9th Period are:

a. Net sales value is adequate (versus First Half) after two low periods.
b. Sales value per ton is high versus prior periods. Sales value is up $19,500 on only two more tons. Material costs, however, chewed up the gain. Standard profit contribution is up only 0.5%. Variances total $2,600 positive much better than 7th or 8th Periods—is there a trend?
c. Quality loss ($1,198) is the remaining loss variance. Paper machine waste and efficiency show large positive variances this period. Both show a three period favorable trend; this should be studied in detail to identify causes for longer-term use.

Graphic presentations of trends are even more desirable if they can be reproduced economically. The graph in Exhibit 11 is made on a Xerox master and is reused each period. It shows the Plant A Income from Operations actual versus assignment for the year. This is a cumulative chart but the effects of Periods 7, 8, and 9 are clearly visible.

Quick reference to the chart shows that:

a. The assignment is $312,000.
b. Plant A started out well, moving ahead of the assignment rate for five periods.

EXHIBIT 11
TREND FOR PLANT A PRODUCTS

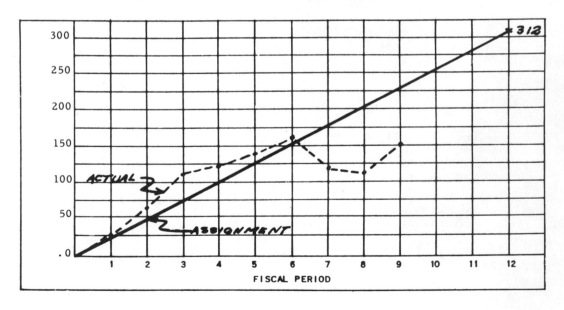

c. In the 6th Period profits leveled out to be almost equal to the assignment rate, as shown by the almost parallel lines.

d. Profits dipped significantly in the 7th and 8th Periods and rose in the 9th. The 7th Period drop was so pronounced that it completely offset earlier gains, causing the actual line to drop below the assignment; this is a valuable index of the severity of the drop.

e. Extrapolation of the current (9 Periods) rate shows that the assignment will not be met unless positive action is taken. If a line is drawn from zero through the 9th period, $151,000, it will indicate only $200,000 for the year versus the assignment of $312,000.

DEVIATION FROM PROFIT PLAN

Every profit center should be given a profit assignment. It should be required to develop a profit plan, as described in Chapter 9, Profit Planning.

Period reports of deviation from plan, by category, are necessary if the plan is to mean anything as a control tool.

Plant A has an assignment to make $312,000 profit this year. To accomplish this, the profit plan calls for sales and costs as shown below. Actual performance to the 9th Period is also shown below:

Profit Plan—Plant A

	Per Year	4 Weeks
Sales	$3,155 M	$ 243 M
Standard Profit Contribution %	39.7%	39.7%
Standard Profit Contribution	1,252 M	96.5 M
Term Costs	(890)M	(68.5)M
Manufacturing Variances	(50)M	(4.0)M
Profit	$ 312 M	24.0 M

Plant A—Actual 9th Period

	4 Week Period	Average/ Week
Sales	S 234,800	$ 58.7 M
Standard Profit Contribution %	38.5%	38.5%
Standard Profit Contribution	90,000	22.6 M
Term Costs	64,800	16.2 M
Variances	10,400	2.6 M
Profit	S 36,000	$ 9.0 M

Deviations from assignment by category must be calculated and reported. Sales and % P.C. (mix) are the responsibility of the Sales Department, while term costs and variances are manufacturing's responsibility; it is important to identify who is responsible. It can be done like this:

	Assigned	Actual	Difference	Effect on Profit
Assigned Profit				$24.0 M
Sales: Volume	243	234.8	$(8.2) \times 39.7\% =$	(3.3)M
Mix (P.C.%)	39.7%	38.5%	$(1.2)\% \times 234.8 =$	(2.8)M
				$17.9 M
Manufacturing:				
Term Costs	(68.5)	(64.8)		3.7 M
Variances	(4.0)	10.4		14.4 M
Actual Profit				$36.0 M

This information can be reported on an each-period basis and on a year-to-date basis to pinpoint current and cumulative responsibility for falling behind assignment. For the 9th Period, it is clear that Sales fell down on the job while Manufacturing was doing better than assignment, resulting in a net gain on assignment. A similar year-to-date comparison can be calculated as follows:

	Assigned Profit	EFFECT ON PROFIT				Actual Profit
		Volume	Mix	Variances	Term Costs	
Plant A 9th Period	24.0	(3.3)	(2.8)	14.4	3.7	36.0
Year-to-Date	234	(130)	(10)	18	39	151

Both of these displays coupled with the trend charts from Exhibits 10 and 11 make a powerful tool to display in quick summary the impact of performance versus assignment, as shown in Exhibit 12.

EXHIBIT 12

MANUFACTURING CONTROL REPORT

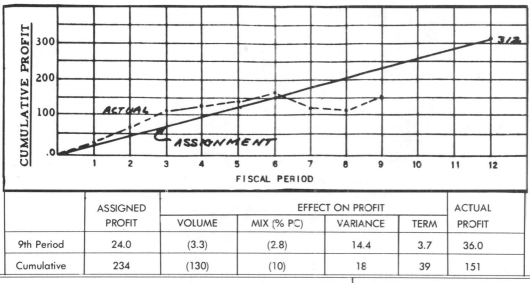

	ASSIGNED PROFIT	EFFECT ON PROFIT				ACTUAL PROFIT
		VOLUME	MIX (% PC)	VARIANCE	TERM	
9th Period	24.0	(3.3)	(2.8)	14.4	3.7	36.0
Cumulative	234	(130)	(10)	18	39	151

SALES & MANUFACTURING SUMMARY	Mill	
☐ Weekly ☐ Period	Period	19

ITEM		7th Period	8th Period	9th Period	10th Period	11th Period	12th Period	First Half Yr.
OPERATING STATISTICS								
Days Run	A	5.1	5.3	5.0				5.7
Days Down-Lack of Bus.	B	1.9	1.7	2.0				1.3
Orders Booked	C	63	50	73				79
Finished	D	59	65	72				79
Shipped	E	52	62	64				79
PROFIT PROJECTION								
Net Sales Value	F	27.1	39.2	58.7				58.2
Sales Value/Ton	G	522	634	918				740
Mfg. Ret. & allow. (Memo)	H	(2.2)	(0.2)	(0.3)				(0.7)
SalesRet. Hallow.(Memo)	I	—	—	—				
Standard Material	J	(13.8)	(20.1)	(30.4)				(28.8)
Standard Direct Cost	K	(2.7)	(4.2)	(5.7)				(6.3)
Standard P.C.	L	10.6	14.9	22.6				23.1
Std. P.C. as % of Net Sales	M	39.1%	38.0%	38.5%				39.7%
Material Variance	N	(3.2)	0.4	1.6				(0.1)
Direct Cost Variance	O	(1.4)	0.9	1.0				0.5
Actual P.C.	P	6.0	16.6	25.2				23.5
Term Cost — Budgeted	Q	(12.7)	(13.5)	(15.0)				(16.6)
Adjustments	R	(1.7)	(3.8)	(1.2)				(0.6)
	S							
IFO	T	(8.4)	(1.1)	9.0				6.2

3

Cost Control Within the
Control Function

If he is to be respected as one who is competent in his field of control, the controller must have a reputation for, and a history of, success, particularly in his own department. Nothing is so damaging to his reputation as the discovery of gross carelessness or waste within the controller's organization.

This subject is overlooked in most of the literature. Perhaps it is considered so obvious as to need no specific comment. In this case, because the need *is* so obvious and because other than conventional techniques can be applied, a specific chapter is devoted to the several aspects of control within the controller's department.

TIME—THE RAW MATERIAL OF CONTROL

Time is to the controller what raw materials are to the operating manager.

The value of his output is a function of the waste/yield ratio of his input material.

As controller, you must effectively utilize your own time. There is too much to be done to waste time in other people's work. This is the value of the completed staff work concept. However, application of that concept requires decisions on what to delegate. Another valuable concept, called by Colin Coffee of Management Development Associates "The Principle of Calculated Neglect," can be applied to this decision-making process.

The Principle of Calculated Neglect is built on Pareto's Law which says that a small proportion of events account for the largest portion of the results. In Chapter 8 this is discussed in some detail. This law applies to your time: 20 percent of your tasks account for 80 percent of your value to your employer. These must be identified and must receive your best effort. The other 80 percent of your tasks account for only 20 percent of your value. If some of these 80 percent of your tasks are *neglected* selectively in order to improve on the top 20 percent, little if any loss will have been suffered.

An A-B-C analysis of your time will help in this identification. To solve a problem, you must first define it. To improve on your time utilization, you must first know how you spend your time. While your secretary could work-sample your time or log your activities, it is far better to log them yourself. You must summarize and analyze the results. This will be more meaningful if you have recorded the data in the first place.

Resolve to record at least two weeks of activities. A shorter sample is too easily biased by single influences such as special meetings or trips. A suggested log sheet for recording, in 15-minute chunks, an entire day on one sheet is shown in Exhibit 13. This may be good enough even though a bare minimum of explanatory information can be recorded. These log sheets are better suited for analyses of clerical and supervisory positions. A better executive time analysis can be made from a day's accumulation of episode (event) sheets, illustrated in Exhibit 14. One sheet is filled out for *each* episode in sequence during the entire day. Appropriate descriptive data can be checked or written on each sheet to fully describe the episode. Critical analysis of these sheets can yield such information as:

a. Too many episodes. Each one is too short to be productive. A reasonable number, including 30-second phone calls, is forty to fifty a day. Even this number means an *average* of about 10 minutes per episode.

b. Excessive phone calls scattered over the entire day. The phone can be an intolerable tyrant when calls continuously interrupt. Have your secretary take the caller's message or number for a return call so that you can have *some* uninterrupted time for thought.

c. Too many short, incoming calls. You are being used as an information center.

d. There are few upward contacts initiated by your subordinates. All the arrows lead from you to them. Communication should be a two-way street. Are you accessible?

e. Certain subordinates receive very little of your time. Are important areas being ignored or is this an example of calculated neglect?

Having summarized the activity, attention now must be given to the A-B-C items, for delegation. A workable definition of A-B-C for classification as you go is:

A—Items which only you have the knowledge to do or
which you do for security reasons.
B—Items which your immediate subordinate can do
about as well as you.
C—Items which a subordinate two or more levels down
can do satisfactorily.

EXHIBIT 13

DAILY WORK LOG

PAPER CORP. SPECIALTY PRODUCTS DIV. DAILY WORK LOG																					DATE DEPT. SECTION NAME			REMARKS
8:00 - 8:15																								
8:15 - 8:30																								
8:30 - 8:45																								
8:45 - 9:00																								
9:00 - 9:15																								
9:15 - 9:30																								
9:30 - 9:45																								
9:45 - 10:00																								
10:00 - 10:15																								
10:15 - 10:30																								
10:30 - 10:45																								
10:45 - 11:00																								
11:00 - 11:15																								
11:15 - 11:30																								
11:30 - 11:45																								
11:45 - 12:00																								
12:00 - 12:15																								
12:15 - 12:30																								
12:30 - 12:45																								
12:45 - 1:00																								
1:00 - 1:15																								
1:15 - 1:30																								
1:30 - 1:45																								
1:45 - 2:00																								
2:00 - 2:15																								
2:15 - 2:30																								
2:30 - 2:45																								
2:45 - 3:00																								
3:00 - 3:15																								
3:15 - 3:30																								
3:30 - 3:45																								
3:45 - 4:00																								
4:00 - 4:15																								
4:15 - 4:30																								
4:30 - 4:45																								
4:45 - 5:00																								
TOTALS																								

EXHIBIT 14

EPISODE ANALYSIS LOG

NAME	EPISODE ANALYSIS	DATE

WHEN?

Started _____ Stopped _____

Interrupted _____

WHERE?
- [ ] my office
- [ ] _____ 's office
- [ ] on the floor
- [ ] out of the office
- [ ] _____
- [ ] _____

WHAT WAS TRANSMITTED?
- [ ] information
- [ ] instruction
- [ ] request
- [ ] plans
- [ ] decisions
- [ ] _____

FROM WHOM TO WHOM?

_____

Sups.

_____   _____

- - - - - - - - - - - - - - - - - -

_____   _____

_____ (You) _____

_____   _____

- - - - - - - - - - - - - - - - - -

_____   _____

Subs.

_____

WHAT KIND OF ACTIVITY?
- [ ] talk
- [ ] phone
- [ ] meeting
- [ ] reading
- [ ] writing
- [ ] dictating
- [ ] listening
- [ ] thinking alone
- [ ] observing or inspecting
- [ ] doing

WHAT SUBJECT?

HOW IMPORTANT?
- [ ] A item
- [ ] B item
- [ ] C item

If you have more "A" items than you have time for, and no "B" or "C" items, you either have neglected to train your subordinates or you are mis-classifying activities.

There is a pattern, obviously, which helps delegation; B and C items should be delegated. Your B items should become your subordinate's A items. His B's are passed down as A items. At the lowest level, some C items are left undone because more important work is done. This is "calculated neglect" at its best!

Time utilization must be carried down the line if this pattern is to be implemented. It is no good for you to delegate your B items to someone who already has and keeps a full load. If he doesn't carry through the same idea, he probably also will not work on A and B items, neglecting C items. Unless he has analyzed himself, he probably does not recognize those kinds of differences in his tasks.

From this same scheme, one more useful concept has been defined. As you move up the ladder of progression, yesterday's A items become today's B items. You can handle the B items in a breeze; the A ones are newer and tougher. A big time and effort waster springs from the fact that, since people are comfortable with things they can do well, they "retreat to the familiar" in times of stress. If an A item is just too tough, one can retreat from it to a cozy B item and continue to be "productive" even though the more important problem waits unattended.

When the number of items to be done grows too long, keeping track of the A items can become difficult. Remember, it *is* the A items you want to keep in mind.

As new items come up, jot them down on a piece of paper. As items are completed, cross them off the list. Immediately, decide which are A items and which are B or C. Note the list accordingly. Alongside the B and C items, note the name of the person to whom the task is delegated.

Start each day by looking over your list of A items. Decide which are to be completed that day. List them in order of priority on a new "One at a Time List" illustrated in Exhibit 15. Date the card. Put the card in your shirt pocket and refer to it as each task is completed. Cross off the completed item and decide on the next one to be tackled. During the day, if new high priority A items come up, add them to the list immediately, revising the priority assignment accordingly.

COMPLETED STAFF WORK

Effective use of subordinates must include the requirement that every subordinate does his job fully, completely, entirely. His job must include the responsibility to exercise independent judgement and make decisions. The executive who lets his subordinates force him to make all the decisions will suffer acute frustration over his inability to free himself from the mass of detail constantly coming over his desk. An executive's productivity is the result of the quality and quantity of his decisions. If he spends his time on minor league decision-making, he will be a minor league manager.

The controller must force his subordinates, *his* staff, to do the complete job. General A. L. Learch (publication unknown) is credited with having described

EXHIBIT 15

ONE AT A TIME LIST

Day		Date	

the concept of "completed staff work." This is the only *real* solution to the problem of effective delegation. Delegation of decision-making is the requisite above. Staff assistants are not supposed to be merely additional sets of arms and legs. A head comes with every set of limbs. Completed staff work requires that the head be thoroughly exercised, as described below.

Completed staff work is the study of a problem and presentation of a solution, by a staff officer, in such form that all that remains to be done on the part of the head of the staff division, or the commander, is to indicate his approval or disapproval of the completed action. The words "completed action" are emphasized because the more difficult the problem is, the greater is the tendency to present the problem to the chief in piecemeal fashion. It is your duty as a staff officer to work out the details. You should not consult your chief in the determination of those details, no matter how perplexing they may be. You may and should consult other staff officers. The product, whether it involves the pronouncement of a new policy or affects an established one, should, when presented to the chief for approval or disapproval, be worked out in finished form.

The impulse which often comes to the inexperienced staff officer to ask the chief what to do, recurs more often when the problem is difficult. It is accompanied by a feeling of mental frustration. It is so easy to ask the chief what to do, and it appears so easy for him to answer. Resist that impulse! You will succumb to it only if you do not know your job. It is your job to advise your chief what he ought to do, not to ask him what you ought to do. He needs answers, not questions. Your job is to study, write, restudy, and rewrite until you have evolved a single proposed action—the best one of all those you have considered.

The theory of completed staff work does not preclude a "rough draft" but the rough draft must not be a half-baked idea. It must be complete in every respect except that it lacks the requisite number of copies and need not be neat. But a rough draft must not be used as an excuse for shifting to the chief the burden of formulating the action.

The completed staff work theory may result in more work for the staff officer, but it results in more freedom for the chief. This is as it should be. Further, it accomplishes two things:

1. The chief is protected from half-baked ideas, voluminous memoranda, and immature oral presentations.
2. The staff officer who has a real idea to sell is enabled more readily to find a market.

When you have finished your "completed staff work" the final test is this:

If you were the chief, would you be willing to sign the paper you have prepared and stake your professional reputation on its being right?

If the answer is in the negative, take it back and work it over because it is not yet completed staff work.

To get completed staff work throughout your department requires leadership. Quoting the foregoing paragraphs in a directive won't do it. Face-to-face discussions with each, and then all, of your staff assistants will get you off to the right start. This is a very simple concept, almost too simple. That very fact may cause your people to miss the profound implications. Completed staff work must become standard procedure. When it isn't delivered, you must reject the effort as insufficient. When a poor job is accepted, you've lowered the floodgates to a lower standard of performance. On the other hand, recognize those who do perform at the highest levels of excellence. Use their example to upgrade lower performers.

This really puts most managers on both ends of the stick. Most of us are staff to our superior as well as chief to our subordinates. Apply the completed staff work concept to your own staff work as well as to that of your subordinates.

The completed staff work concept requires pre-planning and leadership of the manager in assigning/delegating problems to his staff:

1. Define the problem clearly, concisely, unambiguously. If this cannot be done, it cannot be delegated. How would you know that your subordinate is working on the right problem?
2. Give the assignment to one man. Be sure he knows what the assignment is. Be sure that he knows the assignment is his. Tell him what you want done. Is it just information? A recommendation? Several alternative choices of action? Or action with an information report after the action has been completed?
3. Contribute your experience. There is no gain in having him spend time discovering for himself what you already know.
4. Set a target completion date. Accept progress reports. Be alert to misdirected effort, a change in problem definition, or lack of progress.
5. Refuse to do the thinking for your staff. It is their job to furnish proposed solutions or to take action. Your job is to accept or reject their solutions, not to help them find solutions to propose to you.

It has been said: you can either teach your staff to deliver completed staff work or you can develop ulcers doing everyone's job yourself. Both require considerable energy. But management is much more pleasant with completed staff work.

PROJECT MANAGEMENT-BY-ACTION

Follow-up is necessary to insure completion and steady progress on assignments that require several weeks to analyze and complete. A technique called the "Case System" permits your secretary to take care of all of the mechanics of follow-up in a routine manner.

In the Case System, each project assigned to an individual is given a specific case assignment number and is assigned in writing. The case assignment includes the name of the project, the objectives of the project, and sometimes a statement concerning the techniques to be used in the solution of the project.

The original assignment should be made on a ditto master, listing the objectives of the project at the top of the page. Enough copies are to be made to give the person to whom the project was assigned worksheets for all required status reports. The advantage of this is that the original objective is displayed for the writer and for the reader on each status report, facilitating review of progress toward completion.

Periodically, during the life of the project, the person to whom the project is assigned submits a written status report. In this report he gives a brief statement of his progress, his accomplishments, and any difficulties which he has encountered during the week. The purpose of the status report is to inform the supervisor of the current status of every project, to indicate to him those areas wherein an individual is having trouble, and to require the persons to whom projects are assigned to routinely review their progress toward completion of all assigned projects. In addition, the status reports give a chronological history of the project for future reference.

Upon completion of the project, a closing report is written. This closing report restates the original objectives, states which of the objectives were accomplished and which were not, and summarizes the results of the project.

Your secretary can monitor progress for you by sending out status reports when due in lieu of depending on each man to send in reports on time.

As each case assignment is made, a file folder is prepared for the new case number. A copy of the assignment sheet goes into the file. All interim status reports go into the file. On completion of the project, all working papers and correspondence relating to the project go into the same file with the closing report. This gives a complete story in one location of all work done on the project and the results obtained.

Cases are indexed by subject, by case number (by year), and by the individual to whom the case is assigned. These three cross-indexes permit reference to a case in any way desired. One can review all of the cases assigned to any particular individual to determine the number open, the number completed, etc. Or, if it is desired to find out what has been done on a particular subject in past projects, the subject file will permit one to find that information. The chronological index by case number is useful in determining whether a particular case is pertinent to some particular point of interest when only the case number is known (from a piece of correspondence) after the case has been completed.

Exhibits 16 and 17 illustrate the front and back of a case report form. This includes all information pertinent to assigning or reporting a case. Exhibit 18 illustrates a closing report in full.

SELECTION OF ASSISTANTS TO YIELD SYNERGY

One of the most important ways in which a division controller can more effectively utilize his time is through the proper selection and training of his subordinates.

The division controller should be a planner. He should be an innovator. He should paint with a broad brush. He should not have to spend time in detailed calculation and clerical work. He should not have to spend time in day-to-day

EXHIBIT 16

CASE REPORT FORM

CASE REPORT	REPORTING PERIOD	DATE OPENED	ASSIGNMENT ☐	FILE NO.
	WEEKLY ☐	DATE SCHEDULED	INTERIM RPT ☐	
	MONTHLY ☐			
	QUARTERLY ☐	DATE CLOSED	FINAL RPT ☐	
ASSIGNOR:	ASSIGNEE:		DEPARTMENT	

SEE OTHER SIDE FOR INSTRUCTIONS

ITEM DESCRIPTION   A

OBJECTIVE WHAT RESULTS ARE WANTED?   B

ACTUAL ACCOMPLISHMENTS E   WHAT WAS DONE THIS REPORTING PERIOD   C

FUTURE ACTION RECOMMENDED OR PLANNED F   WHAT OBSTACLES WERE MET   D

EXHIBIT 17

REVERSE OF CASE REPORT FORM

INSTRUCTIONS: Assignor: 1. Complete heading and items A and B on copy master. Send copies to assignee (one for each "reporting period") and to your supervisor. Retain master.

Assignee: 2. Each "reporting period" fill in items C and D on one copy and forward to assignor.

3. When case is complete fill in items E and F and forward to assignor along with work papers.

Assignor: 4. Each "reporting period" evaluate progress toward objective with respect to accomplishments and to time schedule. Discuss with assignee when indicated by progress.

5. When case is complete review items E and F, rewrite if needed, have typed on master and distribute (minimum) to your supervisor, assignee, and in the closed case file along with work papers. Destroy interim reports if covered by final report.

All: Check block marked assignment, interim report, or final report as pertinent. Do not check on master except for final report.

EXHIBIT 18

FINAL (CLOSING) CASE REPORT

CASE REPORT	REPORTING PERIOD		DATE OPENED Feb. 28, 19XX	ASSIGNMENT ☐	FILE NO.
	WEEKLY	☒	DATE SCHEDULED March 28, 19XX	INTERIM RPT ☐	61-93
	MONTHLY	☐	DATE CLOSED March 18, 19XX		
ASSIGNOR: A. Smith	QUARTERLY	☐		FINAL RPT ☒	
	ASSIGNEE: L. Cass			DEPARTMENT Controller's	

SEE OTHER SIDE FOR INSTRUCTIONS

A — ITEM DESCRIPTION

B — OBJECTIVE — WHAT RESULTS ARE WANTED?

E C — ACTUAL ACCOMPLISHMENTS — WHAT WAS DONE THIS REPORTING PERIOD

F D — FUTURE ACTION RECOMMENDED OR PLANNED — WHAT OBSTACLES WERE MET

A.   INTIATE PREVENTATIVE MAINTENANCE PROGRAM FOR
      DICTATION EQUIPMENT IN YOUR DEPARTMENT.

B.   1) This program should include testing machines on a routine
            basis.

      2) The purpose of this program is to reduce downtime at peak
            periods and to reduce the chance of processing reports on a
            malfunctioning piece of equipment.

E.   1) This program has been set up with IBM. Only the routine
            scheduling of preventative maintenance work by IBM needs
            to be finalized.

      2) The CENTRAL UNIT has been replaced twice. The first
            replacement had more downtime than the original. The
            second replacement was thoroughly tested in the IBM
            Office before installation.

      3) This maintenance program has already uncovered faulty
            machines before the defect caused incorrect reports and/or
            excessive downtime.

supervisory problems. He should not have to detail exact operating procedures for his subordinates.

In order for him to operate thus, his top-level assistants must be capable of carrying out their assigned duties with the minimum of supervision. They must be innovators and planners in their own right. While the relative proportion of their time spent on planning and innovating should be less than his, nevertheless there should be a relatively high level of capability. Synergism will be the result.

The division controller's replacement should normally come from this echelon. Therefore, the training the people at that level are given is important in the career planning of the division controller as well as in their own career planning. There should always be a logical replacement for every person in the organization, either ready or soon to be ready. This requires that the division controller recognize, select in his own line, and train through proper duty assignments, his replacement. If there are two or more logical contenders for this particular replacement, it is better for them, better for the organization, and better for the division controller that people look upon each other as competitors for any future vacancy. This will result in greater incentive to them to do a better job, to learn more, to grow in their own jobs. The spirit of competition can take over and spur them on to greater accomplishments than they would otherwise reach. In this area, office politics can be dangerous both to the men in training and to the division controller. Individual competition should not be allowed to degenerate into petty political warfare. There are rather obvious clues to this which will be immediately apparent if the controller is alert to the possibility.

Further, in the selection of subordinates there is a category of assistants who may be labeled "staff assistants." It is important in the selection of these people that the controller select only those who complement his own individual talents. A common error is to select people who are similar in background, training, and approach to problems. This results in merely a duplication of the same fundamental talents at different levels in the organization, and, therefore, with different levels of experience. Staff assistants can be immensely more useful if their talents are complementary to those of the division controller. This brings to a problem different outlooks, different ideas, different solutions, and different backgrounds.

These specialized staff assistants are found to an increasingly great degree. Staff assistants can concentrate their knowledge on specific projects for the division controller and thereby provide valuable advisory assistance to him. But, the assignment of too many staff assistants and others reporting directly to the division controller can result in the addition of too much routine to his own job, suppressing creativity in favor of supervision and control of routine. If this comes about, the division controller has defeated his original purposes in selecting the staff assistants.

An additional facet to the problem of selection and training is that of replacement in depth. It is not sufficient to have one or two capable replacements at the top level in the organization. There should be selected, and in training, replacements at several levels down through the organization. In this day and time the professional work force is highly mobile. The classified ads of the newspapers every week contain interesting job opportunity advertisements. There is no way of guaranteeing at what time any individual manager at any particular level of professional accomplishment might decide the grass is greener on the other side of the fence and leave your employ. To the extent that it is economically possible, there should be backups in training for this eventuality. It is true, of course, that replacements could be selected by the same technique: advertise and hire from the outside. The trouble with this is that the man coming in from the outside is an unknown quantity insofar as his professional quality is concerned, is probably less exerienced than the man you lost, doesn't know his way around your organization at all, and perhaps does not know the industry. Better to promote from within. You will know the quality of his work and he will know his way around your organization. All he needs is greater experience.

EFFECTIVE USE OF SUBORDINATES

The controller, personally, does very little actual control work. This is the job for which his staff exists. For this reason, the controller must have an adequate staff in quality and size. It is misplaced effort to reduce the staff for dollar savings directly to the extent that division-wide analysis and control suffers. The 2:1 ratio can easily be bettered by an effective staff. Quality, of course, must be high. The controller should not shelter marginal employees in his department. This is unfair to everyone. The employee knows he is below par and fears eventually being caught up with. Costs are too high. Others dependent on this staff for direction and help get inadequate service. Given adequate quality and quantity, the contoller then has the responsibility of utilizing this staff to the optimum.

The first thing to do is to insure that everyone knows the content, scope, and limits of his job. Job descriptions for major posts are necessary for clear definition. This is particularly true with functional organizations where physical duties are clear-cut, but where responsibilities for corrective action or follow-up may be less clear. For clerical positions, procedural manuals for each job, including detailed job instructions, are preferable to mere job descriptions. Exhibit 19 is an example of the minimum job description content.

Having defined the job itself, the controller must establish an avenue of communication for the routine review of performance of his subordinates from the top to the bottom of his organization. You should start with the basic premise:

**Every person, in his heart, wants to do a
good job and to be recognized as doing so.**

This truism may be rejected by the cynic, but the rejection does not change the truth of it. While there may be surface bitterness, apathy, or indolence, there is within every man the spark of enthusiasm. It is the manager's job to kindle a flame from the spark.

Let your people know what you think they do well and how they should improve. They will try to guess, anyway, and will act on those guesses. How much better it will be when they know what you think!

EXHIBIT 19

JOB DESCRIPTION

CONTROLLER'S DEPARTMENT

Date: October 15, 19_

Job Title: General Accountant—Junior
Name of Person Now Holding Job:
Title of Person to Whom He Reports: General Accountant
Name of Person to Whom He Reports:
Description of Job:

General—

To learn all duties of General Accounting pertaining to Financial Statements, General and Operating Ledgers, Account Analyses, Period Reports, and other miscellaneous work. Under direct supervision of the General Accountant, do the following specific functions:

1. Be familiar with Accounting System as to where information is originated, how it is processed, and where and when it is recorded in ledgers.
2. Know all General and Operating Ledger accounts by name and account number. Know what they contain.
3. Make all Standard and General Journal entries. Know significance of entries.
4. Prepare all Financial Statements required by Corporate Accounting. Release statements after approval by the Division Controller.
   a. Expense Schedules 2, 2B, 3—Collect all expenses by responsibility; distribute Service Department; know basis for such distribution; test expenses for reasonableness versus budget and last period.
   b. Profit & Loss Schedule.
   c. Trial Balance—Take Trial Balance to see that accounts are in balance.
   d. Analysis—Breakdown of all balances to be sure postings have been made correctly.

PLANNED PERFORMANCE REVIEW

Because every manager has three major parts of his job, a performance review of subordinate managers can be patterned after this sub-division of their duties: managing, doing, supervising. While forms, per se, are to be abhorred in performance review because they often degenerate into inequitable, biased check-lists of personality traits, there is merit in using forms as *guides* in planning a performance review interview. Exhibits 20 and 21 give the form and description for one such subjective appraisal in these three vital areas.

EXHIBIT 20

PERFORMANCE APPRAISAL FORM

CHECK SHEET MANAGERIAL PERFORMANCE STANDARDS CONTROLLER'S DEPARTMENT		
About	By:	Date:
INNOVATION: (Search out and define? Communication the problem? Solve or direct solving?)		
DO-ING: (Self-starting, technical knowledge, value judgements.)		
MANAGING: (Communicating, programming and scheduling, controlling and evaluating.)		

EXHIBIT 21

PERFORMANCE APPRAISAL

INNOVATION

1. Does he search out and define areas which require innovation?
2. Does he present the problem convincingly to his supervisor, his colleagues, and his subordinates, so that all concerned come to the conclusion that this is an important matter?
3. Does he either personally or as a leader direct the solving of the problem and, in so doing, utilize available resources of our organization?

DO-ING

1. Is the individual a self-starter and does he follow through himself? In other words, does he get things done, or does he explain to people why he couldn't get them done? Does he have to be reminded to do them? Does he have to be pushed into doing them, or does he start them and follow through on his own?
2. What degree of technical knowledge does he display? An adequate amount for his job? An inadequate amount? Or a superior technical knowledge?
3. What is the individual's record as to value judgement that he makes as a part of his job? Does he understand and consistently support company policy? Does he display emotional maturity? Does he have an appreciation for the significance of precedent? Does he become involved in emotional reactions?

MANAGING

1. *Communicating Skill.* Does he communicate efficiently and clearly both up the line and down the line? An efficient communicator saves his own time and that of others. There is only one measure in clearness of communicating: If misunderstandings arise, then the communicating was not done clearly.
2. *Programming and Scheduling.* That is, does he state clearly a specific sequence of activities to be followed in reaching an objective and in setting time schedules and priorities for these activities? This can be judged from carbon copies of memorandums to his men detailing these things.
3. *Controlling and Evaluating.* This would include establishing yardsticks which are fair, evaluating the performance of his people against these yardsticks, and initiating corrective action whenever it is needed. In this area we also should include his follow-up of the routine under his supervision and his checking of this routine to make sure that it is being carried out as he has planned it.

A different but related approach referred to as the "Managers Letter" may be extracted from Peter Drucker's classic *The Practice of Management.* Get each subordinate to give his answer to each of the following questions, and then point out where you, his supervisor, agree with and differ from those answers. This often uncovers areas of very significant misunderstanding at relatively high levels:

    a. Define the objectives of your superior's job, as you understand those objectives.

    b. Do the same for your job.

    c. List the performance standards you think your supervisor applies to you in your job.

    d. List the things in your department which you believe are major obstacles to carrying out your objectives.

    e. List the things your supervisor does that hamper you and those that help you.

    f. What is your program for the next twelve months to accomplish the objectives stated in (b) above?

A written record of this Manager's Letter, supplemented by notes from personal interviews, serves as fertile ground for successive reviews later the same year. New reports could be prepared each year. New letters should vividly show greater comprehension and better objectives with each rewrite.

Performance reviews should be carried all the way down, but this must be forced or it will not happen. Subordinate managers must be required to plan and implement such a program. Exhibit 22 illustrates a directive issued and followed for a comprehensive review program.

PLANNED PERFORMANCE GOALS

In previous paragraphs, several approaches to conventional performance appraisals were described. Generally, reviews such as those are devoted to a commentary by the supervisor on how the subordinate goes about his job. Improvements are phrased in terms of better techniques, more readable reports, greater accuracy, and the like. Even though checklists are avoided, traits are discussed.

An entirely different approach has been recommended by Douglas McGregor, M.I.T., by W. M. McFeely, Vice-President Organization, Riegel Paper Corporation, and others. Several names have been applied to it, such as "management by objectives" and "planned individual performance." The fundamental difference in this approach to performance review and other traditional ways is that this way is *results oriented*.

The first interview sessions are, in fact, discussions of what the subordinate's job objectives really are. After thoroughly discussing job content, scope, and limits, discussions move to improvements—improvements in results, not personality traits. The subordinate is encouraged and led by nondirective interview techniques to propose work-oriented improvement goals. Whatever he proposes should be accepted without qualification by the supervisor unless the goals are patently too ambitious. To do otherwise would make the goals the supervisor's, not the subordinate's, robbing them of the personal touch. Goals of his own creation, to be

EXHIBIT 22

PERFORMANCE REVIEW PROGRAM

TO: All Department Heads

PERFORMANCE REVIEW PROGRAM

Detailed below is a Performance Review Program which is to be put nto effect immediately. The procedure outlined is an elementary one. It does not nclude the use of any static checklists. It merely requires that you, on a routine basis, sit down wi'h each individual under your supervision and tell him what you think of his performance since the last such discussion.

1. Prepare a schedule listing each person in your section, specifically assigning a particular month of the year for his performance review. Since this s something new, schedule reviews six months apart. This will give you more practice and will give the individuals a better chance to benefit from the discussions. Please give me a copy of your schedule by Friday, July 14th.
2. During the week prior to the specific date scheduled for the performance review, prepare an outline of the comments that you plan to make. Go over your outline with me to see whether I agree with what you have to say, whether I have any additional comments that I can pass on to you from other people in the division, or whether I, personally, have any comments to add.
3. This outline should list two specific areas of greatest need for improvement with specific illustrations of how greater skill would have helped in the past, and two specific areas of superior performance or recent improvement. Future interviews should include comments on previously mentioned areas of improvement.
4. Use this outline in your discussion with the individual. Immediately after the performance review, record the substance of the individual's reaction to the review plus your pertinent comments.

---

reviewed later for accomplishment, will serve as a powerful stimulus for completion. There is a personal commitment to such goals.

The goals should be completed with:n one year. They should be specifically related to the work objectives of the subordinate. Primarily, quantitative (how much) goals should be stressed, although qualitative (how well) goals are also valid. Examples of such goals are:

1. Reduce staff by one clerk by better systems.
2. Reduce supplies cost by 10 percent.
3. Complete period closings within five working days.
4. Reduce payroll errors by 10 percent.

5. Increase computer utilization to 80 percent.
6. Cross-train programmers in all three programming languages for flexibility.

At subsequent interviews, progress should be reported and new goals set for the future.

This approach keeps all attention centered on doing a better job—higher quality, less cost. It removes the individual and his personal idiosyncracies from the interview scene. Results are what count.

Why will this work? Because everyone wants to do a good job. Because everyone has the capacity to do better than he is doing. Because personal involvement and commitment are the incentive necessary to get people to function at those higher levels of performance of which they are capable.

PREVENT COMMUNICATIONS STOPPERS

Effective communication underlies effective controllership. If things are allowed to become routine communications stoppers, the controller and his staff cannot be effective.

This applies to controller-to-subordinate communications as well as to other department contacts. Principles advocated in this section apply equally to both situations.

Written directives are the least effective of several ways of communicating an order. This is primarily due to the complete lack of feedback from the recipient to the sender. The sender is absolutely tied to his written effort to get his point across correctly the first time. There is no opportunity for the sender to observe reaction, to detect by a furrowed brow, a blank stare, a shaking of the head, that the recipient is in trouble with the memo in front of him. How much better it is for the sender to be able immediately to ask for a restatement *by the recipient* of the directive just received orally! If there is any confusion, it will be apparent and can be corrected at once with no embarrassment by either party. Compare this with the corrective action two weeks after a recipient has taken what he thought was proper action based on a written directive he misinterpreted upon receipt.

Perhaps there is some wonderment as to why feedback should be so important. Upon reflection, one often decides that it is strange that we *ever* understand without feedback. Consider that two distinctly different human beings are involved, each with independent experience, motivation, and goals. One wants the other to take some action. We accept that a man is the product of heredity and environment. Man A and Man B come to this confrontation from very different origins. They may be from different national or ethnic groups, with whatever hereditary differences apply. They were educated in two different school systems and attended different colleges, one perhaps liberal arts and the other engineering. One is from the South and one from the North where subtle differences in word denotation and connotation exist in vocabulary. Who knows what subtle and profound differences there are in their immediate home environment—sickness at home, financial troubles, teenage child not under control—that affect each on the particular day in question to preoccupy his mind and detract from his normal level of acuity. Every man reacts and understands within the framework of his own experiences. One cannot be consistently successful in person-to-person communication until he realizes that this is so and conducts himself accordingly. With all this going against a writer, it is surprising that misunderstandings occur so frequently?

By the same token, it should not be surprising that two people often appear to reach different conclusions from identical sets of written data. Typically, debates and arguments ensue over the two conclusions. Don't make that mistake! The very forces we have listed are acting. Arguments at the conclusion level can never be resolved. Agreement must be reached on the premises and the data, first. Having done that, somehow the same conclusion now comes from those who just before were arguing for different conclusions. What happened? One or the other had interpreted the data in the light of his particular experience and had mistakenly inferred some significance to that interpretation. How often one hears, "No, what I meant to say was...." This is the way to resolve differences, by debate over premises and facts, to insure that all parties have the same (complete) facts and that premises and assumptions are acceptable to all. Tell each other what you mean and how you know. Avoid using abstract words when engaged in discussions of fact, premises, and assumptions. Words of this sort must be interpeted because of their very nature, hence involve conclusions in the very processes designed to avoid debates about conclusions. Use words which are specific, have little room for interpretation, are less ambiguous. With persons you know well, or with whom you work frequently, abstract words can be used now and then because your friends have shared these words with you and know the specifics you imply.

MANAGE CONTROL STAFF SIZE

The controller has two elements of cost directly incurred by his department for which tight controls of expenditures must be maintained. One of these is for people on the payroll. The other is expenditures for machine rentals and operating supplies.

The controller should be careful to maintain an accurate log of the people in his department, noting each hire, transfer, promotion, discharge, and quit. He should be able to trace, over a period of time, all of the personnel moves in his department. He should be able to justify any specific increases in the work force and should be very careful to achieve dollar reductions when personnel can be eliminated from the payroll. A simple way to keep track of the people is to use a time log, as shown in Exhibit 23. Ordinary fourteen-column worksheets are quite satisfactory for this purpose. List down the left-hand column the job titles for all of the jobs in the standard work force. In the first column set down the names of all of the incumbents and at the top of the column put the current date. In the next column, list the names, as appropriate, as new people are assigned to each of the existing functions. If it becomes necessary to add functions, add the name of the new function in the first column and write the name of the new incumbent in the "current" column. Quarterly, bring the log up to date, indicating with a check mark those persons who are still in the job, dating the column at the top and totaling at the bottom. The purpose of this is to maintain a *complete* log of all of the ins and outs of each job, and to identify the dates of jobs created and jobs eliminated.

EXHIBIT 23

PERSONNEL STATUS LOG

Title	1/1/x4	2/25/x4	4/1/x5
Controller	Bennett	X	X
Secretary	Grim	X	X
Staff Assistant	Seguine	X	X
Staff Assistant—Added 4/1/x4			Jack
Manager Budgets & Standards	Wilson	X	X
Clerk Typist	Felix	X	X
Cost Analyst	Enright	George	X
Cost Analyst	Frank	Wilchak	X
Cost Analyst	George	Enright	X
Plant Accountant	Eck	X	X
Cost Clerk A	Diehl	X	X
Cost Clerk B	Wilchak	Brown	X
Shipping Clerk A	Fisher	X	X
Shipping Clerk B	Kirk	X	Job Eliminated 3/20/x5
Total	13	13	13

Experience with a log such as this will give the controller invaluable intimate knowledge of the depth of experience of each person in his own department as he traces each person in and out of specific transfers and promotions, and will give him an intimate familiarity with the control scheme which can then apply to all of the salaried positions in his corporate organization. It is a proven fact that, without the existence of a log such as this, it will be absolutely impossible to reconstruct what has happened to a work force which has either grown or been reduced. If the work force has grown, surely at some date in the not too distant future the controller will be called upon to justify the changes. Without the log, he probably won't be able to identify what the changes are, much less be able to justify the individual changes. On the other hand, if there is a reduction in the work force, the controller should be in a position to itemize the whys and where-fores, to give his subordinates credit where credit is due, and to himself receive credit from his superiors.

Controlling machine rental and office supplies expenditures in the controller's department is no different from any other department. Because of the annual or semi-annual nature of expenditures for forms and certain major supplies, a period-by-period variance analysis is not appropriate. In this instance, it is much more useful to compile cumulative budget versus actual comparisons which allow for a dampening effect in the variance figure for lump-sum purchases. Exhibit 24 shows an example of one such useful report on a trend basis. Note that in the First Period there was a large expenditure for forms. In the particular instance this is an annual purchase of a relatively expensive multi-ply order set. This annual purchase was anticipated in the budget but prorated over the full year. The lump-sum purchase falling in the First Period shows a large negative variance for the First Period and also for the year-to-date as of the First Period. However, because there are other lump-sum expenditures which have not yet occurred, the year-to-date variance is not as bad as it might otherwise be expected to appear. The year-to-date figure thus analyzed gives a good basis for control.

EXHIBIT 24

TREND VARIANCE REPORT

PERIOD VARIANCE REPORT   COPIES TO: DEPT. HEAD   FROM: GENERAL ACCOUNTING   DEPT. *Order / Billing*

ITEM	BUDGET $/ YEAR	BUDGET 5 WK PERIOD	BUDGET 4 WK PERIOD	#1 (5 WEEKS)	#2	#3	#4 (5 WEEKS)	#5	#6	#7 (5 WEEKS)	#8	#9	#10 (5 WEEKS)	#11	#12	#13 ADJ.	GRAND TOTAL ACTUAL	TOTAL VARIANCE
SALARIES	96,208	9076	7761	7895	6393	6396	8276	6688	7118	8904	7104							
LABOR OVERHEAD	6844	550	442	550	442	442	550	461	461	516	461							
OPERATING MATERIAL	1130	107	85	1	11	1	1	10	-	230	8							
FORMS & SUPPLIES	10492	984	787	2419	690	588	1533	1552	683	152	436							
RENT & DEPRECIATION	23597	2226	1781	2226	1781	1781	2401	1921	1921	2401	1921							
ALL OTHER EXPENSE	-	-	-	164	353	163	50	-	27	-	411							
GRAND TOTAL	137,208	12945	10356	13264	9670	9370	12810	10632	10210	12863	10377							
VARIANCE THIS PERIOD (OVER) UNDER BUDGET				(309)	686	986	135	(276)	146	82	(21)							
CUMULATIVE VARIANCE (OVER) UNDER BUDGET				(309)	377	1363	1498	1222	1368	1450	1429							

ACTUAL EXPENSE PER PERIOD

Part Two

GENERAL ACCOUNTING DUTIES

4

General Accounting

While internal control consists of a great deal more than merely accounting, a valid and consistent accounting system is the foundation on which any thorough control system must be based.

There can be no equivocation of the necessity for establishing accounting policy at the highest level and insuring that this policy is followed diligently throughout the corporation. Generally accepted accounting principles must be followed in all entries into the books of account. To allow inconsistencies and inaccuracies to enter into the books of the corporation will result, at best, in grossly misleading control reports since the significance of the variances generated therefrom will be entirely fictitious and, at worst, will result in financial statements and books of account rejected by the company's outside auditing firm, by the Internal Revenue Service in its tax audits of the firm's reports, and by other regulatory agencies that have access to the company's financial statements and reports.

CHART OF ACCOUNTS

A well-constructed chart of accounts is an invaluable aid in facilitating coding of transactions for initial entry into the accounts and, subsequently, for the extraction of significant information during financial analysis projects for control purposes. There can be no responsibility accounting without this. The chart of accounts should follow the responsibility accounting concept so that a responsibility code is established for each cost center for which a budget is to be prepared and for which cost variance reports are to be published. This responsibility code number must identify one, and only one, such cost center and should be applied to all transactions which relate to that cost center. For formal entry into the books of account, it is possible to use control accounts that maintain the identity of the profit center without going to great lengths, actually, to record into the books of account the cost of each individual cost center.

Electronic data processing equipment can be used to identify cost by cost center on tabulations prepared subsequent to the period closing without the necessity of each of these cost centers being individually represented in the factory ledger. It is mandatory, however, that costs relating to one profit center be entered in the books of account independently of costs of all other profit centers; the books of account will then show all of the costs and all of the income of each profit center, thereby establishing validly and independently the actual profitability of each such profit center.

In addition to being identified with the code number of the cost center to which the expenditure is to be charged, categories of cost should be grouped by a code number system. For instance, all payroll costs for hourly direct labor should carry a significant cost code. Each other major category of expense should have its own independent code number. Similarly, raw material costs should carry an independent set of code numbers identifying each major category of raw materials.

The purpose of this subdivision within the chart of accounts is to facilitate the generation of homogeneous reports that indicate actual expenditures for comparison with standard expenditures for the same item for a given period of time.

Codes designed for the identification of costs by cost center are illustrated by Exhibit 25. Notice the parallel structure for manufacturing units. For ease in using the code structure, digits can have combined significance in addition to the cost center significance of the three digits. Where possible, this concept should be followed. Proper coding is a major problem; this is one way to ease the burden on the users of the code structure. The code in Exhibit 25 was constructed as follows:

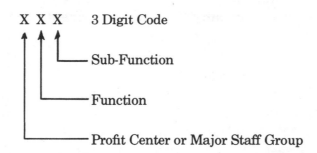

Examine Exhibit 25 to see how this was carried through.

Necessary to cost analysis are account and sub-account codes to be used with responsibility codes to classify types of expenditures for homogeneity in statement preparation and control reporting. Account codes identify major categories of costs such as salaries, rents, royalties, power, and fuel. Sub-accounts identify whatever sub-categories are desired; for instance, within fuel it may be desirable to identify separately coal, oil, and gas. Exhibit 26 shows a partial set of account and sub-account codes.

EXHIBIT 25

RESPONSIBILITY CODES

OPERATING LEDGER

CHART OF ACCOUNTS

Responsibility Codes

Paper Mills

Mill & Code				Department
W	H	R	M	
100			400	PM General
			401	PM #1
			402	PM #2
			403	PM #3
			404	PM #4
			405	PM #5
			406	PM #6
107				PM #7
108				PM #8
	209			PM #9
		310		PM #10
			414	PM #14
			417	PM #17
120	220	320	420	Finishing General
			421	Super Calendars
			422	Finishing Winders
			425	Loading
			426	Receiving
130	230	330	430	Pulp Preparation
133	233	333	433	Material Handling
160	260	360	—	Power Plant
170	270	370	—	Mechanical Maintenance
171	271	371	—	Electrical Maintenance
190	290	390	—	Quality Control
198	298	398	498	Mill General

Administration

	903		Chauffeurs
	904		Purchasing
	905		Traffic

EXHIBIT 25

RESPONSIBILITY CODES (Cont.)

908	Personnel
960	Controllers Department—General
961	Accounts Payable—Billing
962	Offices Services
963	Mill Accounting
964	General Accounting
965	Data Processing
966	Systems Planning
967	Profit Planning

EXHIBIT 26

ACCOUNT CODES

OPERATING LEDGER

CHART OF ACCOUNTS

Account Codes
(Partial List)

001	Salary
002	Direct Labor
003	Term Labor
004	Labor Overhead
005	Depreciation
006	Insurance
007	Property Taxes
008	Operating Material
010	Rents and Royalties

Sub-Account Codes
(Partial List)

Account 010—Rents & Royalties

01	Equipment and Machine Rental
02	Office and Plant Rental
03	(Open)
04	(Open)
05	(Open)
06	Royalty Payments
07	(Open)

These codes are recorded on purchase orders and thence onto invoice vouchers for use in subsequent analysis. For data processing, an eight digit code field may be defined to contain in the codes like this:

XXX	XXX	XX
Responsibility Code	Account	Sub-Account

This abbreviated list of codes is meant to illustrate the type of code construction possible. There could be 100 accounts, each with dozens of sub-accounts, if it is desirable. The author knows of 154 sub-accounts to one "008" account.

An expanded field of 13 digits could be more useful in that it would permit the same punched card to be used for all types of entries, such as all payable entries, journal voucher correcting entries and miscellaneous (nonproduct) sales. This would include routine expense purchases, capital additions and inventory items. General ledger and raw material codes could be constructed as shown in Exhibit 27.

Data would be entered in this field for each category as described below:

	Type	Resp.	Account	Sub-Account	Group No.
13 Digit Field					
Expense	X	XXX	XXX	XX	------
Capital	X	XXX	XXX	XX	XXXX
Raw Material	X	-----	XX	XX	------
Journal Voucher	X	XXX	XXX	XX	------
		General Ledger			
Miscellaneous Sales	X	XXX	===	XX	------

FINANCIAL ACCOUNTING STANDARDS BOARD

The latest in a series of authoritative bodies, the Financial Accounting Standards Board (FASB) replaced the Accounting Principles Board (APB) in 1973. The APB had replaced the Committee on Accounting Procedure in 1960. The goal of the FASB is to restore the integrity of financial reporting by establishing standards of financial accounting and reporting and by narrowing the range of alternative practices. The Board has final and ultimate private-sector authority over the subject, style, content, and substance of financial accounting standards.

The quality and integrity of financial statements has been questioned since the turn of the century. The various bodies named above had their birth in efforts to establish that desired integrity. Unfortunately, the advent of the FASB has not abated such challenges.

When it is said that financial statements have been prepared "in accordance with generally accepted accounting principles" it is assumed that the

EXHIBIT 27

GENERAL LEDGER AND RAW MATERIAL CODES

General Ledger—Examples

Account Number		Account Title
INVENTORIES		
140	—	Raw Materials and Supplies Inventories
141	—	Product Inventories
142	—	Materials in Transit
143	—	Reserve for Changes in Standard Cost
144	—	Reserve for LIFO
PREPAID EXPENSES		
160	—	Fire and Other Insurance Prepaid
161	—	Rents Prepaid
162	—	Airline Deposit
163	—	Employees Cash Advances
ACCOUNTS PAYABLE—EMPLOYEES		
280	—	Collections—State Income Taxes
281	—	Collections—Christmas Club
282	—	Collections—Federal Credit Union
283	—	Collections—U. S. Savings Bonds

Raw Material—Examples

Account #	Material
1–199	Bleaching Chemicals
200–239	Alums
240–259	Not Assigned
260–284	Fillers
285–299	Germicides
300–349	Glues
350–379	Oils
380–389	Pitch Dispersants
390–399	Resins
400–424	Sizes

statements present fairly a firm's financial position, changes in financial position, and results of operations. In practice, because of the way principles have been developed in the past, because of the multiplicity of opinions and lack of objective research, the statement "conforming to GAAP" has not had a uniform meaning.

The APB, like its predecessor, the Committee on Accounting Procedure, was unable to cope with a rapidly changing business and financial environment. Neither group was structured with the flexibility needed to meet these changes.

By the middle of the 1960's, a large number of unsettled financial reporting problems had developed. The work of the APB was diverted from the development of theory to the solution of day-to-day problems.

By the end of the 1960's public confidence in the integrity of financial reporting had decreased, and the APB was being severely criticized for not taking a strong enough position in many areas, for taking a position before hearings and exposure drafts of proposed pronouncements, and for relying on part-time APB members who did not have sufficient time to devote to APB problems.

An AICPA committee, chaired by Francis M. Wheat, recommended a change. The Wheat Report resulted in the creation of the Financial Accounting Standards Board to replace the APB.

Organization of the FASB

The Financial Accounting Foundation, the oversight body of the FASB, appoints the members of the Financial Accounting Standards Board. Trustees of the Foundation itself are appointed by the Board of Directors of the AICPA and selected from the following fields: one trustee is the president of the AICPA; four are CPA's in public practice; two are financial executives; one is a financial analyst; one is an accounting educator. Non-CPA's are chosen from names submitted by the Financial Executives Institute, the Financial Analysts Federation, the National Association of Accountants, and the American Accounting Association. The Foundation is also charged with raising funds for operations and with appointment of members to the Financial Accounting Standards Advisory Council.

The Financial Accounting Standards Advisory Council is composed of 20 members working with the FASB in an advisory capacity. Only one-quarter of the members may come from a single field of activity. Members of the Council assist the FASB in establishing priorities, setting up task forces, reacting to proposed standards, and performing other needed tasks.

The Financial Accounting Standards Board of seven members is appointed by the Board of Trustees of the Financial Accounting Foundation. Four FASB members must be CPA's from public practice, and the other three should have extensive experience in the financial reporting field.

Board members devote full time to FASB work. Members have no obligation to, or dependence on, any other group such as partners, employers, clients, or the AICPA.

The Board is supported by a permanent staff composed of more than 60 persons, including administrative, technical, and research personnel. Research personnel investigate specific issues associated with FASB projects. The research division provides information about specific questions under review and about the impact of alternative solutions.

Operating Procedures

The operating procedures of the Financial Accounting Standards Board are as follows:

1. Topics are suggested by members of the FASB, members of the Advisory Council, and other interested persons or groups.
2. Board members define the problem or topic.
3. A task force, headed by a member of the Board, is appointed to refine the definition, to determine the nature and extent of research needed, and to prepare a Discussion Memorandum. The Discussion Memorandum presents alternatives and covers the advantages and disadvantages of each.
4. A 60-day exposure period is given for the Discussion Memorandum, after which public hearings are held for presentations of all sides to alternative positions.
5. Members of the FASB evaluate the data presented in support of alternatives and prepare a Draft Statement for a period of exposure.
6. Comments, position papers, and other communications on the Draft are evaluated. After approval (by at least four of the seven members), a Statement of the standard is issued which becomes effective 90 days later.

FASB Research Methods

The FASB intends four kinds of research. The first is theoretical research to develop a conceptual framework and then to review and maintain it. The second is empirical research required to assure that those making the decisions will understand the issue and its ramifications and to assure discovery of all the feasible solutions; this research is performed prior to the issuance of a discussion memorandum. The third is research to inform the decision-makers as to the anticipated impact of each possible solution. Finally, research is required to determine the acceptability of a proposed standard; the issuance of an exposure draft accomplishes this fourth kind of research.

To illustrate the breadth and scope of its research, consider *Statement No. 5,* "Accounting for Contingencies," issued in March, 1975 following compliance with all the Board's procedures. The problem which started the project is given in the Statement, as follows:

> Some enterprises now accrue estimated losses for some types of contingencies by a charge to income prior to the occurrence of the event or events that are expected to resolve the uncertainties while, under similar circumstances, other enterprises account for those losses only when the confirming event or events have occurred.

The task force consisted of 16 members from industry, public accounting, the financial community, and academe. The Discussion Memorandum provided examples of various types of contingencies and considered several at length. Research was undertaken in the preparation of the Discussion Memorandum. The research included searching relevant literature, examining financial statements, a questionnaire survey conducted by the FEI, and a study of catastrophe reserve accounting methods; 87 position papers were received in response to the Discussion Memorandum; 212 comment letters were received in response to the Exposure Draft.

Assuming that the Board's mission is to eliminate differences in accounting under similar circumstances, the Board had the choice: to have enterprises that assume risk and do not insure to issue statements either similar to or different from those that assume the same risk, but do insure, at the option of the firm. The FASB decided that, under this rule, its mission would be accomplished by differentiating between companies transferring the risks and those that did not by prohibiting the establishment of reserves for contingencies. Under this rule, the assumption of risk would result in fluctuations in income as irregular losses were incurred. The fact of a risk no longer could be hidden by accruing for anticipated losses of some future reporting period.

ACCOUNTING PRINCIPLES

It should not be necessary to this audience to dwell on the necessity that sound accounting policies be laid down and adhered to. In general, these policies should insure that costs are correctly recorded and documented, liabilities are paid when due, assets are recorded at proper value, sales and income are properly stated, receivables are collected when due, and so forth.

It is not my purpose to restate in this book alternative methods for doing this task. Libraries abound with technical texts on minute subdivisions of the broad categories alluded to. For technical guidance, go to those sources.

The point to be made here is that rules to insure that the selected policies are, in fact, carried out must be written and published. The accountants must know precisely what the policy is in each case. Accounting must be precise; generalities cannot be entered in the ledger. Procedure manuals that define this guidance to the accountant are a personal responsibility of the controller.

CONCEPTUAL FRAMEWORK OF ACCOUNTING

The Financial Accounting Standards Board (FASB) has embarked on a project aimed at developing a Conceptual Framework for Accounting. This has been referred to as the process to develop a constitution for accounting. The

Conceptual Framework project is intended by the FASB to result in the issuance of documents called Statements of Financial Accounting Concepts; these Statements will provide the underlying support and guidance for the future development and application of all financial accounting standards. It is contemplated that four phases of the conceptual framework project will be implemented:

1. There will be developed specific Objectives for Financial Reporting by businesses, such as the identification of objectives of financial statements, purposes of statements, and the general nature of financial reporting.
2. The elements of the financial statements will be better defined, that is, formal definitions of assets, liabilities, equities, etc., are needed.
3. The Qualitative Characteristics of Financial Information will be explored, that is, the FASB intends to identify and clarify the characteristics that should govern the development of accounting standards. These characteristics include such things as reliability, relevance, timeliness, and materiality.
4. The Measurement of the Elements of Financial Statements will be explored. A selective basis for measuring assets, for measuring liabilities, etc., is part of the evolution of the Conceptual Framework.

In November 1978, the Financial Accounting Standards Board issued the first in the Conceptual Framework series. This Statement of Financial Accounting Concepts No. 1 was entitled "Objectives of Financial Reporting by Business Enterprises."

FORECASTS OF PROFITS

The Securities and Exchange Commission has been encouraging companies to issue profit forecasts for a number of years. In 1979, as a further encouragement, the SEC issued what are called "safe harbor" rules and guidelines relative to financial forecasts. These rules and guidelines apply to all public forecasts whether simply included in press releases or included in official SEC filings. The purpose of the safe harbor rule is to limit a firm's liability in the event that a forecast, made in good faith and prepared on a reasonable basis, turns out to be inaccurate and people have relied on the forecast to make decisions. The safe harbor rule puts the burden of proof on the party claiming injury. It is up to that party to prove that the projection did not have a reasonable basis and/or that it was not disclosed in good faith. The SEC has not mandated the content of the forecast, but suggests that revenue, net income, and first year earnings should be included.

The SEC has warned that selective disclosure which might be misleading is not allowed and is not covered by the safe harbor rules; an example of selective disclosure is the public disclosure of a forecast of greatly increased revenues without any mention of whether net income would be increased. The SEC indicates that companies issuing forecasts will have the duty to update forecasts should there be any major changes.

No third party review of forecasts by a public accountant or any other person is required, although such review is permitted, if the firm desires.

FOREIGN CORRUPT PRACTICES ACT OF 1977

The Foreign Corrupt Practices Act of 1977 (FCPA) includes some items of profound significance to controllers, accountants and auditors. The Act, effective December 19, 1977, applies to all U. S. companies and their officers, directors, employees, agents, and stockholders. All of these persons are prohibited from bribing foreign governmental or political officials. Further, all publicly held companies must meet the FCPA's internal control and record-keeping requirements. The requirement that managers maintain internal control is not a new one; what is new, however, is the inclusion in public law of a civil and criminal liability for failure to maintain adequate internal control.

Bribery of foreign officials is defined as a direct or indirect payment or offer to an official which offer is intended to promote business interests. Interestingly, the law does not prohibit facilitating payments to relatively low level government employees. The penalty for violating the bribery provision is a fine to a company of up to $1 million; individuals who are convicted face a maximum fine of $10,000 and/or imprisonment for up to five years.

Perhaps more importantly to controllers (because these provisions apply to all publicly held companies, totally independently of any foreign operations) is that the companies (1) must devise and maintain a system of internal control sufficient, among other things, to provide reasonable assurance that transactions are properly authorized and recorded, and (2) must keep records which "accurately and fairly" reflect financial activities.

The law does not specify what reasonable assurance is; therefore, until specific criteria are established, which unfortunately may come about through case law rather than regulation, management must take appropriate steps to evaluate the sufficiency of their internal control system. Publicly held companies must consider whether their present system provides reasonable assurance, as that phrase is used in the law.

With regard to record keeping, the law places the responsibility on publicly held companies to "make and keep books, records and accounts which *in reasonable detail* accurately and thoroughly reflect the transactions and dispositions of the assets of the issuer." The "in reasonable detail" qualification was included to avoid applying an unrealistic degree of exactness. The Conference

Committee Report of the Congress states that this phrase was added to make the point that the records should reflect transactions in conformity with accepted methods of recording economic events, that "accurately" does not mean exact precision but it means that the records should reflect transactions in conformity with General Accepted Accounting Principles.

The Act requires that companies devise and maintain internal control systems sufficient to provide reasonable assurance of meeting the internal control objectives specified in authoritative literature. The internal control objectives, as set forth in Statement on Auditing Standards No. 1, are now incorporated in Section 13(b) of the Securities and Exchange Act:

a. Transactions are executed in accordance with management's general or specific authorization;

b. Transactions are recorded as necessary (1) to permit preparation of financial statements in conformity with General Accepted Accounting Principles or any other criteria applicable to such statements, and (2) to maintain accountability for assets;

c. Access to assets is permitted only in accordance with management's general or specific authorization;

d. The recorded accountability for assets is compared with the existing assets at reasonable intervals and appropriate action is taken with respect to any differences.

It is, of course, nothing new that management has the responsibility for maintaining internal control. Managers have always accepted this as a management responsibility. The accounting profession has always recognized and reported this to be a management responsibility. However, subjecting officers and employees of firms to civil liabilities and to criminal prosecution under federal law for not having a sufficient system of internal control is a quite significant new development. An evaluation intended to determine whether an internal control system provides such reasonable assurance is a highly subjective process. No clear criteria are available from the law or from the supporting testimony to help determine exactly how this assurance is to be provided.

Corporate "Codes of Conduct" have been developed by many firms in an effort to communicate to all employees of the firm a concern for compliance with the Foreign Corrupt Practices Act; at the same time the codes identify specific things which the firms recognize as *not* being in conformity with the FCPA. Included in such a Code of Conduct for a firm might be the following:

1. Use of any assets of the firm is strictly prohibited for any purpose which is unlawful under the laws of the United States regardless of whether the event is occurring within or without the United States.

2. No unrecorded funds or assets of the firm or any subsidiary of the firm shall be established for any purpose whatsoever.

3. No false entries shall be made on any books or records of the company or its subsidiary.

4. No payment on behalf of the company may be approved or made with the understanding that the payment is to be used for any purpose other than that explicitly described in the source document offered in support of the payment.

5. Any employee having information of any unrecorded funds must, under threat of dismissal for cause, report such information to the Corporate Controller.

6. All managers of the firm are responsible for communication of the policy, for enforcement, and for compliance with the policy.

7. Appropriate levels of management and executive groups will at periodic intervals certify their understanding of and their compliance with the Code of Conduct.

One effect of the internal control provisions of the Foreign Corrupt Practices Act will be that managers will be much more rigorous in their investigation of and challenge to their systems of internal control. Most public accounting firms have developed techniques and systems for the evaluation of the adequacy of internal control. These techniques include the detailed identification of and evaluation of the controls in the transaction processing systems of the firm. Where a control is missing, an evaluation needs to be made to determine if a control should be implemented. Where a control is judged to be weak, an evaluation must be made as to whether it ought to be strengthened. It must be recognized that the internal control provision of the Act does not include references to materiality but to reasonable assurance. The general interpretation is that "reasonable assurance" contemplates that the cost of an internal control procedure must be compared to the value of the benefits. Reasonable assurance does not require an absolute level of control, but neither is reasonable assurance limited to controlling only at the level of materiality. In short, firms must evaluate whether the estimated cost of the possible internal control is justified by the expected benefits.

The Securities and Exchange Commission in the implementation of the requirements of the Foreign Corrupt Practices Act has added rules and regulations not initially included in the act itself. One of these is that the Securities and Exchange Commission has prohibited falsifying any corporate records; further, officers and directors are prohibited from making any materially false statements, whether orally or in writing, to any accountants, internal auditors, or independent auditors. Importantly, the SEC has rejected the idea that *scienter*, that is the specific intent to deceive, is required in a showing that materially false statements have been made or that reports have been falsified.

INFLATION ACCOUNTING

In 1979, the Financial Accounting Standards Board issued FASB Statement No. 33 requiring large public companies to report on the effects of inflation in their financial statements. The Chairman of the FASB described the Statement as being necessary to meet an urgent need for information about the effects of changing prices. He indicated that the Board felt that very undesirable consequences would occur if this information were not required to be disclosed. These consequences included a severe limitation on investors' and creditors' understanding of a company's performance, a limitation on their ability to assess future cash flows of a firm, and an inability of government officials to interpret implications of government decisions on economic policy matters in the business community.

Statement No. 33 requires that certain disclosures on the effect of changing prices be presented in supplementary information in annual reports. The statement applies only to public companies; further, only companies with either $1 billion of assets or $125 million of inventories and gross properties at the beginning of the fiscal year are required to present this information.

An interest in reporting the effect of changing prices has been an item of controversy in the accounting community since the 1930's. No concensus has been reached even to this date. FASB 33 does not resolve the controversy. Instead, FASB 33 requires that companies report under both of two fundamentally different measurement approaches. One approach requires the combination of historical cost with constant dollar accounting to deal with the effects of general inflation. The other approach requires the use of historical costs with current cost accounting, intended to address specific, rather than general inflation, price changes.

The required information must be reported in annual reports to shareholders and in Form 10K to the Securities and Exchange Commission. Information in a specified format for the current year is required; in addition, a five-year summary of selected financial data is also required. Information can be presented either in an unaudited footnote to the financial statements or entirely outside the financial statements, at the option of the firm.

The illustration in Exhibit 28, which shows income from operations changing from a profit to a loss after inflation adjustments, is obviously an extreme example. The actual effect will depend on whether LIFO or FIFO is used in the financial statements, on the age and relative amount of properies in each age bracket, and on the changes in the specific prices of the company's assets versus the rate of change of general inflation.

EXHIBIT 28

STATEMENT OF INCOME FROM CONTINUING OPERATIONS

ADJUSTED FOR CHANGING PRICES

For The Year Ended December 31, 1980
(In 000s of Average 1980 Dollars)

Income from continuing operations, as reported in the income statement		$ 9,000
Adjustments to restate costs for the effect of general inflation		
Cost of goods sold	(7,384)	
Depreciation and amortization expense	(4,130)	(11,514)
Loss from continuing operations adjusted for general inflation		(2,514)
Adjustments to reflect difference between general inflation and changes in specific prices (current costs)		
Cost of goods sold	(1,024)	
Depreciation and amortization expense	(5,370)	(6,394)
Loss from continuing operations adjusted for changes in specific prices		$ (8,908)
Gain from decline in purchasing power of net amounts owed		$ 7,729
Increase in specific prices (current cost) of inventories and property, plant, and equipment held during the year*		$ 24,608
Effect of increase in general price level		18,959
Excess of increase in specific prices over increase in the general price level		$ 5,649

*At December 31, 1980 current cost of inventory was $65,700 and current cost of property, plant and equipment, net of accumulated depreciation, was $85,100.

Historical Costs—Constant Dollar Basis

Constant Dollar accounting is a method of reporting items on the financial statement translated in terms of a fixed purchasing power. This approach attempts to portray the effect of general inflation on the exchange value of the dollar. Statement No. 33 does not require the entire financial statement to be translated; instead, the FASB has focused on those items most likely to be affected by inflation—inventories, property, plant, equipment, monetary assets, and liabilities. The Statement requires disclosure for the current year of the following:

a. Historical Income from Continuing Operations adjusted for average current year constant dollar valuations of costs of goods sold, depreciation, depletion, and amortization.
b. Purchasing power gain or loss on net monetary items.

The Statement does not require items such as investments in affiliates, intangible assets, deferred charges, and credits to be restated. The Statement specifies that the Consumer Price Index for all urban customers is to be used to measure general inflation. This index was selected primarily because a Consumer Price Index is available on a monthly basis.

Current Cost Technique

Current Cost accounting is a method of measuring assets and expenses at a "current cost" as of the balance sheet date. This method is intended to focus on specific price changes for specific assets as contrasted with the price impact of general inflation. Current Cost determinations are to be made for the assets as presently owned and used by a company. This requires some determination of a current acquisition cost for the assets, specifically as currently used. This is technically not the same as replacement cost valuation, which is defined as the cost of replacing current assets with their equivalent, nor it is the exit, that is, disposition value, of current assets.

The Board requires a Current Cost accounting of inventories, property, plant and equipment. Companies are required to disclose for the current year the following:

a. Historical Income from Continuing Operations adjusted for current cost measurements of costs of goods sold and depreciation.
b. Increases or decreases in current cost valuations of inventories, property, plant, and equipment—net of the effects of general inflation.
c. Current Cost valuation of inventories and net current cost of property, plant, and equipment as of the balance sheet date.

The Board has allowed firms a wide range of flexibility in selecting methods of determining "Current Costs." These methods range from indexing historical costs using specific price indexes to specific pricing. Because of the experience which many large companies had under Accounting Series Release No. 190 as mandated by the Securities and Exchange Commission, it is probable that many companies will base their Current Cost determinations on their experience with Replacement Cost data.

For inventories, Replacement Cost measurement can generally be used to determine the Current Cost of inventories and cost of goods sold. As a matter of fact, the cost of goods sold as determined by the LIFO inventory method provides a good approximation of cost of goods sold at Current Cost.

For properties, plant, and equipment, Replacement Cost methods which produced a cost for "replacement in kind" may well be used to determine Current Costs. In those instances where replacement with technologically improved assets is assumed, it may be possible to make adjustments to delete the cost increment for the change in technology in order to arrive at Current Cost data. The most cost effective and probably the most objective method for determining Current Cost is the indexing of historical costs using specific price indexes. Since historical costs must be adjusted for general price index changes, it should be relatively simple to follow the same procedures, substituting specific indexes for the general indexes. It is the individual firm's responsibility to justify specific indexes.

Exhibit 28 illustrates one presentation of the effects of general inflation and specific price changes. A $9,000,000 historical cost profit becomes, due to general inflation, a $2,514,000 loss; specific price changes increase the loss to $8,908,000.

Five-Year Summaries

In addition to current-year information, companies are also required to present a summary for the last five years of certain financial data deemed necessary to aid users in assessing trends and making judgements concerning the future. Of the items required in Statement No. 33, only sales, dividends, market price, and consumer price index disclosures are required to be reported for the years preceding 1979.

A form of Five-Year Summary is shown in Exhibit 29. Note the comparison of price adjusted earnings per share (a loss of $5.94/share for 1980) versus cash dividends paid out of $2.00/share.

Management Responsibilities

The requirement that inflation accounting disclosures be made is directed at management. The disclosures which are required are supplemental instead of being included in the financial statements themselves. Nevertheless, FASB Statements constitute generally accepted accounting principles; it follows, therefore, that some degree of auditor involvement is inevitable. The specific degree of involvement will be determined by the American Institute for Certified Public Accountants. It is likely, since the data is not part of the financial statements, that the data will be unaudited but that the auditors will be expected to review the reasonableness of the disclosures.

EXHIBIT 29

FIVE YEAR COMPARISON OF SELECTED SUPPLEMENTARY

FINANCIAL DATA ADJUSTED FOR EFFECTS OF

CHANGING PRICES

(In 000s of Average 1980 Dollars)

	Years Ended December 31,				
	1976	1977	1978	1979	1980
Net sales and other operating revenues	265,000	235,000	240,000	237,063	253,00
Historical cost information adjusted for general inflation					
Income (loss) from continuing operations				(2,761)	(2,514)
Income (loss) from continuing operations per common share				$ (1.91)	$ (1.68)
Net assets at year-end				55,518	57,733
Current cost information					
Income (loss) from continuing operations				(4,125)	(8,908)
Income (loss) from continuing operations per common share				$ (2.75)	$ (5.94)
Excess of increase in specific prices over increase in the general price level				2,292	5,649
Net assets at year-end				79,996	81,466
Gain from decline in purchasing power of net amounts owed				7,027	7,729
Cash dividends declared per common share	$ 2.59	$ 2.43	$ 2.26	$ 2.16	$ 2.00
Market price per common share at year-end	$ 32	$ 31	$ 43	$ 39	$ 35
Average consumer price index	170.5	181.5	195.4	205.0	220.9

SEGMENT REPORTING

In its Standard No. 14, "Financial Reporting for Segments of the Business Enterprise," the Financial Accounting Standards Board has spelled out a category of significant disclosures describing a company's operations by industry grouping and by geographic area. These disclosures must be included in the firm's financial statements. Statement No. 14 requires that a firm report revenue, profit contribution, and identifiable assets for each significantly different industry segment and for each significantly different geographical segment. The Statement also requires disclosure of export sales, sales to a single customer or a group of customers under common control, and sales to domestic government agencies or to foreign governments if such sales represent 10 percent or more of Consolidated net sales of the firm.

The Securities and Exchange Commission has adopted its regulation S-K intended to coordinate several disclosure requirements including the requirements of FASB Statement No 14. The SEC requires additional information beyond that required by Statement No. 14 with respect to intersegment transfers of product and with respect to interim performance of industry and geographic segments.

Industry Segmentation

The determination of a firm's separate, therefore reportable, industry segments is the basic requirement of FASB 14, and yet this determination is most difficult of implementation. The Statement is flexible with respect to the definition of industry segment. It indicates that the Standard Industrial Classification code and other similar systems might be useful in grouping a firm's products by industry lines, but that these classifications are not sufficient in and of themselves for the determination of segments as required by the Statement. The Statement goes on to recognize that no single set of characteristics is universally applicable nor is any single characteristic determinable across the board. A number of factors, therefore, enter into the determination of segment categories, including such factors as the nature of the products, of the production process, of markets, and of marketing methods. Ultimately, the Statement notes, "Determination of an enterprise's industry segments must depend to a considerable extent on the judgment of the management of the enterprise."

In a 1978 survey of 250 SEC reporting firms, 25 percent of the firms indicated their operations were in one industry segment. Significantly, however, only 20 percent of firms in manufacturing reported as being in only one industry segment.

There appears to be a positive relationship between company size and number of reportable segments. Of 90 firms in the survey with sales of $1 billion dollars or less, 65 percent reported no more than 3 industry segments.

Geographic Segment

FASB Statement No. 14 requires companies to report, in addition to industry segments, information on revenues and profitability by geographic area. A separate geographic area must be reported if either sales to unaffiliated customers or identifiable assets are 10 percent or more of the related consolidated amounts. In addition, factors to be considered in determining geographic segments include proximity, economic affinity, and the relationships of an enterprise's operations in various countries. In the same 1978 survey referred to earlier, close to one-half of the firms reported no reportable foreign segments.

Method of Presentation

FASB requires that information regarding an enterprise's reportable segments be included on one of the following, at the discretion of the firm:

a. In the body of the Financial Statements, or
b. In a footnote to the Financial Statements, or
c. In a separate schedule which is, itself, an integral part of the Financial Statements.

Segment Profitability

FASB 14 requires firms to report operating profit or loss for each reportable industry segment. Operating profit is defined as total revenue minus all operating expenses; included under operating expenses are those that might not be traceable to one specific industry segment but which are incurred for the specific benefit for two or more segments and which must, therefore, be allocated to the segments. Operating expense does not however, encompass such items as general and administrative expense, interest expense, income taxes, and other items listed in the Statement.

Transfer Pricing Disclosures

In the original Exposure Draft, FASB 14 anticipated requiring disclosures of certain specific transfer price information. This requirement, however, was not included in the Statement as issued. Statement No. 14 does not mandate any specific method of pricing inter-segment sales between industry segments or between geographic segments. Rather, it indicates that such sales "shall be accounted for on the basis used by the enterprise to price the inter-segment sales or transfers." The Securities and Exchange Commission has gone beyond the FASB requirement; the SEC requires the disclosure of any inter-segment transfers made at prices substantially higher or substantially lower than the prevailing market price or the prevailing price charged to unaffiliated parties. In the referenced 1978 survey, more than 50 percent of firms reported no material amount of inter-segment sales. Of the other half of the firms, 75 percent indicated that inter-segment sales were priced at the equivalent of the fair market price; the other 25 percent described their policies as being based on cost, cost plus percentage markup, market less a discount, or negotiated rates.

CLOSING SCHEDULE

If a closing timetable designates swift and orderly closings with subsequent timely control reports, an overall closing schedule must be prepared by the controller. The schedule must assign completion dates for all major portions of the closing work load, with specific individuals assigned the responsibility for compliance with each date. It is particularly important that specific dates be assigned for passing information from one department to another, say from payroll to data processing or accounts payable to data processing.

With multi-plant divisions wherein each plant prepares its own control reports, the information flow network becomes quite complex. The author has used the PERT (network) charting technique with some success to define these interrelationships and to establish realistic schedule dates. Details of the techniques are widely published. One particularly good reference is *PERT—A New Management Planning and Control Technique* published by the American Management Association.

While not in classic PERT format, Exhibit 30 shows the general techniques involved. This describes the flow of data from various plants to data processing and finally to the accountant for payroll distribution ledger entries.

TRANSFER PRICES

In the multi-division company wherein each division has a profit motive unto itself, and wherein one division uses as its raw material the finished product of another division, there will be product "sales" between these two divisions. The price at which product is transferred from the manufacturing division to the consuming division can become, if inadequate attention is given to this area by corporate management, a major source of friction and discontent.

Inter-division transfer prices have a pronounced effect on division operations and profits. A clear, definite policy on transfer pricing must be fixed by corporate management with rules specified for implementation, revisions, and

EXHIBIT 30

PERT CLOSING SCHEDULE

PAYROLL DISTRIBUTION

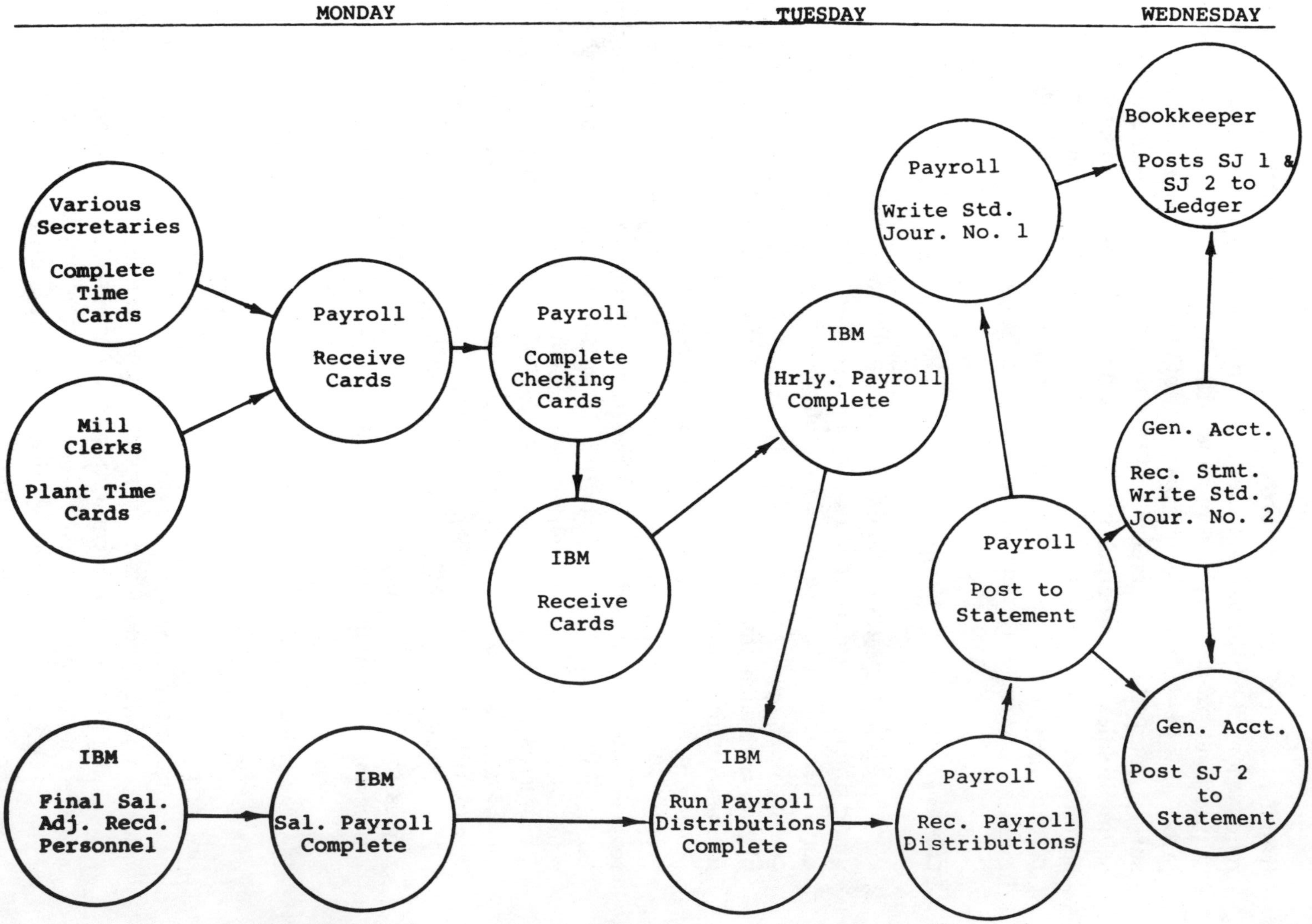

114

appeal. The policy statement should relate pricing policies to profit objectives and to a basic philosophy of any decentralization of profit responsibility.

Invariably, the selling division wants more for its product than it receives and the consuming division wants the product cheaper than it is currently getting it. If left to their own devices, the individual divisions can find a multitude of reasons to offer as justification for their positions. If encouraged in initial appeals to central management, the divisions can spend an inordinately large portion of managerial time debating prices on inter-division sales.

In situations such as these, the corporate controller can often take an early, strong position to establish equitable transfer prices between divisions and to eliminate the atmosphere for time-wasting transfer price debate.

Transfer prices must not in any way work to reduce return on investment. If possible, they should create the opposite effect: an increased return on investment. To do this, division goals must be synonymous with corporate goals.

a. Where market prices are used, a special concession negotiated with an outside vendor should not be used against another division. This is shifting profit, not increasing profit.
b. The true corporate profit must be readily discernible. In the case of items marginal in one division, profits must be audited closely so that the corporate best interest is served in deciding to keep, improve, or reduce market position.
c. Management and clerical time must not be wasted on inter-division pricing debates.
d. Division profit motives must be supported. Cost reductions achieved by one division should remain with that division and not be spread to others.

If the product of the manufacturing division is one that is sold both inter-division and in the marketplace, an easy and equitable solution to this problem lies in establishing the principle that market prices will apply on inter-division sales. The consuming division is allowed to buy the product at the same price that the manufacturing division sells it to an outside customer.

In the case of the product transferred at market price, there should be provided an avenue of legitimate appeal to corporate authority for price relief in the same way that an outside customer can use competitive situations to bargain for special price relief. The mechanics for this should be specifically spelled out with the corporate controller designated as the primary control point in this scheme. Further, this appeal should be restricted to a once-a-year opportunity.

With autonomous, profit-oriented divisions, an arms-length relationship is desired, the kind of relationship found in a competitive market buyer-vendor situation, where prices are negotiated between independent, willing, and able buyers and sellers. Since this cannot be in an integrated company, platitudes to the contrary notwithstanding, there will be *inter*-dependence, not *in*dependence.

There are cases where the product is not sold to an outside customer in the same form as it is sold inter-divisionally. An example is a secret chemical made exclusively for another division. The two divisions could be allowed to negotiate transfer prices. This, however, also leads to the unfortunate situation where divisions spend too much time trying to justify why the prices should be changed. A better solution to the problem is to establish fixed rules in advance, which rules are then applied in a fairly routine manner as subsequent transactions occur.

One such rule which has gained fairly wide acceptance is to allocate the total profit available on the final sale to the customer in proportion to standard conversion cost or value added within each of the divisions. In Exhibit 31, $3.27 of total profit is allocated 84 percent to Plant A and 16 percent to Plant B.

An alternate, but also widely accepted, solution to the problem is to have the first division sell the product at its standard cost plus a standard profit. This profit can be, for instance, a specified return on investment for the assets involved in the manufacture of the product. The calculation of this return on assets can be simplified. A "return-per-machine-hour" rate can be developed which can be applied in the same manner as "cost-per-machine-hour" rates to get both profit per unit of sales and cost per unit of sales. Exhibit 32 shows the derivation of such a rate and its use in a specific price calculation, to include $1.57/unit profit at the rate of 10 percent R.O.I.

There are instances known to the author wherein the products of one division are transferred to the other division at *cost* with all of the profit in the total transaction accruing to the division making the final sale to the customer. This is most undesirable. If the first division has no chance of making a profit on its operations, then there obviously is no profit motive to that division in that portion of its total activities involved in manufacturing products for inter-division sales. This is contrary to all rules of good professional, scientific management. The only incentive remaining to that division is that of operating efficiently, at minimum operating variances. Unfortunately, in the absence of very strictly enforced rules to the contrary, the first division can eliminate its variances, not necessarily by good management, but by sharp cost accounting. By careful preparation of standards, particularly standard machine speeds and standard waste factors, standard costs can, over a period of time, be made to closely approximate actual costs, resulting in the elimination of manufacturing variances. Any of the other plans are preferable to the transfer of product at cost, either standard or actual cost.

Having glibly described two "easy techniques" for establishing transfer prices in the absence of true market prices, it is important now that pitfalls and disadvantages of the techniques be also pointed out. Both have serious shortcomings.

EXHIBIT 31

ALLOCATE PROFIT IN PROPORTION TO CONVERSION COST

Calculation of Profit Split:

Conversion Cost	#1	$6.98	=	$8.31	=	84%
Conversion Cost	#2	1.33	=	8.31	=	16%
TOTAL		$8.31				

Standard Profit	=	$3.27			
Profit #1	=	3.27	×	84%	=	$2.75
Profit #2	=	3.27	×	16%	=	$ .52
TOTAL		$3.27	/cwt.		

Yield Operation #2 = 90%

Profit/Unit in Transfer Price is

$2.75 × 90% = $2.48

Check:

Operation #1 Mat'l Cost	Opn #2 Yield	$ 7.84	90%	=	$ 8.72
Operation #1 Conv. Cost	Opn #2 Yield	6.28	90%	=	6.98
Operation #1 Profit	Ope #2 Yield	2.48	90%	=	2.75
Sub-Total Transfer Price		16.60	90%	–	18.45

	$18.45
Material Cost (in addition to transferred matl.)	.72
Conversion Cost Operation #2	1.33
Profit Operation #2	.52
Discount	.93
Selling Price	$21.95

117

EXHIBIT 32

CALCULATION OF RETURN PER MACHINE HOUR RATES

	Installed Asset Value	Allocate Common Chem. System (1)	Allocate Working Capital (2)	Total Assets	10% of Assets	Standard Activity	10% Return Per Hour
Machine 1	$ 21 500	———	$ 39 600	$ 61 100	$ 6 110	2 000 Hrs.	$ 3.05
2	39 600	$ 19 300	175 000	233 900	23 390	2 000 Hrs.	11.69
3	55 500	25 700	233 300	314 500	31 450	2 000 Hrs.	15.73
4	196 000	———	272 100	468 100	46 810	2 000 Hrs.	23.40
Chemical System	45 000	(45 000)					
Total	$357 600	-0-	$720 000	$1077 600	$107 760		

(1) Basis: Production per year. Machines 1 and 4 do not use this system.
(2) Basis: Sales per year.

Use of Rate

Assume one unit of product costs $15.21 for material and $12.23 for conversion.
Standard production on Machine 3 is 10 units per hour. The transfer price should be:

Material	$15.21/Unit
Conversion	12.23/Unit
Profit ($15.73/hr. ÷ 10 Units/Hr. =)	1.57/Unit
Tranfer Price	$39.01/Unit

118

In the case of the proration of profit, the following problems may arise:

1. Standard costs used to prorate profit have to be derived the same way in both divisions or an equitable division can't be made. This may not be possible, particularly if the selling division is process oriented and the buying division job-shop oriented.
2. Standards must be equally "tight" in both divisions. The one division with tight standards will be penalized because its standard costs are "lower," hence its allocated profit will be "low" in comparison with the division with "loose" or easy standards.
3. The division pricing the product to the customer may price it too low for the other division to get, through allocation, what it considers an adequate profit. This leads to friction when the unhappy division balks at continuing to produce at low profit levels, but the selling division continues to take orders.

In the case of standard cost plus fixed profit or markup, a different list of objections exists:

1. Individual calculations are required for each lot, resulting in high clerical costs.
2. Pricing of new products is difficult until valid standards are derived.
3. True risk may be over- or under-compensated since the rule is constant for all products, new and old.
4. A 10 percent markup as defined in Exhibit 32 may leave zero profit for the buying division.
5. Routine standards revision wipes out the gain from process improvement for the division creating the improvement.
6. High-cost machines could be used to produce inter-division products with costs and profits assured by the captive customer. This could leave lower-cost machines available for the production of direct customer products. The captive division customer has a strong incentive to involve himself in a scheduling problem of the other division under this situation, an unhappy event.

INVENTORY CONTROL

In the spectrum of general accounting, the one area most misunderstood by operating management and the area for easy profit manipulation is inventory valuation and control.

Operating managers get balled up in the application and significance of valuation reserves. Further, it makes for far fewer operating problems if a high inventory of every item is available in the plant. So what if an item sits unused for six months before it is used? It was right there, available, when the machine broke down, wasn't it?

Loose control at the level of corporate inventory valuation rules and controls makes it possible for divisions to manipulate reported profits by manipulating total inventory valuations. In addition to physical audits of inventories, controls on methods of valuation are required. Written procedures should give exact rules for initial valuation and for reserves as necessary to reflect current true value.

One technique for control over inventory quantities is to establish a standard value for each major category of inventory and then require the operating manager to justify any excess over that standard. The responsibility for such a justification must match the authority to change the quantity. If the purchasing agent buys fuel, for instance, don't demand the justification for an over-standard quantity from the plant superintendent. If such responsibilities are not clearly assigned, the controller should get the ambiguity resolved. For one paper mill operation, responsibilities are assigned as follows:

Purchasing Agent	Fuel
	Fiber
	Additives
	Pack & Ship Material
	Operating Supplies
Plant Superintendent	In-Process Inventory
Sales Managers	Finished Product

A technique useful with a profit center manager is to establish "return on investment" control index of performance, with inventory included in the total investment. Inventory will often be the major part of total investment; when this is true, a substantial improvement in return on investment can be made by reducing that inventory. High inventories can be brought in line by simply cutting back on purchases while consuming at the normal rate. The relationship of inventory to R.O.I. is clearly shown in the chart in Exhibits 33 and 34.

Exclusion of inventory and other working capital from the return on investment calculation results in a high R.O.I. as shown in Exhibit 34. On $1,500,000 sales and $1,500,000 in fixed assets a 20 percent return on investment is indicated. This is not acceptable, however, because working capital is very much an asset "invested" in these same sales. In this case, high inventories are required for fast service and immediate delivery in several geographic areas. In fact, working capital may total $1,500,000, the same amount of money invested in plant

EXHIBIT 33

RETURN ON INVESTMENT

RELATIONSHIP OF ELEMENTS INVOLVED

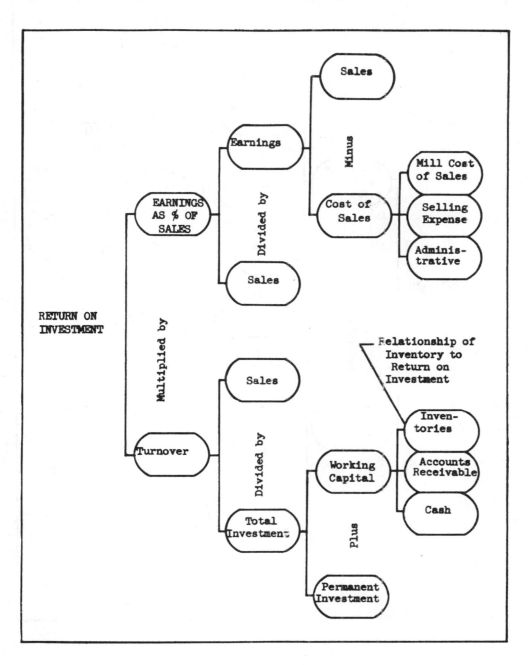

EXHIBIT 34

R.O.I.—PERMANENT INVESTMENT

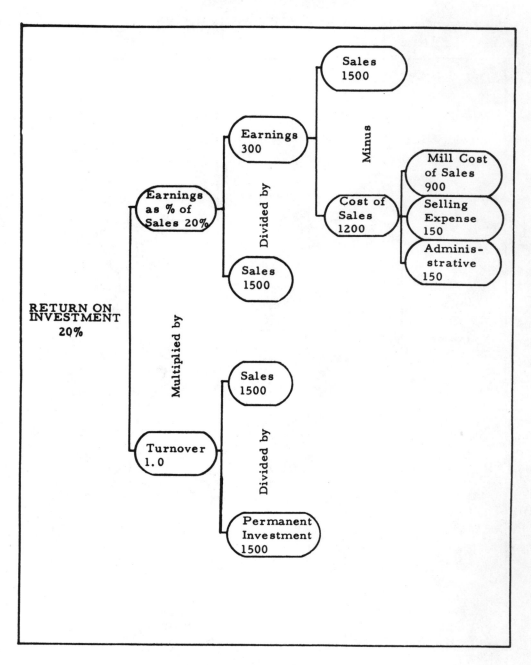

and equipment, a not unusual situation in retail and service oriented divisions. Exhibit 35 includes this investment; clearly the 10 percent R.O.I. shown here is a much better measure of performance than the 20 percent cited in Exhibit 34. With return on investment becoming a widely used control statistic, it is important that the complete measure be performed.

INVENTORY VALUATION

Raw material and product inventories represent a major portion of the total assets of a manufacturing organization. Therefore, it is vital that the value which these inventories represent is adequately and accurately stated in the books of account.

Raw material inventory is made up of items bought by the division with payment recorded through the accounts payable account. The value, then, of the inventory should be that recorded value paid. In a falling market, though, new purchases can be made at lower prices. It would be overstating the value to keep the inventory at that higher price. The value has deteriorated, another hazard of carrying high inventories to satisfy manufacturing's whim.

Product inventory is worth the manufacturing conversion cost and raw material cost of getting it into product inventory. It is preferable to use current standard costs to value current production. But in a falling market with declining raw material prices, a product made from higher priced components is no longer worth that standard cost. It is now worth current, lower costs.

In both cases, this amounts to saying that all raw material, process, and finished goods inventory should be valued at the lower of original cost or current market.

Provision must be made for reducing the valuation on certain categories of raw material process and finished inventory. An expedient way to do this is to use valuation allowance contra accounts which, in effect, reduce the total inventory valuation to some lower "true value." Allowances often established for this purpose include damaged stock, obsolete items, and loss items. If standard raw material prices are used to value raw material consumed, a standard versus actual purchase price variance account has to be set up through which to take variances in purchase price of material. If product inventory is valued at standard cost, reprice allowances must be set up through which to charge reprice differences in product and in raw material.

A determined effort should be made to teach the significance of these allowances to operating management. Profits are affected by many things that happen to and in inventory. Decisions which result in too much finished inventory create the opportunity for inventory to become old and then obsolete. Money initially paid for material and manpower is written off just as surely as if the item

EXHIBIT 35

R.O.I. INCLUDING WORKING CAPITAL

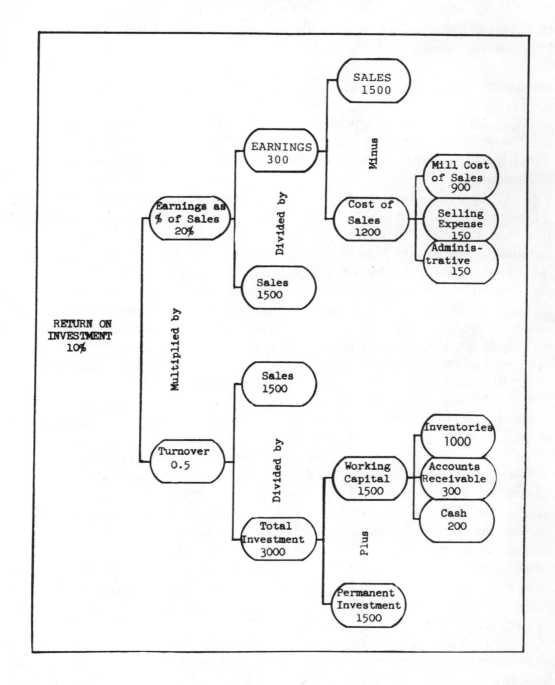

had been physically junked as it came through the manufacturing process. Inventory is damaged in handling and rehandling while it sits in the warehouse, in the way of the shipping crew and unwanted by any customer. As prices change and processes improve, standard costs change. This year it may cost 5 percent less to produce one unit of production. All of the inventory produced at the higher price is written down to its new, lower value. That excess value added—an unhappy phrase—is lost value which cannot now be passed on to the customer. It represents time and material wasted last year in building too much inventory.

PHYSICAL INVENTORIES

Physical counts of all inventories are required to insure that what is reported to be on hand, actually is on hand. If it were known that no actual count were ever to be taken, those so inclined would be certain to steal without fear of discovery. Those charged with record-keeping could fabricate production records without leaving the comfort of the swivel chair. Fictitiously high book inventories could be generated to create the appearance of low production costs and high profits.

Precautions to prevent inventory fraud must include at least annual physical inventory counts by people not ordinarily involved in normal reporting and production of the inventory being counted. Semi-annual and quarterly counts are more desirable, if not too costly.

A control scheme for the physical count must be prepared by the controller. Elements to be included are as follows:

a. Written instructions should be published to include:
   1. Date and time allocated for inventory taking.
   2. Name of inventory supervisor.
   3. Names and duties of personnel, crews, etc.
   4. Proper classification of items to be inventoried.
   5. Physical rearranging or housekeeping necessary before inventory is taken. This should be done sufficiently in advance to permit the work to be done in an orderly manner.
   6. Clear delineation of location and category responsibilities.
   7. Method of identification of items.
   8. Forms used, including tag color, marking method, or inventory identification.
   9. Control instructions on tags and forms.
   10. Method of determining quantities. Included in this are such things as what instruments to use, or what techniques to use to measure the material.

11. Means of verifying count.
12. Details of accounting check.
13. Method of adjusting for work flow occurring during the inventory, who will adjust, cutoff times, etc.
14. Dividing line between this inventory and preceding or subsequent ones (for example, between work in process and finished goods).

b. A form for recording the count and identifying the item must be invented to satisfy the needs of the specific situation. It should facilitate the following:

1. Recording identification and count.
2. Insuring return of all forms used. Serially prenumbered forms which can be sorted serially after the count are best for this purpose.
3. Marking the item to show that it has been counted.

One scheme devised to accomplish this involves the use of a colored punched card, as shown in Exhibit 36. The identification data and count are written in the blanks provided. A serial number is punched into and printed on each card; an adequate supply is so numbered ahead of time. Cards are key-punched from these inventory cards. A sort and listing is made to determine that all cards are returned. Gaps in the key-punched deck must be accounted for in unused, returned cards. The supervisor assigned to each area is held responsible for cards issued to him. The perforated stub on the left end of the card is glued or taped to the item when the card is filled out on the floor as the item is counted. A quick visual check for stubs, say orange-colored this month, will reassure the controller that all units have been recorded.

Note the construction of the card in Exhibit 36. This is not an expensive, perforated card. The perforation is made by punching all twelve positions in Column 16 of a regular IBM card which has been preprinted on the back, as shown. This is a very good example of ingenuity, of adapting a common item to a complex, multi-purpose need.

EXHIBIT 36

INVENTORY CONTROL TAG

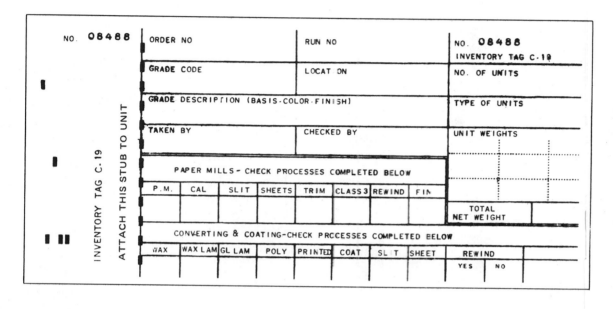

5

Treasury Duties

In the smaller company, the same man often must wear both the controller's hat and the treasurer's hat. This is a truism which, however, requires some definition.

All treasurer duties do not automatically go this route.

Those activities connected with bank relations, stock issues, and other sources of funds are often the direct responsibility of the chief executive officer and are therefore beyond the scope of this book.

Other treasurer's duties can properly be within the scope of the controller, particularily in the smaller company.

ACCOUNTS RECEIVABLE

Protection of receivables is a vital function, particularly where cash sales are a minor portion of total sales. While functions may be subdivided, control encompasses the entire order acceptance-invoicing-accounts receivable-cash receipt cycle. The steps in the process are identified in Exhibit 37.

Before an order can be accepted, it must be approved at the credit desk, either literally or through the mechanism of an approved credit list. Credit policy must be liberal enough not to discourage orders but restrictive enough that bad debt losses are held to a tolerable level. As with any control scheme, zero losses are bad because this represents a too tight policy which does not allow sufficient risk taking, which probably means a few good risks are being rejected as well as poor ones.

Credit investigation and approval schemes must provide for regular and prompt review of new orders with a minimum of delay for good risk customers. An approved list of customers whose orders can be processed without limit and without delay can be published, at least on the best customers. A second list with dollar credit limits can also be published; use of this list requires a feedback from the accounts receivable function to order-entry to permit identification of over-limit customers in order for this scheme to work smoothly.

EXHIBIT 37

ACCOUNTS RECEIVABLE SCHEME

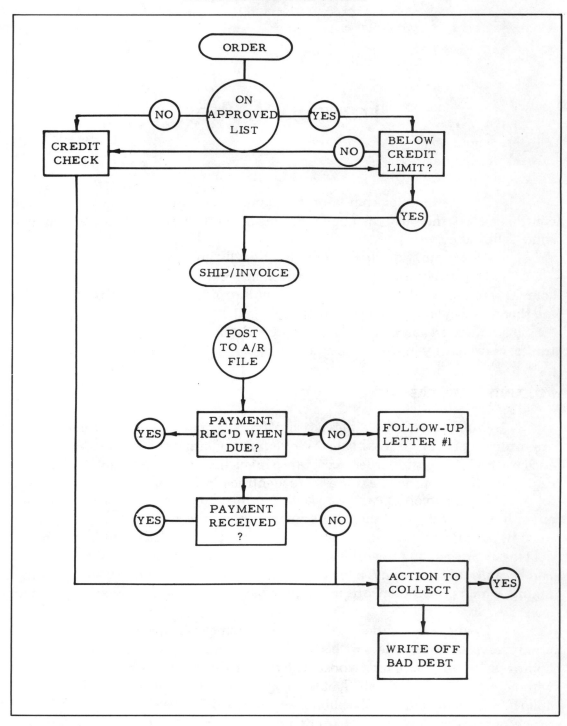

The accounts receivable scheme must provide, at least, for up-to-date posting of invoices and receipts to each customer account, for over-limit reports to order-entry, for actionable information on past due accounts, for prompt handling of adjustments, for enforcement of cash discount terms, and for writing off of bad debts.

A useful index of control is "average number of days accounts are outstanding" or "receivables as a percent of sales." Both measure the same thing. If receivables are 10 percent of sales, this is the same as saying receivables average 36.5 days outstanding:

$$\text{Ratio} = \frac{\text{current (or average) receivables balance}}{\text{annual sales}}$$

Average days outstanding = Ratio x 365

Two comparisons are important:

a. The trend in number of days outstanding, and
b. Actual days outstanding versus the net due terms. Even though your terms are 2 percent 10, net 30, you may find a 40 day average outstanding balance. This means you are supplying 10 extra days' working capital for all your customers, on the average.

For evaluation of credit terms and policies, the ratio of bad debt write-offs to total sales and the ratio of orders rejected because of credit problems to total orders are useful. A high ratio of bad debts means loose control in general or one particularly bad actor not spotted in time, while a ratio too low means inadequate risk-taking. A high ratio of orders rejected could be confirmation of inadequate risk-taking.

The foregoing was written primarily about customer receivables, but it also applies to employee receivables, notes receivables, freight claims receivable, insurance claims receivable, and non-product sale receivables. Each such sale or claim should be set up as a receivable in order that complete follow-up procedures can be assured.

CREDIT APPROVAL

Every prospective new customer to whom goods are to be shipped on terms other than cash in advance or C.O.D. must be rated and approved as a credit risk.

The sales department will typically come to the Credit Manager with an order in hand, requesting approval of the credit risk involved. It must be clearly established that the Credit Manager has a reasonable time allowed to investigate the potential risk before giving his decision. The gathering of information on which to make that decision will include one or more of the following:

1. Financial data supplied by the customer. This will be an important source of credit limit data particularly with small and privately held firms.
2. Credit bureau and similar investigatory firms. Character evaluation of owner-managers is important.
3. Personal visits by the Credit Manager are particularly important in new growth customer accounts.
4. Dun and Bradstreet reports are a must in credit management, supplementing all other data.
5. Discussions with other suppliers can confirm and elaborate on D&B credit line and experience data.

No rule of thumb can be given to assist in deciding to accept a credit risk. The key word is "RISK." There is some risk in every credit sale. The task of the Credit Manager is to achieve a balance between the cost of credit management and a reasonable bad debt loss experience. There must be some bad debt loss. If there is none, too many orders are being refused credit approval. Potential profit on disapproved orders is being lost because of excessive conservatism.

PAST DUE INVOICES

One routine report should be an Aged Account Analysis, showing by major customer or summary by division or product the current balances as well as those over 30 and, say, 90 days past due. A trend chart showing total dollar values past due should accompany each statistical report, as shown in Exhibit 38. In this case, corrective action should have been initiated when the chart jumped up in March. No results show, however, because the past due line has continued upward through the current month.

Corrective action includes direct contact with past due customers, first and foremost. If a poor risk is involved, corrective action to improve your relative position versus other supplier creditors must be taken. Demand notes are one favorite device often used. Owner-managers frequently are willing to give personal notes pledging personal assets against their business debts.

A minimum action would be to insure that cash discounts are not taken on past due invoices. Interest should be charged for the past due period. It is not sufficient as salesmen often think to allow the discount but to charge interest. A 2 percent, 60 day term is actually 12 percent annually; interest at 12-14 percent is the greatest one could expect to charge past due accounts in most industries.

EXHIBIT 38

AGED RECEIVABLE BALANCE BY PLANT

		Past Due		
	Total	30 Days	60 Days	90 Days
Plant A	125,000	11,000	3,000	1,500
B	175,000	14,000	5,000	3,500
C	300,000	26,000	7,000	4,000
D	90,000	7,300	2,500	1,700
Total	690,000	58,300	17,500	10,700
	100%	8.5%	2.5%	1.5%

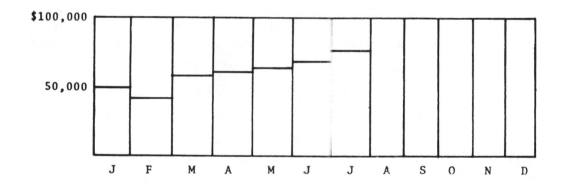

BALANCE SHEET ANALYSIS

A very few words on balance sheet analysis belong somewhere in this book. Because of their relevance to risk evaluation in credit management, they will be put here.

There is no deeply profound technique for this analysis. The numbers are there; no detailed explanations for the balance sheet figures are readily available to outsiders, even to suppliers from whom credit is being requested; one must infer from trends and from ratios whatever he can about current and future risk.

The Current Ratio is the ratio of total current assets to total current liabilities. Most analysts would like to see a ratio of at least 2:1. Anything less than this casts doubts on the ability to meet short-term obligations. Because inventories are part of current assets and inventories may not be readily convertible to cash, the Net Quick Assets Ratio is a better test of short-term liquidity. This is the ratio of total current assets less inventories to total current liabilities. This ought to be at least 1:1.

Inventories may be too large for the volume of sales. The dangers in this are the exposure to losses in the event of material price reduction, selling price reductions, style changes, and obsolescence. Inventory Turnover, which is annual sales divided by inventory value, analyzed for trends and compared with like companies is a valid indicator.

Capitalization Ratios are useful in analyzing the extent to which debt is already being used to finance operations and growth. The Debt Ratio is the ratio of total long and short-term loans, including bonds, to the sum of debt, stock, surplus, and retained earnings. Trend is important. Total annual interest cost versus net profit is important. The ratio of short-term to long-term debt is important.

However, footnotes to financial statements are more revealing than any of these items. In these can be found changes in accounting methods, methods of treatment of start-up and development charges, inventory reserves, pension funding methods—all of which can be used to tailor the appearance of the balance sheet.

MANAGEMENT OF FUNDS

Having arranged for funds from his bank, the chief executive might delegate to the controller the responsibility to manage the use of those funds. It would be his duty to balance receipts against disbursements, keep adequate balances in every bank account, and use borrowed funds as necessary when receipts lag or disbursements jump up.

Important to this is accurate daily information on cash received from customers in payment for products sold. A daily total of receipts must be given by accounts receivable to the controller. Without this daily input, there is no adequate way of knowing that enough funds are available to be in the right place at the right time.

Similarly, disbursements must be reported as made, both for payroll and for accounts payable. This is the notification to the controller that checks have been written against certain bank accounts so that he can transfer funds if necessary to cover the disbursement. Notification must be made the same day in order for transfers, if required, to be made at the same time.

To conserve cash by reducing "float," consideration should be given to the use of lock boxes which permit more frequent pickup of payments from customers. This gets money into the bank hours or days earlier than if mail were delivered in routine mail deliveries. A change from checks to drafts also permits more effective use of funds. Funds must be deposited in the bank the same day checks are issued. In effect, the money lies there idle until the check arrives via normal bank channels as a charge against those funds. When drafts are used, instead of checks, no funds are transferred until the draft arrives at your bank to be honored. This gives you the full use of your funds during the interval they would otherwise be idle in your checking account.

To gain a lead-indicator on the need for and availability of cash, use two readily available sources of information.

Invoices are a leading indicator to cash receipts. Terms of cash discount coupled with invoice date give an acceptable prediction of cash receipts, day by day. Billing totals are required for control; in any case, they can be used to predict receipts at very little additional expense.

Payroll disbursements are fairly predictable from history. In most cases, hourly payrolls fluctuate within narrow ranges. Salary payrolls are known exactly in advance except for non-exempt overtime, a small percentage of the whole. Payroll dates are known exactly. Purchase orders issued indicate total funds to be needed for accounts payable, although timing is not specific. A moving average of purchase orders written, used in combination with actual payroll disbursements, should predict, adequately, this part of the equation. If it is necessary to level out expenditures, a limit can be placed on allowable purchase orders to be written each week. Once this limit is reached in a week, only emergency orders approved, say, by the controller can be written. Other orders are deferred to the following week. This procedure can also be followed to eliminate expenditures not really necessary. With a maximum dollar limit not to be exceeded each week, a greater selectivity will be followed in insuring that the really necessary purchases are made and that less necessary ones are deferred or eliminated entirely.

A daily status report of cash received and disbursed should be prepared, summarizing the transactions and balance for each day, as illustrated in Exhibit 39.

CASH MANAGEMENT

Cash management is the term used to describe the process whereby an organization attempts to maximize the benefits that can accrue from the effective use of its cash resource. The success of an organization's efforts can be determined by looking at how well it: (1) has funds available to meet disbursement needs; (2) eliminates all unnecessary borrowing; and (3) invests all idle cash. Full considera-

EXHIBIT 39

DAILY CASH STATUS REPORT

Daily Cash Report: June 21, 19__

Balance June 20, 19__	$3,325,270
Receipts	721,000
Disbursements	824,000
Balance June 21, 19__	$3,222,270
Bank Balance:	
First State Bank—Payroll	$ 824,000
Second National Bank	2,398,270
Total	$3,222,270

tion must be given to the specific elements that affect the availability of funds. To meet this objective, the following aspects must be well-managed:

Cash Inflows

> Terms of collection
> Billing process
> Collection of cash and timeliness of deposit

Cash Outflows

> Terms of payment
> Timing of payment

Utilization of Cash

> Short term investments
> Debt reduction

Use of Financial Institutions

> Service availability
> Selection of services
> Payment for services
> Contract-bid and award
> Measurement of relationships

Cash Forecasting

As anyone who has ever paid or received interest knows, having a dollar today is worth more than having a dollar sometime in the future. Cash management is the business of arranging one's finances to make the most of the use of the money on hand and to minimize the money borrowed and, hence, the interest paid for it.

In simple terms, effective cash management means collecting money as quickly as it is due—by billing for it on a timely basis and by efficiently processing receipts. Cash management also means ensuring that one pays bills and makes other disbursements on time—not early or late. Finally, good cash management means making sure that the money that accumulates between receipt and disbursement is put to work—either by earning interest or by repaying short-term debt and eliminating interest on debt.

The benefits from effective cash management correspond proportionately to the size of the cash flow being managed. For example, if a firm has $100 for three days, it is difficult to invest it; however, with accumulations of $100,000, or more, there is a ready market in which such large amounts can be profitably invested for periods as short as overnight. Similarly, in large organizations with decentralized units that receive and disburse money, the cumulative effect of many small savings can result in a substantial benefit.

The author was a consultant in 1978 to a White House study of cash management practices in the Federal Government. This work resulted in interest savings of one *billion* dollars per year to taxpayers.

The primary goal of cash management is the saving of interest on debt and the earning of interest on investments. Detailed activities to achieve this goal include the following:

a. **Accelerating the inflow of receipts.** There may be opportunities to collect money that is due in a more business-like way, including collecting money more frequently and sending out bills in a timely manner. For large receipts, there are sophisticated methods of receiving funds through Electronic Fund Transfers, which eliminate the transit and processing time on money.

b. **Streamlining receipt processing.** Accelerating the cash inflow is only a valid objective if the firm then promptly receives and processes payments. At times, either the uneven flow of receipts, administrative bottlenecks or inattention by management delays the processing of receipts. Such receipt bottlenecks may be broken by streamlined receipt processing, through work simplification, and by techniques such as lock boxes.

c. **Controlling disbursements more closely.** The firm should pay its bills and other obligations on time—not before or after.

d. **Eliminating excessive idle cash balances.** While any organization needs some operating cash for day-to-day needs, the amount should be kept to a minimum. One should seek opportunities to decrease the levels of working capital cash and invest funds at the highest feasible rates.

e. **Establishing policies, authorities, and responsibilities to ensure institutional cash management excellence.** In addition to identifying and benefiting from short-term cash management improvement opportunities, one should institutionalize these improvements.

A checklist of specific cash management improvement ideas is presented in Exhibit 40.

EXHIBIT 40

CASH MANAGEMENT CHECKLIST

I. **Purpose of review**

    To reduce interest cost and to increase interest income.

II. **Activities to be reviewed**

    A. Cash Inflows
        1. Terms and billing procedure for:

            a. Receipts for goods and services, licenses, etc.
            b. Unpaid bills
            c. Loan repayments
            d. Other

        2. Collection procedures

            a. Receipt by firm or agent
            b. Process of acquiring "good" funds

        3. Other

    B. Cash Outflow

        1. Procurement process

            a. Payment terms of purchase
            b. Scheduling of disbursement

        2. Loans

        3. Other

    C. Utilization of cash

        1. Knowledge of availability of cash

        2. Decision process for utilization

            a. Investment process
            b. Debt liquidation process

EXHIBIT 40

CASH MANAGEMENT CHECKLIST (Cont.)

    D. Relationships with financial institutions

        1. Services acquired

        2. Selection of institution

        3. Means of payment (compensating balances or charges)

        4. Monitoring of payment

    E. Cash Forecasting

III. Interview Questions

    A. What are the policy and procedure statements governing the functions?

    B. Are cash management activities constrained by other factors?

    C. Which executive has the responsibility for operating policy and procedures? What are his operating policies and procedures?

    D. Which manager has the responsibility for operating practices? What are his operating practices?

    E. What are cash management relationships with respect to Corporate versus Division executives?

        1. Policy

        2. Procedures

        3. Responsibility

        4. Practice

    F. What cash management initiatives have been undertaken recently and what has been the effect? What cash management initiatives are contemplated for the near-term future?

    G. With regard to terms and billing procedures (including loans and loan repayments)

        1. Terms

            a. How are payment terms determined?

            b. How is the time value of money considered in determining payment terms? price?

            c. What late payment penalties or discounts are in effect?

            d. What specific form of payment (check, cash, wire, etc.) is specified?

        2. Billing procedures

            a. How is billing schedule determined?

            b. What inter-period follow-up is made for past due accounts?

            c. How is timeliness of payment monitored, and penalties assessed?

EXHIBIT 40

CASH MANAGEMENT CHECKLIST (Cont.)

H. With regard to collections

1. What functions are performed at the point of entry?

2. At what point *is* payment (check, money) separated from the accounting document?

3. At what point *can* payment be separated from accounting document?

4. Is there a clerical audit of payments for timeliness of payment, penalties, interest, etc.?

I. With regard to availability of "good funds"

1. What is the elapsed time between each function, i.e., receipt to deposit?

2. How/where are proceeds deposited?

3. When are funds "available"?

4. How/when does the corporate treasurer know about location and availability of funds?

5. Does the firm use EFT for receipts? How? Why/why not?

J. With regard to relationship with financial institutions

1. How is the decision made as to what services to acquire?

2. How is the financial institution selected?

   a. Fee or balance compensation
   b. How is cost vs. compensation monitored?

3. Does the firm monitor the quality of services, especially funds availability versus deposit date?

K. Is there an investment function? Describe.

L. Does the firm have debt outstanding?

1. Can it be repaid at the discretion of the firm? In increments?

2. Is debt level adjustable by reborrowing more or less?

M. Outflows

1. Purchasing

   a. Does the firm have a central purchasing function?
   b. Does the purchase order specify payment terms?
   c. How does time value of money enter into consideration of terms? pricing? discount?
   d. Does the firm use EFT for payment? How?

EXHIBIT 40

CASH MANAGEMENT CHECKLIST (Cont.)

N. Debit

1. Does the firm borrow?

   a. Direct from banks?
   b. Bonds?
   c. Sell Accounts Receivables?
   d. Other

2. What is decision process as to when and how much to borrow?

3. Is borrowing in anticipation of need or after the fact?

IV. **Specific Data Requirements**

A. Descriptive Information

1. Dollar values and timing—by category (type of payment or collection)

   a. Inflows
   b. Outflows

2. Develop a flow chart depicting flows into and out of the organization

B. Collection procedures/data

1. What is the geographic and time pattern of receipts, by source, including volume and average size? Is there a potential for lock box or regional processing?

2. What is point of entry to the firm? (including lock box, etc.)

C. Utilization of funds

1. What cash balances are held in what banks?

   a. How much?
   b. Why?
   c. Where?
   d. In what form?
   e. Under whose control?

V. **Cash Forecasting**

Does the firm do cash flow forecasting?

1. At what level? period?

2. For what purposes?

3. To whom is forecast communicated? For what purpose?

4. How accurate are forecasts?

5. What actions are taken vs. inaccurate forecast?

CASH CONTROL

Embezzlement or misappropriation in cash handling is an ever-present danger. Adequate controls must be set up by the controller to remove temptation from the honest employee and to thwart the outright dishonest employee.

The basic rule to be followed is to separate the handling of cash so that at least two people are involved, one functioning as a check on the other. A third party is desirable to receive control information from each and to verify that independent clerical data indicates the same action. Exhibit 41 shows this three party control over salary payroll disbursement.

EXHIBIT 41

THREE PARTY CASH CONTROL

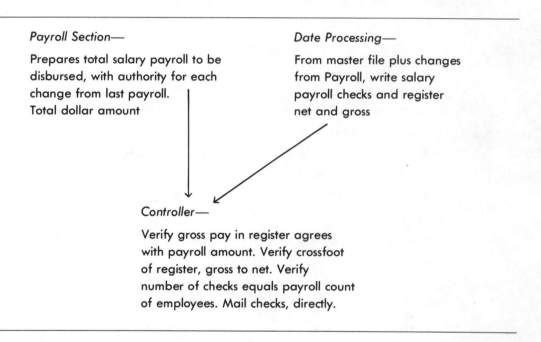

Payroll Section—

Prepares total salary payroll to be disbursed, with authority for each change from last payroll. Total dollar amount

Date Processing—

From master file plus changes from Payroll, write salary payroll checks and register net and gross

Controller—

Verify gross pay in register agrees with payroll amount. Verify crossfoot of register, gross to net. Verify number of checks equals payroll count of employees. Mail checks, directly.

Following this principle, the following minimum separation of duties must be set up:

1. Purchase orders are to be written by one person, physical receipt to be acknowledged by a second, and accounts payable disbursement by a third.
2. Accounts payable matching of vouchers is to be done by one person with a verification that all necessary documents are present by a second person before payment. Documents are to be stamped or perforated to prevent a second use.

3. Billings are to be reported to accounts receivable and to the general accountant for entry to the books of account. Cash receipts are to be deposited with a copy of the deposit slip sent to the general accountant for entry in the books. Receivables credits to customer accounts must tally with cash receipts.

4. Tight control over check forms must be exercised. All checks must be serially numbered. Every number must be accounted for, either by a valid voucher or by the presence of a void check. If signature plates are used, the plate must be available under controlled conditions with every revolution of the signer machine accounted for by a valid or a void check. (See Exhibit 42 for a sample plate control sheet.)

5. Separate petty cash disbursements from petty cash receipts.

6. Bank reconciliations are very important. Every check issued must be accounted for when received back through channels. When done by someone not involved in disbursements or receipts, this serves as an audit on both of those functions. In addition to verifying that the checks were validly issued by your company and to accounting for still outstanding claims, deposits and disbursements should be checked against entries in the books of account.

7. Everyone whose signature is accepted on checks should be bonded. Petty cash funds should be reimbursed weekly through accounts payable. All vouchers received for disbursed funds should become part of the accounts payable file in support of that payment.

EXHIBIT 42

SIGNATURE PLATE CONTROL SHEET

		Checks Used (Inclusive)		Void	Valid	Voided After			Meter	
Initial	Date	First	Last	Checks	Checks	Signing	Signatures	Start	End	Turns
J. V. B.	1/12	0026	0127	4	98	4	10ꞏ	1000	1101	101
J. V. B.	1/13	0128	0128	—	1	—	1	1101	1102	1
J. V. B.	1/14	0129	0228	5	95	—	95	1102	1197	95

PETTY CASH

Petty cash funds fit in the category of necessary evils. While it is desirable that payments be made by check, this often is not practical. Petty cash funds will exist, of necessity, for reimbursement of emergency purchases, travel expenses, and cash advances for travel. They are not to be used for routine purchases to circumvent normal purchasing procedures.

A particular employee should be designated petty cash custodian. He will be held accountable for the cash in his care. Specific procedures should be published spelling out in detail forms, approvals, and reimbursement.

Exhibit 43 illustrates a form for reimbursement of emergency purchases. No one should be reimbursed without the signature of a designated approval authority. This form provides for an adequate description of the circumstances of the expenditure as well as approval and accounting code for the charge. When used for travel advances, the "amount received" block will be initialed, as well.

EXHIBIT 43

PETTY CASH VOUCHER

PETTY CASH DISBURSEMENT VOUCHER NO.	**1283**

PAY TO J.E. BENNETT	DATE 2/8/XX

AMOUNT *Two hundred and Fifty—* DOLLARS _____ CENTS
(PLEASE WRITE AMOUNT)

Description	AMOUNT
Travel Advance — trip to	250	00
Pittsburgh — to investigate	
complaint	

ACCOUNT CODE 183		TOTAL	250	00

EXPENDITURE APPROVED	AMOUNT RECEIVED

The form for weekly expense reporting and reimbursement will be governed to a large degree by Internal Revenue Service rulings concerning deductible business expenses. Exhibit 44 illustrates a form with adequate expense control information including space for compliance with Internal Revenue Service rulings. Be sure that your form adequately describes entertainment, etc., to the satisfaction of those regulations, as you interpret them.

INSURANCE COVERAGE

This is a checklist of types of insurance coverage necessary to most manufacturing firms. The reason for the policy will be apparent from the descrip-

EXHIBIT 44

TRAVEL AND ENTERTAINMENT VOUCHER

		WEEK ENDING 6/22/XX	NAME J. V. BENNETT DEPARTMENT CONTROLLER							MAILING _____ ADDRESS _____		

EXPENSE REPORT		DAY	SUN. A	MON. B	TUES. C	WED. D	THURS. E	FRI. F	SAT. G	H TOTAL	K ACCOUNTING USE ONLY
		DATE		6/17	6/18						
	PLACES VISITED	FROM		Md.	Md.						
		TO		NYC	NYC						
MILEAGE				32							
OWN CAR @ $.20/MI	1			6 40						6 40	
CO. CAR @ ¢/MI	2										
TOLLS & PARKING	3										
GAS, OIL, CAR WASHES *	4										
BUS, TAXI, ETC.	5			14 50	14 70					29 20	
RAILROAD	6										
AIRPLANE	7										
MEALS	8			27 90	32 40					60 30	
LODGING	* 9										
TELEPHONE	10										
ENTERTAINMENT	11										
TIPS, BAGGAGE	12										
GIFTS	13										
	14										
	15										
*RECEIPTS ALWAYS REQUIRED TOTAL 1 - 15	16			48 80	47 10					95 90	

SPEEDOMETER READINGS - LEASED CARS		ITEMS BILLED DIRECT TO RPc		LESS TEMPORARY ADVANCE	—
MILEAGE END		AUTO *	$		
MILEAGE BEGINNING		AIRPLANE *	$	DUE	—
MILES TRAVELLED		RAILROAD *	$	DUE EMPLOYEE	95 90
LESS PERSONAL MILES		TELEPHONE *	$	EXPLAIN PURPOSE OF EXPENDITURE BELOW.	
NET COMPANY MILES			*	CROSS REFERENCE BY LETTER AND NUMBER.	

EXPLANATION OF ENTERTAINMENT EXPENSE. INCLUDE (1) NAME, TITLE, AND COMPANY OF ALL PERSONS ENTERTAINED, (2) PLACE AND TYPE OF ENTERTAINMENT, AND (3) BUSINESS REASON FOR ENTERTAINMENT.

[ ] INDUSTRY OR PROFESSIONAL MEETING

[ ] CUSTOMER COMPLAINT

[X] OTHER (SPECIFY)

8-B Includes lunch R J Talbert and HB, Discussion & M.I.S. re Profit Forecast

Reports re trip and further work M.I.S.

APPROVED BY: _____ CHECKED BY: _____ CASH RECEIVED BY: J.V. Bennett

EMPLOYEE'S COPY

tion. Whether it is necessary to a specific company depends on the risk versus the cost of protection.

Fire. A premium-saving device in ordinary fire insurance is a minimum loss, say $2,000, below which losses will not be claimed. This amounts to self-insurance for the smaller losses. Some larger companies completely self-insure; many of these carry catastrophe policies for losses of, say, $2,000,000 or over. Generally, an inspection service is a part of the insurer's service to the policy holder. Premiums are lower when the inspector's recommendations are carried out because risks are reduced.

Business interruption insurance is often included in this coverage to cover for lost income and to pay continuing costs during plant shutdown and repair following a fire loss.

Coverage generally includes damages incurred by fire, water, sprinkler systems, lightning and windstorms, smoke, and certain explosions.

Boiler and Machinery coverage applies to heat and power generating equipment, not covered under the fire policy. A deductible is common here, where all losses are reported but where the first, say $2,000, is deducted from the payment.

Coverage includes property damage to the equipment, and use and occupancy of the production equipment and buildings for actual losses sustained.

Workmen's Compensation requirements are typically statutory.

General Liability coverage to protect against any and all claims for personal injury and property damage is necessary. Coverage should be on an "occurrence" and on an "aggregate" basis. This can be particularly pertinent to consumer products where claims of adverse effects from use often arise. It is also pertinent to industrial products used as components of a subsequent product, where a contingent liability claim might arise from either a consumer claim or from apparent failure or quality rejection of your product in the production process of your customer.

Valuable Papers coverage on files, records, and storage vaults is good to have for repair, replacement, or payment in case of damage or destruction. This might include technical papers, tax records, asset records, central file storage, etc.

Transportation and Marine Export product protection is necessary. This covers products sold on a delivered basis. In addition, it can cover machinery, patterns, your property to be worked on in the premises of others, property in public warehouses, and property on exhibition.

Crime Insurance coverage protects against such things as employee dishonesty, loss of money or securities through disappearance, robbery, etc., loss due to acceptance in good faith of counterfeit money or money orders, depositors' forgery, and theft of office equipment and tools.

Airplane Insurance is a separate policy. Because liability claims can be very high and because aircraft are very expensive, this coverage comes separately. Personal bodily injury and property damage liability is included as well as hull damage to the aircraft.

6

Accounting Services

This chapter serves briefly to describe the staffing and security problems of that group of accounting functions not previously covered in this book. In this section, there will be notes about:

> Order Entry
> Billing
> Accounts Payable
> Payroll

Organizationally, these activities do not have to be associated with any other specific function or with each other. The major requisite is to assign a relatively strong individual to be in charge of each at the lowest echelon feasible, with simultaneous setting up of security precautions amenable to easy and frequent audit. This relieves higher supervisors of the chore of routine supervision without sacrificing control.

Particularly in payroll and in accounts payable, the controller should exercise some personal audit in connection with check signature control.

ORDER ENTRY

Order entry initiates the corporate life cycle.

Often there is a tendency to disregard the order writing procedure as a necessary chore in order to get on with the really important business to be done. In fact, however, the order cycle is the entire reason for being in business. Full and careful attention must be given to the swift and accurate translation of the customer's needs into a physical shipment and billing. This area can be short-changed only at the peril of the continued profitable existence of the business.

Orders are received either in the form of a purchase order written on the customer's form or in the form of an order written out on an order blank by a company salesman according to his understanding of the customer's needs. Two things should happen very quickly:

1. The order should be written up as an internal sales order, for order picking or manufacture as necessary.

147

2. For orders not ready for immediate shipment, an acknowledgement of the order should be sent to the customer. In addition to confirming to him the details of the order as you understand it, you should also give him a shipment date which he can count on to be reliable.

As a general rule, both of these steps should take place the same day the order is received. Anything less than this level of performance is a compromise with good service.

For telephoned orders, customers may send in written confirmation of the order. This will be received after your acknowledgement has been sent, one purpose of which was to confirm to the customer your understanding of his order. Even so, you must check this confirmation against your entry of his order. This, too, must be done with dispatch, for the initial order has gotten into the manufacturing backlog and may be near to entering the physical production cycle by the time the confirmation comes in.

At the time the order is written up for internal processing, copies will have to be sent to all action departments to be involved in the cycle. While this does fill up file cabinets, it is necessary that all action departments know that some action is required of them. The trick is to hold down the information copies. Among those with valid claims to copies are the following:

> Customer (Acknowledgement)
> Salesman
> Sales Manager
> Production Planning
> Data Processing
> Quality Control
> Traffic/Shipping
> Billing
> Order File Clerk

Before any copies of the order are sent out of the order department, careful attention must be given to an accurate write-up of the order. The clerk who performs this order writing function can be likened to an editor, in that he must edit and proofread his copy for logic and clerical errors. The order must be a feasible one or he must reject it for further clarification. That is, it must be for a real product, with realistic time and delivery conditions. Further, it must be checked against the original for clerical errors in write-up or typing.

A reasonable order processing procedure should include these steps, in whole or in part:

1. Count and date-stamp orders, as received, for control.

2. Verify customer's name, address and code, and salesman's name and code against the master file.
3. Initiate credit check.
4. Get traffic routing.
5. Assign order number.
6. Enter price and terms of sale from price list.
7. Get shipment date from production planning.
8. Type order.
9. Proofread against original document. A good technique is to have the editor of this order read aloud to a second editor holding the original document. If some item has been misread, this is the best way to catch that error.
10. Separate the order set, sending copies where needed.

In one central location, there should be a complete file of every order. The best place for this is at the order entry section. The file can be very valuable in processing future orders, if it is complete. When the billing file and the order file are merged, this becomes the complete file for all practical purposes except for miscellaneous correspondence.

Order editing requires a particularly conscienticus supervisor and staff. They must assume nothing. Everything must be documented. All discrepancies must be resolved for them by someone in authority. They must be ready to question everything that looks suspicious, no matter the source or the circumstances. The controller must back up their responsibility to so operate. He should set the stage for this questioning attitude by eliminating resentment and impatience in those to whom the editors must turn for guidance.

BILLING

Billing is the payoff phase of the product life cycle. The customer's needs have been identified and fulfilled. Now, in accordance with the terms of the sales agreement, he must pay for the product he has received.

While he knows, or could find out, what he owes, the dictates of good control require that you tell him what he owes. This establishes one of the necessary documents for his payables control—the invoice—while also setting up your control over the total amount due—accounts receivable.

When the billing copy of the sales order was received, this set up an open item in the billing file. Upon receipt of notice of the fact of and quantity of shipment, an invoice can be written. Ordinarily, a weight list details the quantity the shipping department says was shipped and a bill of lading, signed by the carrier, indicates the fact of shipment.

A control to insure that every shipment is reported for billing is necessary. Serially numbered forms prepared by the shipping clerk, used by the loaders, signed by the carrier, and delivered to billing represent one adequate technique.

A preferable technique is to have the shipping department prepare a weight list from finished production scale sheets or quantity records and the customer's order when the order is ready for shipment. Then, when it is released for actual shipment, the shipping department should prepare a bill of lading with the necessary information to identify the date of shipment and the specific customer's order. The shipping clerk should check the weight list against the physical shipment for accuracy. The loading crew should get the bill of lading signed; this document should go directly, then, to the billing section. At the end of each day, the accumulated weight lists for the day should be totaled by the appropriate unit of measure, the total logged, and the tape sent with the weight lists to billing. Billing, then, matches weight lists with bills of lading and uses the tape total as their control total to insure 100 percent billing. The shipping log should be spot checked against the billing records by the internal auditor to insure adherence to this control check.

One violation of good practice to be alert for is the partial shipment not properly reported. The weight list may show the full order on one document even though the loading crew was unable to get the full quantity loaded. This can happen, for instance, when several orders are being consolidated in one truckload shipment. The bill of lading will not agree with the weight list. This should be handled as two separate shipments because it actually is two shipments. If there is a freight cost to the customer, it may not be appropriate to bill the customer for the excess freight costs of two shipments; this, of course, has nothing to do with either the fact of two shipments or with the cost of two shipments.

Organizationally, the billing section must be independent of shipping, receiving, and receivables, to insure checking of one person's work by another and to reduce the possibility of collusion. Work loads in billing can fluctuate dramatically. One day's shipments may be large quantities on a few big orders while the next day may be a smaller total quantity but on myriad small orders. Therefore, there must be some flexibility in the size of the billing staff with adequate personnel to handle the peak loads but with postponable tasks assigned to fill the valleys between peak loads.

Billing's daily tasks are as follows:

1. Match the weight lists against the signed bills of lading.
2. Check weight lists for arithmetic accuracy.
3. Match weight lists to the sales order.
4. Get transportation charges to be invoiced on each shipment from the traffic department.
5. Prepare invoices. The invoice date should be the date of physical shipment;

this requires that invoices be speedily processed and mailed to the customer so that he can avail himself of the discount terms offered.

6. Check total quantity invoiced against the control total from shipping. After reconciling any differences, send invoices to the customer and to other internal departments. With the copies to accounts receivable and data processing, send the tape of the total value invoiced for the day.

Prices applied to invoices should be as authorized on the original sales order or as amended by formal change orders. This also applies to terms of sale, freight allowances, discounts, commissions, and the like. None of this should originate directly within the billing section in order that the principle of separation of duties is maintained.

Customer credits may be issued from billing but also must be approved in writing by proper authority before this is done. Credits should be included in the control totals issued to data processing and accounts receivable. When debit memos have been written by the customer and he has deducted the amount from his remittance, no credit memo should be sent to him, but it is necessary that one be routed internally from billing to clear the books.

These requirements are sufficiently flexible to permit efficient, low cost billing operations while maintaining adequate controls necessary to minimize the possibility of error or collusion.

ACCOUNTS PAYABLE

In the operation of an accounts payable section, a large degree of routinizing is possible which permits utilization of lower grade, hence less expensive, clerical labor as well as routinized supervision. The important control aspects in accounts payable are matching of documents which establish liability and timing of payments to take cash discounts without early payments which waste cash.

As in other operations, the matching of documents is to be done by other than those responsible for purchasing, receiving, or ledger posting.

Documents necessary to establish liability are purchase order, receiving report, and invoice.

a. One copy of the purchase order goes directly to accounts payable at the same time that it is sent to the vendor. This creates an open item file which is held for subsequent matching. The organization of this file is important to low clerical costs. All orders should be filed alphabetically by vendor since this will be the easiest way to match subsequent documents; the invoice and the packing list attached to the receiving report both are easier to relate to the vendor name, first, than to order number, item ordered, or any other reference.

b. Upon physical receipt of the ordered item, a receiving report is prepared by the recipient, indicating full or partial receipt of the item ordered. This requires him to compare the shipment against his copy of the order. The receiving report goes with the packing slip attached directly to accounts payable for matching against the order. This really presents two opportunities for clerical savings:

1. The recipient's copy of the original order can be sent to accounts payable with the receiving report, eliminating the need to match documents in accounts payable.

2. The purchase order copy can be designed to be the receiving report, as well. This eliminates matching at either receiving or accounts payable.

c. All invoices should be delivered unopened from the mailroom to accounts payable. Because this is impractical when other mail cannot be distinguished from invoices, opening in the mailroom is acceptable when this operation is done separately and with great care to insure that none are lost or missent from the mailroom.

Immediately upon receipt in accounts payable, each invoice should be date stamped and code block stamped. In this same operation, the original must be carefully noted to distinguish it from copies so that the copy is not paid as well as the original.

The next operation is to match the invoice against the order/receiving report. With the file organized alphabetically, the invoices should be so sorted by vendor before going against the open file. This sort may appear a worthless extra step, but the file search will go much faster and more than save the sort time versus the random file search otherwise required.

Warning: do not use paper clips! Staple papers together. Paper clips result in extra papers accidentally attaching themselves to the bottom of the pack. This can result in completely losing track of important papers; time-consuming, frustrating searches for lost papers, lost discounts, and embarrassing correspondence. An alternative is the use of a separate file folder for every order, but this makes for a very slow and difficult file search.

After order, receipt and invoice are matched, the payment can be made. Following the physical matching of documents, a comparison of order and invoice is made to insure the correctness of:

Item Ordered	Discount Terms
Price	Freight Terms
Quantity	Special Conditions

The quantity is also checked against the receiving report, bills of lading, freight bills, and other evidence of receipt. Freight bills are checked against order freight terms. All discrepancies should be resolved. As a practical matter, when there is a price or terms discrepancy, pay in your favor and resolve the discrepancy later. This insures the cash discount for you and saves you clerical cost. If your purchasing department has given the wrong high price versus the invoice price, you are correct. If the invoice is wrong, let the vendor incur the clerical cost of correcting his own mistake. On the other hand, if the invoice is higher than the purchase order and you take the lower order price, it is purchasing's responsibility to unravel the difference. The order was at a given price, not at the higher invoice price. Accounts payable should not take upon itself the responbility of the purchasing department.

Similarly, short quantities should be deducted from the invoice immediately. The receiving report is the quantity authority. Accounts payable is not responsible for checking between the vendor and Receiving on quantities invoiced and quantities received.

Any efforts to reconcile all the differences will result in slow payments, lost discounts, and high clerical costs. Better to pay immediately and let the responsible departments exercise their own responsibilities.

For cost distribution, responsibility codes and account codes must be recorded in the ledger posting operation as previously indicated on the purchase order. In this same operation a cumulative accounts payable control total is generated. Each day's total postings are recorded for comparison with checks issued, to insure that no checks are issued which are not also posted to the ledger.

Before checks are written, an audit of extensions and document authorization must be made as an independent verification of the matching requirements. For economy, the arithmetic should be visually audited on invoices of less than $100, but actually should be completely recalculated for invoices over $100.

Following payment, invoices should be stamped "PAID" or perforated or otherwise be clearly cancelled. Some very specific cancellation is necessary to give assurance that the same matched documents are not used a second time for payment.

Exhibit 45 illustrates the separation of functions required for good control. Note that some separated services can be performed by, say, secretaries in other departments. It is not necessary that all these things be done by "accounts payable" people. That kind of provincialism leads only to jurisdictional disputes between clerks and their supervisors, inevitably leading to lower moral and higher costs. The controller must guard against this insidious thinking; separation of payables functions is a good area in which to begin.

EXHIBIT 45

ACCOUNTS PAYABLE—SEPARATION OF FUNCTIONS

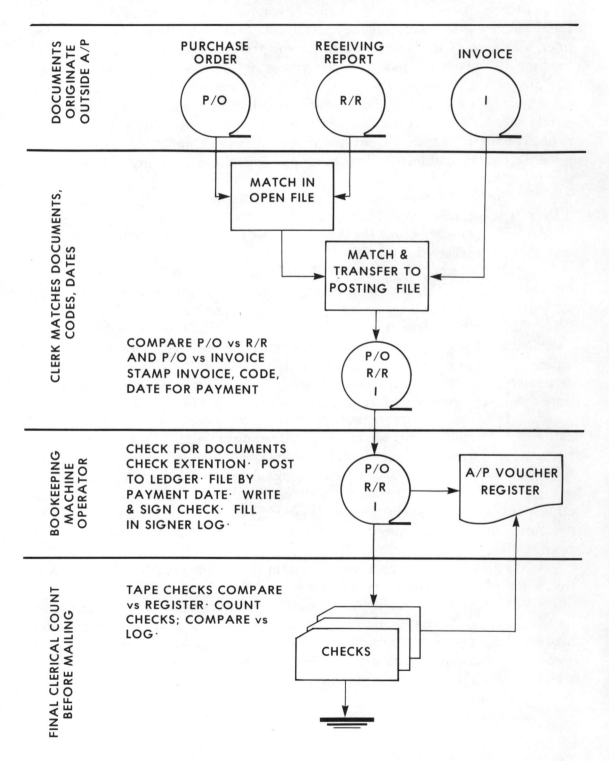

PAYROLL

Of all the accounting services, the staff for payroll requires those with the greatest sense of responsibility and security. Payroll checks represent management's most tangible, most sincere recognition of the worth of the individual. The sanctity of the paycheck must never be violated by careless arithmetic or, with confidential salary payrolls, by careless talk.

Payroll security will be the main theme of this section. Hourly payroll security begins with the regulations for the reporting of hours worked. Salary payroll security begins with the document establishing a pay record at a specific salary for a new employee.

The time card reporting hours worked is the basic document, the security of which must be preserved. If time clocks are used, care must be taken to prevent a person from punching someone else's card. If this is allowed, no one can have confidence in hours actually being worked. Every person on the job must punch his or her own card when he arrives and when he leaves. Anyone else punching a card either early or late does so only because the owner is not present—he is either late arriving or has left early. This is a prima facie case of theft of payroll because time is being reported that was not worked. It should be treated accordingly.

Time cards are not necessary. Foremen can be required to report the number of hours worked by each of their men. This a good foreman knows. If a foreman does not know the hours each man works, a requirement that he find out and report daily may upgrade the overall quality of foremanship.

For proper responsibility accounting under either scheme of reporting hours, the foreman must report transfers of labor from one responsibility code to another. If he fails to report it, the cost will be charged to the man's regular department by default. This causes two costs to be wrong—one too high and one too low.

Every time card must be approved by the foreman's signature before it is accepted by payroll. This gives the foreman a final check for false reporting of hours, for labor transfers, for time worked at a higher rate, for excused absences with pay such as funeral leave, for invalid cards such as a terminated or fictitious employee, or for guaranteed hours as may be provided for by a labor contract for call-in time or the like. Any card not so signed by the foreman should be bounced back to him immediately.

Total hours worked for each batch of cards is a control to be established early. This total will then be used in payroll and in data processing to insure that all cards get processed as reported. A similar control total on hours to be paid is also a valuable control total.

Every pay thus calculated must be posted to an earnings record before disbursement is made. There must be a valid open record for each time card reported. If there is none, either a fictitious card has been reported or the personnel department has failed to report a new employee. In either case, a serious breech of security has occurred that demands immediate attention!

Similar security must surround the reporting of overtime for salaried non-exempt employees. It is important that hours be carefully reported. Supervisors must sign all hours reports. Open pay records must be in the system by the time any hours are reported for payment.

When his signature plate is used to sign payrolls, the controller is obliged to check on the following, personally, to each time re-emphasize the importance of security:

1. The number of impressions of the plate as metered must agree with the number of checks issued. See Exhibit 46 for a sample control sheet.
2. Checks must be serially numbered and 100 percent accounted for as issued or void.
3. The total value of the actual payroll must agree with a predetermined total value. This is easier to obtain for salary payrolls than for hourly; for hourly, the total hours can be the control, with reference to the last payroll as a test of reasonability.

EXHIBIT 46

PAYROLL SIGNATURE CONTROL SHEET

Date	Check Numbers Used	(Void) (Handsigned)	Voided After Signing	Total Checks Signed	Meter Start	Reading Stop	Impressions	Payroll	Approval
3–29–X8	1001–1093	(1)	1	94	1932	2026	94	9,300.00	
4– 4–X8	1094–1180	—	—	87	2026	2113	87	8,700.00	
4–12–X8	1181–1271	(4)	—	87	2113	2200	87	8,700.00	
4–19–X8	1272	(1)	—	—	2200	2200	—	100.00	

Part   Three

MANAGERIAL AND
COST ACCOUNTING DUTIES

7

Cost Accounting

Good management imposes stringent demands on the controller to provide well-based, accurate, and consistent cost accounting systems. Control reports are based on actual versus standard comparisons. Cost reduction starts with high cost areas identified through cost accounting. Standard costs define premises for capital expenditure evaluations. Product pricing decisions are based on detailed unit cost analyses. Cost accounting reports, which are believed by operating management, exert a profound influence on the present and future profitability of an operation.

For accounting techniques relating to job shop costs and process costs and variance accounts, refer to standard handbooks on cost accounting. This chapter will, instead, describe how the controller should use the *output* of the cost accounting system.

TYPES OF STANDARD COSTS

Cost accounting is typically described from the 2 x 2 matrix:

	Process Costs	Job Shop Costs
Standard Costs		
Actual Costs		

The type of manufacturing operation determines whether a process or a job shop cost system will be used. One will not be satisfactory where the other better fits the operation. For basically different operations, the choice will be clear cut. A continuous polymerization operation run around the clock, seven days a week, obviously calls for process costs. A custom furniture manufacturing plant obviously needs job costs. But many operations change character somewhere between raw material input and shipment to the customer. For instance, a paper mill running continuously is a process operation. But a subsequent converting

159

operation in which the web from the paper machine is waxed, printed, laminated or coated to the specific requirements of a specific customer must have control reports based on a job cost system.

Standard costs give better bases for cost control reports than actual costs, alone. It is expensive, however, to develop and keep up-to-date operating standards upon which standard costs are based. Because the process remains fundamentally constant over a period of time, standards for process industries are easier and cheaper to keep up to date. If there is high repeatability in the job shop or if major functions are the same even if materials are different, standards can be economically set for job shop operations.

Where it is at all feasible, the use of predetermined direct costs as the basis for cost control is recommended.

RESISTANCE TO CHANGE

Process and products are always changing, never static. If standards are to reflect a uniform level of attainability, standards must be changed with time to reflect deliberate changes in process, process knowledge, product content, and equipment changes incorporating new design and capabilities.

But revisions suggested to incorporate more subtle changes are hard to document and are equally hard to get operating management to accept. A plant manager who learns to make his product 100 fpm faster wants the benefit of the sweat of his brow to show as favorable variances. And rightly so. He deserves recognition for a job well done. When the standard is changed, the higher speed now attainable merges into the background with everything else routinely expected of that manager, some of which he may not yet be able to do and on which he shows negative variances.

One suggested technique for diluting that resistance to change is the publication of a routine report dedicated *only* to giving recognition to those kinds of changes. Each speed or yield or waste or other change is translated into annual dollar value and is listed in the report. The change is incorporated in the standard when the report is issued. This insures recognition of a job well done, overcoming general resistance to change. Exhibit 47 illustrates such a report.

If standards are "loosened" at the request of the plant manager, this is also duly recorded in this report, serving to dampen enthusiasm for this approach to variance improvement.

SOURCES OF STANDARDS

Having decided to use predetermined standard costs, a major next hurdle is the determination of sources of standards to be developed.

EXHIBIT 47

CHANGE OF STANDARDS REPORT

Distribution: General Manager
                 Plant Managers
                 Technical Director
                 Chief Industrial Engineer

From: Controller

		Savings Dollars
Plant A		
White Powder	Increase speed 30 fpm	$ 800
Khaki Rope	" " 20 fpm	770
Black Crystal	" " 50 fpm	1,950
Jersey Insulating	Reduce speed 15 fpm	(350)
	Total	$3,170
Plant B		
None		
Plant C		
None		

A figure does not operate as a performance goal merely because the controller calls it a standard. It does so only to the extent that an operating executive accepts it as a fair and attainable level of performance. An operating executive is inclined to accept a standard only if he is satisfied that the standard level is reasonably attainable and the variable it measures is controllable by him. If any of these factors are missing, the standard is not accepted as a valid measure. When an operating man is in the position of justifying his performance in the face of a standard he doesn't regard as fair, he can either strive to attain that performance anyway or work to change the standard. He probably regards current performance as adequate but the standard unfair; in this case, he almost always will try to change the standard.

In those activities wherein standards can be expressed in physical units, executives typically make more use of variance data expressed in physical units than variances expressed in dollars. The obvious reason for this general preference for physical units is that operating men have to take action in terms of the physical world; they don't have to translate to units when loss time is reported in terms of machine hours, yield in pounds lost, and efficiency in units of production. If the controller is willing to report data in physical units and to relate variances to physical units, there will generally be a high level of interest and cooperation by operating executives.

Almost every operating man has his own set of little black books in which he keeps what he considers the most pertinent manufacturing information. If the controller can find out what is kept in those books and can translate the contents into his operating reports, he will have the greatest degree of success in getting the enthusiastic cooperation of the operating group. This is the best source of items for which standards should be set. Often a norm is already established in that same set of books, although its author may never have thought of it as a standard in the sense that the controller uses the word.

Regardless of source, a standard must be reasonable to attain on the average throughout the year under normal conditions and *with good management*, but not so easily attained that good management is not necessary. Abnormal conditions should be corrected, not incorporated into the standard. The standard must be representative of current conditions, technical knowledge, and installed equipment. Standards must be consistent among products, operations, and plants with respect to their ease of attainment. For the general knowledge of everyone involved in setting, using, and being measured by standards, these points should be expressed in a written "policy statement." Exhibit 48 is one such policy statement issued over the joint signature of the operating manager and the controller of a national company.

Certain types of standards should be established from time studies by industrial engineers. Generally, these are manual, operator-paced jobs such as machine shop bench work, mechanical assembly, and packaging operations. Continuous-machine speed standards should be set by speed trials held jointly by operating management to monitor quality and by engineers to assure that excess speeds are, in fact, reached before quality fears are allowed to be limiting. Other standards may be simply derived from history, provided that records are good enough and that the good management element is considered in the historical review.

All departments can and should contribute to the development of a complete set of standards. Exhibit 49 shows a typical array of standards required versus the department responsible for originating the standard. In all cases, the top operating or sales executive and the controller retain final approval over any recommendation. Both should approve. Neither should be able to impose a standard, arbitrarily, against the will of the other.

DIRECT COSTING

Because it is such a valuable tool for financial analysis and because it fits in a discussion of cost accounting, the next several pages will be devoted to an examination of direct costing.

EXHIBIT 48

STANDARDS PROGRAM

STATEMENT OF POLICY

The standards program has the following principal objectives:

1. To provide the means for management planning and control at all levels. Not only must everyone be informed of the proper facts related to the area of his responsibility, but those facts must be presented relative to a standard of performance for purposes of evaluating the effectiveness of each segment of our organization and to indicate areas for corrective action.

2. To provide a means of consistent product costing which recognizes all inherent differences between products without recognizing chance or abnormal elements which occur from time to time but which are not inherent in the operation or product. These product costs are used:
   a. As a principal factor in determination of sales prices.
   b. To aid in making decisions which involve choices between raw materials or operations so that the lowest overall product cost results.
   c. To aid in making decisions regarding capital expenditures.
   d. To aid in the improvement of product patterns from the standpoint of profitability.

3. To provide normal production rates for all products for purposes of production planning, scheduling, and control.

4. To provide a means of summarizing the basic economic facts of our business in such a manner that costs of proposed products and revisions to operations can be estimated prior to actual manufacture or operation.

In order to accomplish these objectives, the established standards must be:

1. *Consistent* between products, operations and mills with respect to their ease of attainment.
2. *Representative* of current conditions, knowledge, and equipment.
3. *Reasonable* to attain on the average throughout the year under normal conditions and good management. But not so easily attained that good management is not necessary. Abnormal conditions should be corrected, not incorporated in the standard.

First, what is it? It is a technique for identifying with units of product only those costs directly associated with and proportional to each unit of production. All other costs—overhead, burden, term—are costs of a period of time and are charged against that period, not against production.

Generally, only material costs and production labor costs can be accurately classified as directly variable costs; all others are usually term costs. There are situations in which one can validly include power for motors, heat for cooking or drying, labor for inspection, and certain operating supplies as direct costs. There is no merit in going beyond this by attempting to allocate "variable overhead" costs in order to include a fraction of such costs in each product cost.

EXHIBIT 49

RESPONSIBILITIES FOR ORIGINATION OF STANDARDS

AUTHORITY	FREQUENCY	STANDARD
Chief Industrial Engineer	Annual	Standard Downtime
Chief Industrial Engineer	Annual	Standard Efficiency Level
Chief Industrial Engineer	Continuous	Standard Speeds
Chief Industrial Engineer	Continuous	Elemental Times and Manual Operation Times
Chief Industrial Engineer	Quarterly	Standard Work Force
Chief Industrial Engineer	Continuous	Operation and Running Waste
Chief Engineer	Quarterly	Standard Power Demand and Standard Boiler Efficiency
Manager Budgets and Standards	Annual	Standard Material Usage
Manager Budgets and Standards	Annual	All Mill Losses not Specified by Chief Ind'l. Engineer
Supervisor of Packaging, Shipping, and Receiving	Continuous	Standard Packing Materials
Manager of Sales Services	Annual	Planned Rate of Activity for Prime Machines for Budget Purposes
Traffic Manger	Quarterly	Transportation Costs Materials — In Transportation Costs Materials — Out
Value Analysis Committee	Continuous	Raw Material Specifications

164

The following calculation will illustrate the difference between absorption costing and direct costing. A budget for Plant A is prepared as shown below.

Budget

Salaries	$ 20,000 / Month
* Hourly Operators	75,000 / "
Hourly Indirect Labor	40,000 / "
Operating Supplies	20,000 / "
Labor Overhead	12,000 / "
Depreciation	7,000 / "
* Power	8,000 / "
Selling and Administration	20,000 / "
Total	$202,000 / Month

Plant A has fifty machines operating forty hours a week, three shifts, for a total of 24,000 machine hours a month.

In conventional absorption costing, the machine hour rate would be:

$$\$202,000 \div 24,000 \text{ Hours} = \$8.42/\text{Hour}$$

The direct cost rate, however, includes only the *asterisked* items because these are the only costs which are directly proportional to machine hours of operation. Total direct costs are $83,000. The direct cost rate is:

$$\$83,000 \div 24,000 \text{ Hours} = \$3.46/\text{Hour}$$

The difference between the whole cost rate ($8.42) and the direct rate ($3.46) is the allocation of term costs ($4.96) charged to each hour of machine operation.

Assuming a production rate of two units per hour, the cost of one unit would be:

Whole Cost $8.46/Hour ÷ 2 Units/Hour = $4.32/Unit
Direct Cost $3.46/Hour ÷ 2 Units/Hour = $1.73/Unit

Of course, costs such as depreciation and operating supplies can be identified as being directly chargeable to the production machines. As such, these are not allocated costs. Neither, however, should they be treated as direct costs because they are a function of being in business, hence are time-related, rather than a function of the number of units of production.

Absorption costs using well-thought-out bases of allocation do serve as convenient tools for cost estimating for pricing and for inventory valuation. There are good and sufficient reasons for not eliminating absorption costing, entirely, within the company. For one thing, the Internal Revenue Service will rarely accept direct cost valued inventories for tax purposes. Tax accounting requirements should not prevent the controller from using direct costs, however. The benefits of direct costing are sufficient to justify the additional clerical cost of calculating direct costs and whole costs.

Cost comparisons of two plants or two machines or two products should be made on direct cost values. Term costs will continue in total, unaffected by management decisions as to which machines are to be used to produce which product. Arbitrary allocations of term costs cannot be allowed to influence management decisions. For example in the following problem, the plant manager wants to know which machine he should use to produce 1,000 gizmos:

	Whole Cost Rate	*Direct Cost Rate*	*Gizmos Per Hour*	*Waste*
Machine A	$50.00/Hr.	$ 5.00/Hr.	150	10%
Machine B	$20.00/Hr.	$10.00/Hr.	100	10%

a. Using absorption costing, Machine A costs $0.323/gizmo versus Machine B at $0.20/gizmo. On this basis, Machine B would be used.
b. Using direct costing, Machine A costs $0.032/gizmo versus Machine B at $0.10/gizmo. Machine A would be used.

Which is right? What should the plant manager do?

Direct costs, by definition, are out-of-pocket costs. If Machine B is used, the plant manager's out-of-pocket costs will be $0.068/gizmo higher than need be. On 1,000 gizmos, this excess cost would be:

$$\$0.068 \times 1,000 = \$68.00$$

Overhead costs will be unchanged regardless of the scheduling decision. Direct costs must be the controlling data. Over- and under-absorption of term costs relate only to whether total volume is above or below the break-even point. Excessive direct costs actually force the break-even point to move to higher total volume.

It is a basic responsibility of the controller to be sure the best data is supplied for decision-making. He should refuse to provide whole costs when direct costs are indicated.

An important concept in direct costing is profit contribution. Profit contribution is that income left after material and direct conversion costs are paid for. It is a "contribution" toward payment of term costs. If total profit contribution from all sources is greater than total term costs, a profit has been made. If not, a loss has been incurred. Exhibit 50 illustrates this well. Plant C has the highest

EXHIBIT 50

PLANT COMPARISON—PROFIT CONTRIBUTION

Item	Division Total	(Memo)	Services	Selling	Admin.	Plant A	Plant B	Plant C	Plant D
Customer									
Less: Customer Returns and Allowances									
Inter Division									
Total Net Sales	3405	3405				695	350	1210	1150
Salaries	401		10		161	15	15	30	40
Wages	314		20	130		39	35	70	150
Labor Overhead	32		2			4	4	7	15
Raw Materials Consumed	1959		48			467	152	740	600
Beginning Inventory	2100					100	300	700	1000
Total				20		625	566	1547	1805
Less: Ending Inventory	2100			30	20	100	300	700	1000
Total Direct Cost	xxx	2383				525	206	847	805
Profit Contribution	xxx	1022				170	144	363	345
Operating Materials	118					10	10	20	30
Rents and Royalties	35					5	—	—	10
All Other Expense	95					10	10	10	15
Power, Coal, Oil and Gas	60					10	10	20	20
Depreciation — Straight Line	255					20	25	130	80
Insurance and Taxes	35					2	3	20	10
Total Plant Term Cost	xxx	480				57	58	200	165
Plant Income from Operations	xxx	542				113	86	163	180
Less: Services, Selling & Admin. (Memo)	xxx	441	(80)	(180)	(181)	80	36	165	160
Income from Operations	101	101				33	50	(2)	20

dollar profit contribution of all four plants at $363,000. But after plant term costs and allocated term costs, Plant C is reported as operating at a loss for the period. Income from Operations is no valid measure of the worth of Plant C; had it not operated at all for this period, the entire contribution of $363,000 would have been lost to the division. The *division* would have shown a *loss* of $262,000 instead of a profit of $101,000.

SECURITY OF PRODUCT COSTS

Careful attention must be given to a plan to insure adequate safeguards in the handling of product costing and pricing information. Pricing strategy is one of the most important secrets of a company. The company that most effectively prices its products in relation to costs is, in the long run, going to outlive its worst competitors and make higher profits than the better ones. This pricing secret should not be allowed to leak out to competition through careless handling of standard product cost books and reports.

Documents of this nature should be classified "Company Confidential." Strict security measures should be taken with them.

A record should be kept, by serial number, of product cost books and other such volumes. When superseded, each old issue should be recalled, logged in, and destroyed.

Employees terminating employment or being transferred should be required to turn in such confidential information issued to them, as a condition of their exit interview.

COST ESTIMATING FOR PRICING

It is the ultimate prerogative of the Sales Department to establish prices to be quoted to potential customers. The basis for this quotation, however, should be cost work done under the supervision of the controller. He should establish the cost of each and all operations necessary to produce and deliver the product. His is the sole authority to issue official cost and profitability data.

Effective pricing requires close cooperation between the sales manager and the controller if each is to discharge well his duties.

Sales must elicit from the customer exact information about his product needs. This information has to be faithfully transmitted to the controller. Failure in this communication guarantees ultimate failure with the customer. Either the right product will be quoted at too high a price (no order) or at too low a price (no profit). Both are disasters, so far as this customer contact is concerned.

Having received complete information, the controller must translate it into raw material components and conversion operations. This will require the cooperation of the manufacturing, engineering, purchasing, and technical departments. With all pertinent information collected, material quantities and costs can be calculated and conversion costs determined. A break-even price can be specified. Target profits or P.C. ratios (profit contribution divided by sales value) should be applied to give the Sales Department sales value and profit data from which to quote, bargain, bid, or otherwise maneuver as the marketplace dictates. All this must be done with dispatch. The customer is waiting and he will not wait forever. Considerable judgment must be exercised by the controller to know how much time can be taken to develop the optimum estimate, tempering the desire for greatest accuracy with the need for haste.

An often overlooked duty of the controller is to insure that Sales asks the proper pricing question. Too often, the question will be, "How much does it cost to make item 'x'?" After some probing, it develops that Sales wants to quote on a piece of business that will have to be made in a plant already running six days a week. This new volume will have to be made on Sunday which, for Plant A, requires double-time wages. If this business is accepted, item 'y' from Plant B will no longer be needed by this customer. To have allowed a routine answer to the first question would have been negligence on the part of the controller.

While pricing is basically a sales responsibility, the controller also has a responsibility in this area. This responsibility is to audit the records of the sales manager to insure that established rules are being followed and adequate records maintained. If rules governing pricing and pricing files do not exist, the controller should take action to have certain minimum rules established.

One useful idea is to require a price control file which would contain summary information on each product including descriptions of product, customer, and end use. A chronological history of prices and dates would be entered. Competitive information would be entered; this is vital when prices are reduced to meet competitive situations. Customer response to initial and subsequent quotations should be included. To insure that the maximum feasible price is being charged, all prices must be reviewed routinely as well as when major raw material prices change.

The controller should audit this file for price control and for compliance with federal and state laws governing pricing.

STANDARD VERSUS ACTUAL COSTS

Control reports describing variance from standard in summary format have been discussed earlier.

Variances, however, cannot be calculated in summary. Standards must be calculated in minute detail for each product and each operation. Actual costs can be calculated in detail. Variances can then be identified in detail, isolating exactly what and where standard performance is bettered or missed. Or actual costs can simply be calculated in gross total and compared with the summation of standards; these differences are non-actionable summary differences and should not be dignified as "variances."

The whole point of variance calculation is control. Control requires identification and actionability. A system that does not exactly isolate trouble spots generates alibis and excuses but not control.

An example of identification of trouble spots is this set of standard and actual cost data on a hypothetical product. Notice how the source of the variance jumps out at you:

	Actual	Standard	Variance
Selling Price	$22.00	$22.00	—
Direct Conversion Cost	.71	.64	(.07)
Material Cost	19.33	19.39	$.06
Profit Contribution	1.96	1.97	(.01)
Term Cost	2.13	1.92	(.21)
Profit	($.17)	$ .05	($.22)

	Actual	Standard
Raw Material A Price	$20.00	$20.00
Raw Material B Price	9.46	9.72
Waste	10%	10%
Downtime	4 Hours	4 Hours
Machine Speed	450	500
Production/Day	27,000	30,000

Obviously, two things stand out:

1. One raw material component is cheaper, reducing costs by $.06.
2. Production/Day is below standard because the machine is running below standard speed by 50 fpm. This causes direct and term costs per unit to be about 10% higher than standard.

Compare this with the following display of (essentially) the same information. Assuming the same system was used to collect the actual cost data, the value is lost in the obscurity of the display. Rather than the direct, measured figures above, derived data is presented in typical accounting jargon:

	Actual	*Standard*	*Variance*
Selling Price	$22.00	$22.00	—
Material Cost	19.33	19.39	$.06
Direct Cost	.71	.64	(.07)
Profit Contribution	1.96	1.97	(.01)
Term Cost	2.13	1.92	(.22)
Profit	($.17)	$ .05	($.23)

Raw Material A Purchase Price Variance	Zero
Raw Material B Purchase Price Variance	$.26
Selling Price Variance	Zero
Overall Yield—Standard	125.8%
—Actual	125.8%
—Variance	Zero
Machine Efficiency	90.0%
Downtime Efficiency Variance	Zero

The material price variance apparently accounts for the $.06 difference in material cost.

Machine efficiency at 90 percent accounts for the higher conversion cost. But why was it 90 percent? What needs to be attended to? Was waste high, leaving less good production per hour? Could be, but if it were, an excess weight of material had to make up the waste loss because the total yield was equal to standard. If this happened, material costs would have been high, which they were not. Waste, therefore, must have been standard. Was the loss of efficiency due to lost machine time for repairs, or lack of material, or operator absenteeism? Or was it due to running at a slower than standard speed? Since the downtime efficiency variance is zero, machine speed is finally identified as the source of the trouble.

It is much better to capitalize on the results of the cost accounting system with simple, straightforward reporting than to obscure and discredit a good system with vague, ambiguous reporting.

EXPECTED VALUES

Seldom are costs predictable to an extreme accuracy. While we use standard costs as explicit values which, we hope, will be attained on the average, we recognize that there will be random variation around the standard cost; we expect actual values which should equal the standard, on the average.

Given certain conditions of uncertainty, we may be less sure of the average expectation. We may, for instance, believe that there is a 50 percent probability that the standard will be met, on the average, but that leaves a 50 percent probability that it will not be met. This aspect must be dealt with. The controller can, for budgeting and forecasting purposes, calculate a statistical "expected value." Given the following expectations, for instance:

> Standard cost $4.25, 50% probability;
> Possible cost $5.30, 25% probability;
> Possible cost $5.60, 25% probability;
> $4.25 \times 50\% = 2.125$
> $5.30 \times 25\% = 1.325$
> $5.60 \times 25\% = \underline{1.400}$
> Expected value $\underline{\$4.850}$

Given the three circumstances and their possible effects on costs, the Controller must expect a cost of $4.85 as the best estimate.

In a different set of circumstances, possible values can be applied in a decision-tree format to calculate the expected value. Consider the following simplified research and development situation:

> A new product is being considered. If R & D is undertaken, the cost will be $100,000; it is believed that there is a 70% probability of R & D success. If R & D is successful, a test market program will be undertaken. If very successful, incremental revenue is expected to be $800,000 and if moderately successful, $200,000. The test program will cost $200,000. The probability of a highly successful test is believed to be 40 percent and of a moderate success 50 percent.

The expected value of the overall program is the summation of costs, incremental revenues and their probabilities, as shown in the decision-tree in Exhibit 51. In this example, the expected value of action is $47,000, the combined values of each possible outcome. This can be compared with the expected value of *not* undertaking R & D, which, of course, is zero. Whether one acts on such information depends on the confidence one has in the premises—as always; the key figures are the stated probabilities.

LEARNING CURVES

It is often the case that variable costs do not vary with changes in volume in a direct proportion that remains constant over time. Instead, the variable cost declines on a per unit basis as workers become more familiar with their tasks, becoming increasingly efficient. That is, workers can accomplish their given labor tasks in less time and with less effort because of experience. This experience factor has come to be known as the "learning curve" effect.

EXHIBIT 51

EXPECTED VALUE—DECISION TREE

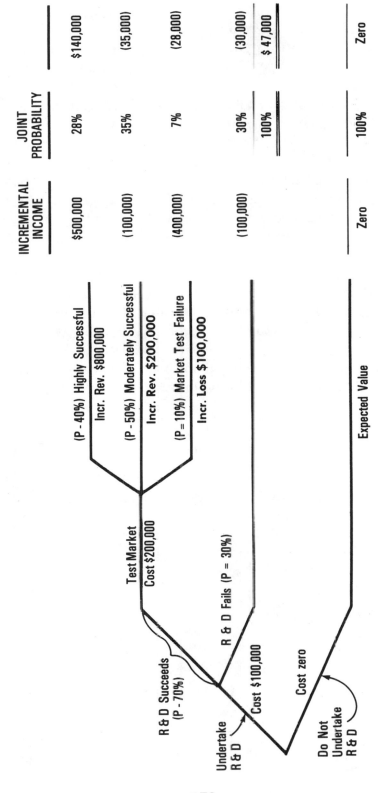

	INCREMENTAL INCOME	JOINT PROBABILITY	
(P - 40%) Highly Successful Incr. Rev. $800,000	$500,000	28%	$140,000
(P - 50%) Moderately Successful Incr. Rev. $200,000	(100,000)	35%	(35,000)
(P = 10%) Market Test Failure Incr. Loss $100,000	(400,000)	7%	(28,000)
R & D Fails (P = 30%)	(100,000)	30%	(30,000)
		100%	$ 47,000
Expected Value	Zero	100%	Zero

173

Learning curve data is expressed in terms of the average hours of production per unit as the number of units increases. The average hours will decline at a constant percentage rate. Assume that it has been established that the cost per unit will decline on an 80 percent learning curve basis. Exhibit 52 shows this learning curve effect in both tabular and graphic form. Assume that for the first lot of 1000 units, the average hours of production per unit are 100; the total production hours will be 100,000. Assume that the next production lot is twice the size of the first, that is consisting of 2,000 units; the average hours of production per unit will be 80 percent of the first lot, that is 80 percent of 100 or 80 hours per unit. The total production hours for this lot of 2,000 units will be 80 times 2,000 or 160,000 production hours. As production increases so that the next production lot consists of twice as many units as the preceding lot, that is, double 2,000 or 4,000 units, the average hours of production per unit for this third lot will be 80 percent of 80 hours or 64 hours per unit. The total production hours for this lot of 4,000 units will be $4,000 \times 64$ or 256,000 hours. Note that without the learning curve effect, the total production hours of this third lot of 4,000 units would be $4,000 \times 100$ hours or 400,000 production hours, versus the expected 256,000 production hours.

This learning phenomenon can occur at any percentage rate although the 80 percent rate is a widely found one. Calculations for the learning curve effect can be reduced to the following formula:

$$A_i = A_1 R^{(i-1)}$$

A_i is the average cost per unit for the ith lot
A_1 is the average cost of the initial lot of production
R is the rate of learning

If you were to apply this formula to the above calculations, A_i is the average cost of the, let's say, third lot; A_1 is the 100; $R^{(i-1)}$ is $.8^2$. Therefore $A_3 = 100 \times .8^2 = 100 \times .64 = 64$ hrs/unit.

EXHIBIT 52

LEARNING CURVE

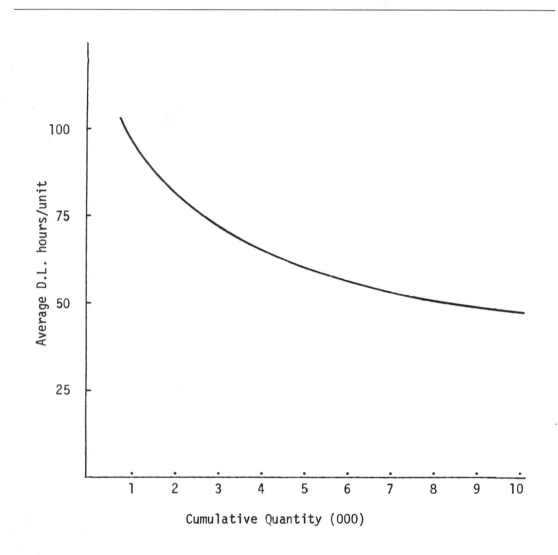

Lot	Quantity Per Lot	Cumulative Quantity	Avg. D.L. Hours/Unit
1	1000	1000	100.0
2	1000	2000	80.0
3	2000	4000	64.0
4	4000	8000	51.2

8

Cost Reduction

Cost reduction is the active, improvement-oriented phase of controllership. Cost control implies adhering to budget, keeping costs in line with a plan or modifying the plan, maintaining the status quo. Cost *reduction* implies *action* to upset the status quo, shifting plans toward ever-more-profitable levels.

Cost reduction implies drastic change. People inherently resist change. Therefore, cost reduction implies resistance, objection, personnel problems, even subversion.

There is no such status as "giving lip-service to cost reduction." Either there is an active plan or there is none at all. That phrase, lip-service, really means someone upstairs has told us to reduce costs, but we are not going to bother. We will mislead him into thinking that a program is under way. Then, after a while, we can all just let the program die a natural death.

This is just what cost reduction programs often come to—an early, natural death, unmourned and unmissed. Those closely affected are happy to see it pass from the scene. Many never heard of it at all, hence could hardly be expected to miss the program now gone.

DIVISION-WIDE PLAN

Sooner or later in the life of every division comes the genuine need for a thorough, rafter-rattling cost reduction campaign.

During a period of high profits and rapid growth, the organization became fat and happy. Marginal activities were added because they could be afforded. Large staff departments were required to engineer and to build new facilities necessary to keep up with booming demand. Old activities were not chopped off because no one had time to recognize them as obsolete. But now, the growth curve has flattened out. Supply has caught up with demand and price competition is being felt. The "second profit squeeze" is beginning to nibble away at profits, which have actually begun to drop even though sales are still rising slowly.

Or, your company has just taken over a financially distressed operation and you have been assigned to eliminate the excess costs, to make a profitable operation out of what is now a drain on profits.

Both situations call for action. Aggressive, division-wide, top-to-bottom action. The general manager must motivate his managers to forget their inherent fear of change in favor of their love for job continuity which can come only through the results of a division-wide cost reduction plan. Hopefully, this will be done before the general manager's own job security is threatened. Late action often brings indiscriminate, across-the-board slashes which are quite harmful to long-range success. Across-the-board slashes by edict are not cost reduction plans and are definitely to be condemned except as a last resort after organized plans have failed to achieve desired results.

It is not advisable to create a special cost reduction coordinator to administer the cost reduction plan. This makes cost reduction "someone else's" job. The program should make cost reduction the number two responsibility of every manager, ranking just barely behind keeping the production flowing. It should come ahead of training, morale, safety lectures, systems improvements, long-range planning, and the like. The controller or the chief industrial engineer should be "in charge" of the overall program as a number one duty, with all else subordinate.

Formal plans and reports are required. This gives emphasis and timeliness to the effort. Every department head should be required to write a list of cost reduction objectives for his department. The sum of these individual lists becomes the overall plan. Periodic reports of progress, oral and in writing, should be made to keep the program current in everyone's mind. Exhibit 53 is an extract from a report on one such plan.

Some review of individual task-lists is necessary to insure reasonably uniform effort in all departments. No one should be allowed to set "easy" goals for himself. This may call for rejecting a first proposed list, requiring that it be made as difficult as the task-lists of other managers. The importance of this shouldn't be overlooked. Because of the implied threat to job security, it is not equitable to threaten one manager more than the next. To put it in a positive frame of reference, the man who meets his objectives completely merits a reward. It would be inequitable to reward one who met completely an easy objective while withholding a reward from someone who failed to complete a much more difficult objective. Peers will quickly recognize differences in difficulty. It would be much better if the superior saw them first and leveled them immediately.

STAFF DEPARTMENT PARTICIPATION

As a general rule, staff departments look upon cost reduction programs

EXHIBIT 53

COST REDUCTION PROGRAM

"While with du Pont at their (deleted) plant, I had a chance to see this program in operation. I can testify to the effectiveness of it and to the great amount of interest and enthusiasm generated among the salary-roll people toward obtaining specific cost reduction dollar goals.

"There was no supervisory suggestion and award system at this plant. As far as I know, no supervisor was ever specifically compensated for a suggestion which he turned in. This, however, did not detract from the effectiveness of the program. During the time that I was there, the plant accomplished something slightly under $5,000,000 in annual cost reduction, including labor and material savings.

"To outline very briefly how the system at that plant worked: In December of each year, the plant prepared their cost reduction goals for the following year. Each area supervisor prepared his own specific list of cost reduction items which he anticipated being able to accomplish during the following twelve months. The two manufacturing plant superintendents collated the reports from their subordinates and submitted their plant cost reduction programs to the plant manager. Simultaneously, the staff departments prepared their own cost reduction programs. The distinguishing feature of these programs was that each and every cost reduction was to be accomplished through some specifically listed item. There was a target date on each one of the items to indicate at what point during the year the savings should be in effect. The plant manager approved these plans. With this forecast as the yardstick for the following year's performance, progress toward these goals was measured on a monthly basis. Each area supervisor, once a month, got together with the industrial engineer for his plant and reviewed his progress toward his goals. He would report on each specific item in the original list (plus any additional items that might have become known during the year) in a written memorandum to the plant superintendent. There was a monthly cost meeting at this particular plant wherein costs for the previous month were discussed by the two superintendents, with all of the area supervisors and staff supervisors present. At these meetings, one of the supervisors would report on the progress of his section toward his cost reduction goals. This worked out to a report from each supervisor once a quarter. The plant manager was always in attendance at these cost meetings and most often had questions for the superintendents about their specific progress.

"With this intense interest on the part of top management, the interest of the area supervisors and their foremen never failed to be quite strong. Much time, thought, and effort was devoted toward the preparation of reasonable goals and the attainment of these goals."

---

as an activity of the operating departments which increases the work of staff, hence requires additional staff.

Not so! Every staff department should be required to produce a list of individual departmental objectives, with assigned dollar reductions from current costs.

Only if *everyone* participates will a program be accepted as a sincere effort to really improve profit. If, while operating and control departments are cutting out the fat and eliminating marginal activities, Personnel hires a training coordinator, Industrial Engineering hires a green, new college graduate, and Technical adds an assistant librarian, you can be sure that petty jealousies will grow, friction will begin to be observed, and the steam will be gone from the program.

Staff departments must pay their own way or they should be discontinued. Under normal circumstances, a good rule of thumb is that every dollar of staff cost should save two dollars elsewhere. This insures that, even with poor results—at times as low as 50 percent—the staff department will at least break even. Objectives set for staff departments must be result oriented, not activity oriented. It is worthless to give a systems analyst the objective "analyze clerical systems." The objective should be "reduce clerical costs $16,000/Year."

Under normal circumstances, the rule is 2:1 savings. When an intensive division-wide cost reduction program is under way, the normal ratio does nothing to give an urgency to the staff man's job. So the ratio should be raised, say to 3:1, for a specific period of time, say one year. This gives a readily identified results-goal for the department.

It also opens the door for cost reduction *in* the department. Now is the time to weed out the deadwood. Every department has low producers who aren't quite bad enough to let go—under normal circumstances. But normal was a 2:1 ratio. Now it is 3:1. Can the guy who has been at 1:1 be expected to come close to 3:1? Be brutally honest. As controller, you have to be. If the low producers are allowed to drift, can the overall be up to 3:1? And even if it *could*, wouldn't it be better to achieve 4:1, the level attainable before the low producers dragged the average down? Discharge or transfer of the man who is not producing results will be a morale booster, too, to those who are at 4:1 and who certainly recognize the inadequacy of the 1:1 man. This is the only effective (or valid) answer to the complaint, "Why should I continue to knock myself out when Joe Zilch loafs his time away?"

With higher objectives established, reductions in staff size will not reduce the total benefit to be realized:

Last Year	*This Year*
10 Men, Cost $100,000	Objective Ratio 3:1
Savings $190,000	Staff Reduction 2 Men, at $20,000
Savings To Cost Ratio 1.9 to 1.0	Budget, 8 Men, at $80,000 Cost
	Potential Savings, $240,000 @ 3 to 1 Ratio

In this example, the potential savings are $240,000 at the 3:1 ratio even after two marginal producers were dropped from the department. Assuming that these were 1:1 men, the ratio would be only 2.6:1 if they were allowed to remain in the department.

Cost	Ratio	Savings
8 Men @ $ 80,000	3:1	$240,000
2 Men @ 20,000	1:1	20,000
$100,000	2.6:1	$260,000

There is no merit in swapping dollars to support 1:1 people. A tight ship where everyone pulls together is much to be preferred.

ORGANIZATION FOR COST REDUCTION

No coordinating or advisory or special committee should be allowed to usurp the responsibilities of the general manager and his primary assistants. They should run the cost reduction program.

Every organization should have a written profit plan, as described in Chapters 9 and 10. The cost reduction program has to be an integral part of that profit plan. Because of his role in the preparation of the profit plan, the controller has to be the one to define for the general manager the required dollar savings necessary to bridge the gap between profit forecast and profit goal. This total dollar gap when "allocated" to specific areas to be made up defines the cost reduction assignment for the division and for each department.

This assignment should be clearly transmitted down the organizational lines, dividing up the total needed so that each manager knows what is expected of him. Every department should have some share of this assignment, however small. The sub-division should not be on an across-the-board percentage basis; this is inequitable. All departments will not be at the same level of efficiency. Some managers will already have done a good job of running a taut ship and their costs will have been trimmed. To require them to reduce costs, say 10 percent, the same as the slothful, fat departments would be a gross injustice to the good manager. It is the duty of the controller and the senior operating managers to know enough about the organization to make allocations that are equitable.

In some corners it will be argued that this approach will fail of its own weight. Cost reduction must be assigned to a specifically selected professional staff, because if cost reduction is everyone's job, it is no one's job.

Nonsense. This argument really goes to the motivation for cost reduction. The reason professional-type staffs succeed is that failure is a direct, immediate, obvious threat to their job security. There is no other reason but cost reduction for them to be on the payroll. This same motivation can apply to the department managers. If they are told that they must attain their assigned goal for cost reduction and that failure to do so threatens salary and job security, the department managers will feel fully motivated to get the job done.

This is certainly not a case against industrial engineers for the plant or against systems analysts for the office. Both are very necessary for professional, detailed assistance to the department manager. And they will have plenty of demands on their time when the managers have the responsibility and the motivation.

PRIORITIES FOR COST REDUCTION

Having decided to reduce costs, how does the manager decide where to start? The controller can give valuable guidance to the manager through the use of a few rules of analysis.

a. Where have costs increased the most over the last five years? This change may indicate a trend to inefficiency, excessive growth rates, a process gone out of control, or a laxity by management.

b. What costs have had the least attention in recent years? Those areas watched most closely are probably fairly well under control. Areas which have received little attention probably represent the most promising areas for high payoff.

c. Apply Pareto's Law. Pareto's Law says that a very few items account for most of the effect while a majority of the items account for a small portion of the result. For instance, in your personal checking account, 20 percent of the number of checks you write account for 80 percent of the total value of your checks while the remaining 80 percent of your checks account for the remaining 20 percent of the money.

This 20/80 rule applies to an almost unbelievable number of situations. Use this to concentrate on the 20 percent of the causes, and you will be changing the 80 percent of the results. Concentrate on the:

20% of the operators who cause 80% of the inefficiency
20% of the products which incur 80% of the rejects
20% of the customers who buy 80% of the product
20% of the machines which cause 80% of the scrap (Exhibit 54)
20% of the people who initiate 80% of the grievances

This is the same thing often referred to as the "ABC concept," particularly in inventory control schemes in which 20% of the products account for 80% of the items and 20% of the items account for 80% percent of the value.

Exhibit 55 graphically depicts the "ABC concept."

THE SCIENTIFIC METHOD

There is no substitute for hard work and imagination in uncovering cost reduction ideas. No checklist is adequate as a complete roster of potential schemes.

EXHIBIT 54

PARETO'S LAW/ABC CONCEPT

APPLICATION OF PARETO'S LAW TO WASTE

PRODUCED BY 25 OPERATORS

Operator 1	1.4 Lbs.	6	11.5 Lbs.	11	19.3 Lbs.	16	9.3 Lbs.	21	1.1 Lbs.
2	.7 "	7	53.1 "	12	60.5 "	17	6.5 "	22	9.3 "
3	205.0 "	8	10.0 "	13	2.0 "	18	0.5 "	23	15.2 "
4	175.0 "	9	4.8 "	14	400.5 "	19	265.2 "	24	3.5 "
5	60.5 "	10	11.7 "	15	10.1 "	20	47.6 "	25	6.2 "

Waste in Sequence

Lowest to Highest	Cumulative Lbs.	%	Lowest to Highest	Cumulative Lbs.	%
.7	.7	—	16.5	124.5	9%
1.1	1.8	—	19.3	143.8	10%
1.4	3.2	—	19.3	163.1	11%
2.0	5.2	—	47.6	213.7	15%
3.5	8.7	—	53.1	266.8	19%
4.8	13.5	1%	60.5	327.3	23%
6.2	19.7	1%	60.5	387.8	27%
9.3	39.0	3%	175.0	562.8	40%
10.0	49.0	3%	205.0	767.8	54%
10.1	59.1	4%	265.2	1033.0	73%
10.5	69.6	5%	400.5	1433.5	100%
11.5	81.1	6%			
11.7	92.8	7%			
15.2	108.0	8%			

This section is included solely to guide you toward potentially worthwhile general areas, while being sufficiently specific to inspire, hopefully, original variations from these stated themes.

First, the general scheme of selecting areas by priority should be followed. Having assigned priorities, the following schemes, tests, and checklists should be applied first to priority area #1. When #1 has been thoroughly worked to completion and time becomes available, move to priority area #2. Do not try to do too many things at once. Concentrate your talents on a few ideas at a time. Too many projects under way simultaneously lead to dissipation of effort and minimum results.

In going through this process, apply the scientific method to your analysis.

The scientific method refers to techniques in the observation and collection of facts together with their arrangement and analysis to make conclusions of

EXHIBIT 55

CHART OF PARETO'S LAW

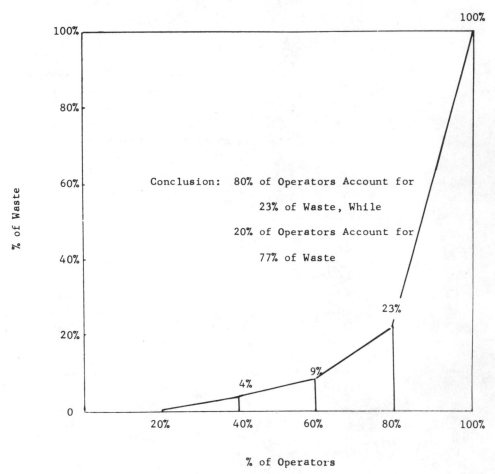

% of Operators

their true significance, including inferences, verification of inferences, and their application to final solutions. Be alert to maintain a careful, scientific attitude in your analysis. Analyze your own methods and data to test for those which run counter to common sense or which are unreasonably non-uniform. Often, the observer himself will be a variable producing inconsistent observations. Never assume any data or fact; test and measure everything. Exhibit 56 lists the steps to follow in applying the Scientific Method.

SALARY COSTS

In applying Pareto's Law to actual cost data, salary costs are bound to be near the top of the priority lists. While the energetic efforts of industrial engineer-

EXHIBIT 56

THE SCIENTIFIC METHOD

1. Recognition that a problem exists.
2. Definition of the problem in terms of known causes and observed effects.
3. Statement of premises and assumptions.
4. Library and literature search.
5. Data collection:
    Commonly observed mistakes in this process include:
    omission
    carelessness
    interdependence not recognized
    habit
    inattention
    abnormal conditions mistaken for normal
6. Validation of data, common sense, consistency, history.
7. Classification of data for subsequent analysis.
8. Analysis. Diagnosis. Prognosis.
9. Inference.
10. Validation of inferences. Simulation tests for validation.
11. Development of general principles from inferences.
12. Application of general principles.

ing coupled with the advent of automation have served to hold down if not actually reduce the number of production man-hours per unit of product, salary costs per unit of product have increased tremendously, because:

a. Government control and reports, including tax reporting, require greater staffs.
b. Customers demand greater service assistance per unit of product.
c. Products are growing more complex, requiring more technical talent in the manufacturing process.
d. Product life becomes ever shorter as research laboratories change, improve, and make obsolete old products at increasing rates. A company must increase its own research efforts equal to that of its most challenging competitor or its markets will be taken away.
e. Data processing and computer installations produce control information never before available but require new staffs to operate them.
f. Automation in manufacturing requires degrees of skill higher than skills of those previously on the payroll.

In analyzing for excessive costs in the salaried areas, a recommended first step is to require of every department head a report detailing what steps he would take to carry out an edict to reduce salary costs by 10 percent. This will uncover departments with fat, to be sliced from the payroll immediately. There should be little hesitation to act in these cases; often the only obstacle consists of how to handle long service employees who deserve consideration over and above routine severance pay policy. The rest of the 10 percent reduction should be identified with reports or procedures to be first eliminated to permit reduction in force. These decisions, in some cases, can easily be resolved. In others, some studies will have to precede the decisions to eliminate duties.

In addition to the 10 percent technique, some fundamental rules can be applied by higher management to evaluate, independently, the relative fat in subordinate departments.

   a. Too many levels of supervision indicate a Parkinsonian excess of middle-level supervisors and secretarial help, and dilution of effort. Lines of communication are too long, causing delay in action and feedback.
   b. Span of control can be too wide or too narrow. It may be a contributing factor to (a). Consider combining two groups into one at the lowest level at which the span is too narrow. This will work all the way up the pyramid. Conversely, at higher levels, the span can be so wide that communication is poor, resulting in misdirection of effort and waste of manpower.
   c. Coordinators and assistants-to are sure warning signs of organizational weakness. Managers should be capable of cooperating without a coordinator to intercede one with the other. Check for ill-defined responsibilities. Or check for a weak supervisor who has chosen to assign a coordinator in lieu of facing up to a problem somewhere within the area to be "coordinated." An assistant-to can be a very useful function in just the right circumstances, one of which is that the man to whom he is assistant must be a relatively unusual man who knows how to use an assistant-to. Most executives do not know how to do this. Again, check job descriptions. Is this assistant a glorified secretary-clerk, or is a genuinely useful executive role being fulfilled?

9

Profit Planning

Why bother to plan? There is no crystal ball available to foretell the future! No one can predict with certainty what events will transpire in the future. In the face of such utter and complete uncertainty, why waste company resources in "planning" for the unknowable?

In fact, the very existence of that uncertainty and unpredictability is the best reason one could advance in favor of planning.

The essence of planning is experimentation, simulation, assuming, even guessing concerning possible uses of company resources under differing sets of possible future conditions and subsequent effects of those uses. Properly done, selected sets of assumed conditions will bracket actual conditions. This done, risks are minimized because planning has recognized the possible condition and a feasible course of action has already been designed. Physical resources are not committed in planning; only ideas are used, testing against assumed reactions.

Planning should not be done simply because it is currently a popular fad. Unless there is a conviction that formal planning is worthwhile, the formal process should be deferred. Instead, attention ought to be devoted to creating the atmosphere within which planning can and will be accepted as a necessary activity. Among the valid reasons why planning is and should be begun are the following:

a. Corporate crisis. Things are suddenly in chaos because of an unanticipated event that no one was prepared to react to and cope with. Suddenly, your major product is obsolete. Competition has moved in and taken over your largest customer. With no warning, your customer has changed his process, eliminating the need for your product. Certain key executives are suddenly lost due to ill health or because of recruiting by another firm.
b. The research department has begun to turn out in quantity a stream of valuable, potentially profitable new product ideas. In order to capitalize on them, a systematic approach to bringing them into production, financing their growth, and developing the new marketing organization must be devised.

187

c. It is better to act, to lead, to be prepared, than it is to react, to follow, to be caught unawares. The uncertain future can better be faced if one does all he can to anticipate what is coming, to organize to get an early warning system in operation, to identify trends as early as it is possible to do so. Changes in technology are reported in trade journals; changes in world politics, world economics, and national politics will occur; the range of possible change (high, low) can be guessed at and plans made for either eventuality. All business is more competitive; this trend will continue. Assumptions can be made about the extent, kind, and timing of greater competition and plans made accordingly. Greater capital investments coupled with galloping technological change and short product lives require greater efforts to reduce the actual risk; planning is such an effort.

In summary, one is better prepared to face future eventualities having already gone through the process of considering possible events, effects, and corrective actions.

WHAT IS PROFIT PLANNING?

Profit planning is the creation of a strategy for the continuation and improvement of a business. It involves the following steps:

1. Setting out, specifically, the objectives of the business during the time span of the plan.
2. Identifying the factors important to the continuation and improvement of the business. Setting up an information system to generate data on the quantifiable factors. This includes information about external forces as well as internal developments and operations.
3. Developing sets of premises to bracket possible future events concerning product obsolescence, competitive forces, political and economic trends, and the like.
4. Preparing action plans designed to accomplish the stated objectives under each set of premises developed under (3).
5. Regular, almost continual updating and revision of premises and action plans, in the light of current events.

In some of these the controller is a spectator, in some a participant, and in some the prime mover.

DEFINING OBJECTIVES

The objectives of the business must be defined by the board of directors and the chief executive officer. They are the ones who must state what it is that the company is to be two, three, five years from now.

An assumed objective is that of continuing to exist. Even this objective requires considerable planning because it implies continuing in current markets at current volumes at current profit levels, utilizing current resources. As a first objective this could serve adequately to get the planning process under way. A full-scale plan to maintain the status quo requires the full exercise of all the listed steps in the planning process. It probably would result in the best-ever picture of what the company really is, right now. Full, complete, comprehensive data would be generated on customers, facilities, competition, market strengths and weaknesses, and the range of potential adverse and favorable developments.

The entire planning process is a vast feedback-feedforward loop. Having fed forward that first objective, the planning process would generate the first plan designed to keep the company in business. This plan, fed back to the originator of the objective, should trigger an in-depth review of the soundness of that objective. In this review, it may become clear that probable competitive action dooms future existence in current areas. Or it may be that your competitive edge is such that nothing short of substantial growth is an adequate objective.

In either case, the objective should be reviewed and restated for a second iteration of the planning process.

HOW LONG TO PLAN FOR?

Five-year plans are the current vogue. This is a compromise between desire and capability. It would be nice to plan ten, fifteen, twenty-five years ahead. But such is clearly beyond our present capability to handle the uncertainty of the future. With a too-long span, assumptions build on premises based on inferences to the point of absurdity.

The response time of your business is one controlling factor in deciding the time span to include. If you are in fashion soft goods, five years in the future probably is beyond comprehension in terms of fabric, print, style, etc. A basic steel converter, on the other hand, can look ahead five years without fear of complete product obsolescence, although a worry could be a technological breakthrough by a competitive material, say plastics, with a shorter facilities construction lead-time. In still a third category are defense equipment suppliers subject to the whims of government procurement agencies and world politics.

In summary, the span of the long range plan should:

1. Be long enough to cover the re-order cycle of your customers. This requires some knowledge of and statement of the customers' product life cycles.
2. Cover your product life cycle, including the rate of technological development and the lead-time to bring a replacement product to market.

3. Provide for the full cycle of recovery and reinvestment of funds required by the product cycle.

PLANNING INFORMATION REQUIREMENTS

If the desires of managers and owners were all that governed operations, planning as described here would be unnecessary. Managers would have their own knowledge of everything pertinent to future developments. Because external factors are controlling and because complete knowledge is impossible, planning for information is vital to success. In this sphere of influence, the controller should be able to contribute as much as any other person.

Information basic to long-range planning includes gross national product, consumer income, consumer spending, consumer price index, balance of payments, tariff rulings, and much other economic data published by federal and state governments. Much of this information the controller is accustomed to using in his routine short-term forecasting. It should be relatively easy to select the data in this category useful to marketing and other executives in long range planning.

Considerable knowledge of industry trends, technological developments, and competitive direction can be gleaned from readily available literature. In order to be on top of the competitive scene, a company should devote time and talent to an organized analysis of other firms' efforts. This is intelligence effort, not undercover espionage. Magazines and newspapers abound with bits and pieces of useful information. Personnel moves are very widely publicized; such moves coupled with knowledge of the strengths, talents, and experience of competitive personnel often indicate shifts in emphasis or new product activity. Trade journals, association meetings, and technical societies are veritable gold mines to the alert, informed listener. Salesmen who call on you and your competitors have with them information you could use concerning their volumes of purchases, new items being used, trends, plans for the future, recent conversations with their executives on current business conditions, and the like. All of this is available to your company if you organize to harvest it. If only superficial attention is given, no one will catch the significance of the executive transfer. Association meetings will be educational and social gatherings only, devoid of intelligence overtones. Your puchasing agent, a busy man with many people trying to see him, will not "waste" his time in idle conversation with salesmen who otherwise might be willing to chat about Mr. Competitor.

Here is another application for the Scientific Method. Organize to collect strategic intelligence. This duty may be the controller's but more often will be a separate activity under marketing. The controller, in any case, can contribute to the effective organization of the function. Staff adequately to handle, sort, sift, and categorize incoming data. File data to that it can be readily retrieved for comparison and analysis with new data. Cross-index and catalog to facilitate retrieval. Train salesmen, engineers, and buyers in the art of intelligence collection. Get them accustomed to listening for the significant bit in the flood of verbal garbage. Require them to report after visits to customers and meetings *without* pre-selecting and editing out the waste; better to report as much as possible with editing just before filing. Often two seemingly insignificant remarks assume tremendous significance when coupled together by an informed analyst. None of the above is intended to endorse espionage, industrial spies, or theft of competitive information. Strategic intelligence gathering is both legal and ethical and should be done. If you don't and your competitor does, you are doubly in trouble.

Exhibit 57 lists several additional types and sources of planning information with which the controller is concerned. Column 1 lists data which should be supplied by the controller. Column 2 lists data which the controller could be assigned to provide. Column 3 lists data more readily available from someone else.

EXHIBIT 57

INFORMATION FOR PROFIT PLANNING

To Be Supplied by the Controller	Available via the Controller	Available from Other Sources
Product Costs	Economic Indexes	Potential Markets
Profit Contribution	Government Statistics	Prices
Variance Analysis	Strategic Intelligence	Volumes
Break-even Data	Value Analysis	Distribution Requirements
Return on Investment	Construction Schedules (PERT)	Advertising Value
Rent or Buy	Production Schedules	Personnel & Labor Relations
Make or Buy		Staffing Requirements
Funds Available		Plant design, Location, Costs
		Material Sources
		Product Developments

PREMISES

Having established a flow of information, that information should then be used to hypothesize possible future events, external and internal.

The intent is not to predict exactly what is to happen. It has been agreed that this cannot be done.

It is intended that premises bracket the future event. In good naval gunfire procedures, the first two shots fired will always miss the target. One will be high; one will be low. This bracketing of the target establishes the exact distance to the target much more rapidly than any other technique (prior to radar). With upper and lower limits established, the formation can quickly begin to fire for effect.

Your premises which bracket future happenings will similarly establish the response best suited to the event and insure that the response is given quickly because you are prepared rather than surprised. You can act for effect, immediately.

Premises thus developed at the top levels define, to an extent, premises to be developed at lower levels. Certainly, the framework within which lower level premises are to be established will be defined. It would be sheer folly to allow lower levels to plan independently of higher level planning.

Premises must be reduced to writing. Only thus can the author of the premise be sure that he has crystallized the premise in his own mind. When he sees it in writing, he may not like it and may reject it in favor of different wording. With premises in writing, it will be easier to test the continued validity of plans as events assumed actually come about, as time passes. Because premises, by definition, are assumptions about the future which, by definition, are not all going to be correct assumptions, one's concepts of facts versus premises must be sharpened and clarified.

General acceptance of premises is necessary before detailed plans are formulated. Discussion and feedback result in better premises, greater validity, and more complete coverage.

ACTION PLAN

For every major set of premises, an action plan for an appropriate response must be prepared. This is the heart of the planning process. This is what gives profit planning life, impact, value. Unless action plans are detailed, the rest of the process is wasted.

It is not necessary that the actual response be the same as the planned response when the time comes. Probably, it will not be the same, but will be a better response because a prior, partial response had already been prepared.

Proceeding from the premises, the complete action plan will include the following:

1. Reasons why action is required. This might be a summary of the potential results of inaction.
2. Specific steps to be taken under the action response. Who is to act. What facilities, manpower, resources are to be used.
3. The end effect to be obtained as a direct result of the interaction of the event that triggers a response and the response, itself. The timetable for action

and effect. The timetable enables management to control the overall situation and to monitor the rate and adequacy of response at predetermined checkpoints. (A useful device for controlling progress on a plan such as this is the PERT Chart technique.)

REVISION OF PLANS

Profit planning is a dynamic process, not a static document produced once every three to five years. Regular, almost continual, revision of the action elements of the plan is necessary to insure that the latest thinking is incorporated.

In practice, a "moving five-year plan" is a good title for the planning scheme. Each year, the current year passes from plan to event to history. The remaining four years are revised to reflect current events and revised objectives. A fifth year is added to the far end of the plan.

Revision may range from minor to total. There is no shame in scrapping an entire plan. The benefit comes from the planning exercise in which the future is assessed and plans drawn, not from the document that represents the product of the planning process. If the situation demands it, throw out the document and repeat the process.

SHORT/LONG RANGE PLANNING

Short range and long range plans are part of the same process. Long range plans are dependent on short range plans and actions. Short range plans are better defined, more exact, near-term phases of long range plans.

Current operations—the current year—require greatly detailed programs and budgets, as described in the next chapter.

Years two through five pick up where short range plans leave off, integrating objectives, forecasts, marketing schemes, facilities plans, financial arrangements, research programs, personnel problems, and production schedules into an orderly, scientific approach to the management of uncertainty.

10

Short Range Planning

For adequate control of the current year's operations, the current year increment of the long range plan must include much more detail than the increment for future years. The short range plan is more than a plan; it is a statement of control strategy and control tactics for the next twelve months.

Strategy is consistent with the basic strategy of the entire plan. Tactics supplement the strategic plan, giving operating direction and implementation to the plan. Strategy defines why and what; tactics define who, where, and when.

Elements of the comprehensive short range plan include:

1. Marketing Plan
2. Operating Plan
3. Expense Budget
4. Research and Development Plan
5. Capital Expenditure Plan
6. Profit Forecast
7. Cost Improvement Plan
8. Profit Plan (Assignment)

These are elements, to repeat, of an integrated comprehensive plan. To consider each an independent exercise in control is to achieve a minute portion of the full potential benefit. There must be feedforward, feedback, modification, and continuing study of the constantly interacting forces of each element on all other elements. Probable effects of changes must be anticipated rather than discovered after the fact. The interaction of elements on each other is illustrated in Exhibit 58 by the direction of the arrows.

MARKETING PLAN

Basic to any and all short range plans is the marketing plan for operations and sales. Immediately available customers and share of market data are controlling for the short term.

EXHIBIT 58

INTERACTING ELEMENTS OF SHORT RANGE PLAN

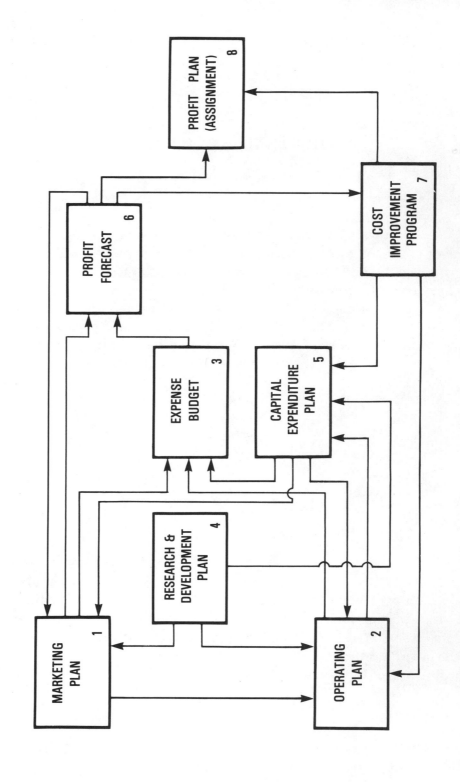

Market position is a company's most important asset. Good relations and good quality coupled with good service give a competitive edge over competition. The primary emphasis in short range plans must be to maintain and strengthen direct customer ties. Operating schedules, R & D, and capital plans must first and foremost meet this requirement.

To this end the marketing plan must provide the necessary information on customers, products, quantities, timing, and prices, so that resulting integrated plans provide the required equipment, manpower, and raw materials at the right time, place, and cost.

Each salesman should be required to forecast sales to each of his customers, giving product volume and price detail. The controller should provide sales history detail on which these forecasts will be based. While salesmen are responsible for detecting trends and unusual changing conditions in each of their accounts, they should not have to accumulate statistics personally. A suggested format for this report to salesmen and for their forecast is shown in Exhibit 59. (Note the inclusion of comparative historical data for information on the same form on which the forecast is to be reported; this is a good example of paper-work simplification.)

The forecast thus received can be summarized in several ways for use by others in preparing their individual plans.

a. Total volume forecast by product when summarized tells Manufacturing the operating activity they will be required to staff for. This can further be exploded into raw material needs, manpower requirements, and equipment schedules. Obviously, these affect the expense budget and capital expenditure plans.
b. Sales management uses the forecasts to identify growth customers, areas of possible losses, lagging salesmen, those whose volume requires additional help for adequate coverage, and so forth.
c. R & D efforts might be directed toward products trending down (reduce costs, improve quality) to regain lost position or toward new products catching on (reduce costs, improve quality) in an effort to capture a larger share of market.

Marketing costs for the forecast level of sales are a direct input to the expense budget.

Total sales dollar volume forecast is a direct input to the profit forecast.

OPERATING PLAN

Given the physical plant as it exists, the marketing plan converted to units of product defines the level of operations to be required of manufacturing.

EXHIBIT 59

SALES HISTORY AND FORECAST SHEET

Salesman: J. Smith   001

Customer	Code	Item	Code	History Year Before 1Q	2Q	3Q	4Q	Last Year 1Q	2Q	3Q	4Q	Current Price	Price	Forecast 1Q	2Q	3Q	4Q
ABC Company	007	Product A	001	32	30	40	60	75	75	60	50	21.00					
		" B	002	50	48	52	47	51	45	48	53	32.00					
		" D	004	120	100	145	200	300	350	340	350	10.50					
XYZ Inc.	834	Product A	001	75	80	50	100	45	90	82	37	21.00					

This activity level defines most of the variable elements of the operating plan:

a. Standard work force. The number of men to be assigned to each cost center on each shift.
b. Supervision. The number of foremen and supervisors required by the above work force.
c. Fuel and power required to operate equipment.
d. Raw materials. Each product exploded into a bill of materials then extended for the total quantity to be produced defines the raw material requirements. This is often the controller's responsibility, working from the elements of the standard cost scheme. Purchasing then takes over to arrange sources, prices, and delivery schedules.

All of these elements are direct inputs to the expense budget.

If sufficient capacity does not exist to produce the forecast sales, an input to the capital expenditure plan is generated with a high priority for action. Desirably, this will not have to be done on a crisis basis but on the basis of carefully projected capacity needs via the long range planning function.

RESEARCH AND DEVELOPMENT PLAN

Based on its charter from top management, the research and development department works constantly toward improving product quality, reducing product costs, and developing new products.

Some of these new products will be additional sales volume to the company. In this area, the controller must stay on top of developments to assist in the overall financial evaluation of such new product lines. Often a significant capital expenditure program has to be undertaken in support of such a new product. These cases involve economic justification of the investment and financing of the project.

On the other hand, some new developments will obsolete current product lines. This is desirable. Better for you to obsolete an item by development of a better one than for your competitor to do it for you. This situation imposes different problems on the controller via the marketing and operating plan. A new (more expensive) marketing plan will have to be devised to replace the old product with the new. Operating plans may have to be revised to provide the different manufacturing equipment and raw material configuration.

R & D activities require increasingly larger staffs as technology gets more complicated. Greater numbers of products are being given increasingly quantified test specifications. Dimensional limits are reduced as the trend to compactness and miniaturization continues.

The R & D plan must take all these things into account, provide the manpower and physical facilities to keep developments moving, and control the rate of progress toward assigned goals. The controller can aid in setting up such a program:

a. Projects should be accepted only after the economic worth is established. This involves projecting potential sales and costs to indicate potential profit contribution, comparing that with expected costs of development. This comparison establishes the net worth of the project.
b. Assign projects so that accomplishments expected are clearly identified. Periodic reviews establish progress achieved. Corrective action is taken immediately when warranted.
c. A cost control program on R & D teams insures against development costs running out of control.

CAPITAL EXPENDITURE PLAN

Capital funds are needed to replace equipment as required to stay in markets at current levels of volume and profitability and to increase profitability through reduced costs and new product exploitation.

A first category is that of replacement of worn-out assets. This is capital money that must be spent in order to maintain plant and equipment in a reasonable condition. This also includes money for new, not replacement, equipment necessary to continuing in business in certain market areas, as well as legal and insurance requirements.

A second category concerns improvement in profitability through cost reduction capital investment and new equipment needed to get into market production of new product developments. In this sphere of the capital expenditure plan, the controller has a primary responsibility. It is he who must assess the value of expenditures for these ends, as measured by return on investment. In Chapter 12, considerable attention is given to his role in this evaluation process as well as specific detail of the content of the capital expenditure plan.

The capital expenditure plan can, in the feedback loop, influence the content of several previous and subsequent plans. Added depreciation from new investment is an input to the expense budget. New product facilities installed in response to a signal from the R & D plan generate changes in the marketing and operating plans. In response to the Cost Improvement Program, cost reduction (automation) equipment may trigger changes in the operating plan.

EXPENSE BUDGET

Through the mechanism of the expense budget, all expectations of sales and of manufacturing are translated into cost data. It is the unique contribution of the controller to translate all of the complexities of the marketing and operations plans into economic reality.

The controller is the sole official source of cost and financial data. As such, he is responsible for receiving plans from other departments to be integrated into an operating expense budget. The basic scheme of collecting expense data and of allocating costs to profit centers is described in this section. Figure 60 is a flow chart of a typical budget preparation.

Salary costs are within limits relatively independent of changes in operations. The budget for this cost is derived from last year's budget, adjusted for changes in staff as approved during the past year plus approved additions not yet actually hired. The budget should provide:

> Base Salary
> Vacation Pay
> Overtime Premium at Budget Activity
> Bonus/Incentive Pay
> Merit/General Increases

Wages must be calculated for each cost center based on the standard operating activity of that center, the number of employees on each shift, and the rate for each job on each shift. A "standard work force" recap is very useful for budget preparation and for subsequent control See Exhibit 61.

Benefits include group insurance, pension plans, and workmen's compensation insurance costs. It also includes payroll taxes such as F.I.C.A., State unemployment and disability coverage, and the like. Costs of non-productive time such as vacation pay for time off and unworked holidays also comes under this heading. If the company operates an employee recreation center or country club, the cost of that activity is also a benefit.

Taxes, Fire Insurance, and Depreciation are straightforward annual costs readily ascertained. State franchise and property taxes are dependent on statute and local government financing needs. Fire insurance policy costs are relatively fixed from year to year. Depreciation charges are a function of asset value and current federal income tax requirements.

Supplies, Rents, and Royalties include a very broad category of expense items. Last year's budget versus actual expense, tempered by changes in activity, is a starting point for budgeting this item. Within the category, individual expenses should be explicitly identified with a minimum in a miscellaneous group-

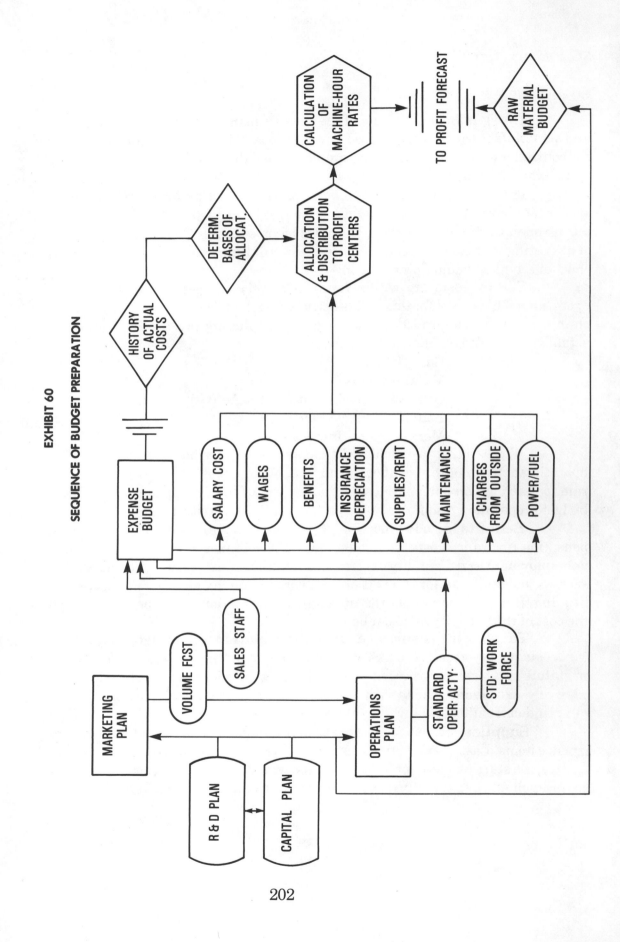

EXHIBIT 60

SEQUENCE OF BUDGET PREPARATION

EXHIBIT 61

STANDARD WORK FORCE

Resp. Code	$ Paid/Man Week	Description	Rate/Hr.	No. Shifts	Hours Worked/Week	Hours Paid/Week	Total No. of Emp.	Total $ Paid/Week
8101	224	Waxer Operator	4.31	3	48	52	3	672
8101	226	Waxer Operator	4.35	3	48	52	3	678
8101	216	Waxer Helper	4.15	3	48	52	3	648
8101	216	Waxer Helper	4.15	3	48	52	3	648
8101	216	Laminator Helper	4.15	3	48	52	3	648
8101	216	Laminator Helper	4.15	3	48	52	3	648
8101	226	Laminator Operator	4.35	3	48	52	3	678
8101	226	Laminator Operator	4.35	3	48	52	3	678
							24	5,298
8102	209	Waxer Mix Man	4.26	4	42	49	4	836
8102	225	Ammonia Plant Oper.	4.55	1	46	49.5	2	450
							6	1,286
8981	217	Winderman A	4.43	4	42	49	20	4,340
8981	209	Winder Helper	4.26	4	42	49	12	2,508
							32	6,848

ing. Once-a-year purchases of supplies and forms must be recognized as well as those which are incurred quite regularly. For sensible budgeting, the sub-accounts described in Chapter 4 in the discussion of the Chart of Accounts are invaluable. If the controller has spent $300,000 in this category last year, he wants to know something of the detail. He should be aware that the $300,000 is composed of

$ 85,000	Computer Rental
20,000	Cards and Forms
110,000	Office Supplies for All Departments
35,000	Printed Multi-Part Forms
25,000	Professional Fees
15,000	Travel and Training
10,000	Miscellaneous
$300,000	Total

so that he can apply some judgement to the adequacy of this figure for next year. If he plans to reduce the salaried clerical work force by $45,000 via an additional $15,000 in computer costs, this must be intelligently budgeted.

Maintenance, Charges from Outside, and **Power and Fuel** must similarly be budgeted as individual items of expense, based on the best estimate of next year's expectations.

All of the foregoing relate to expenditures by cost center. To distinguish this category from allocations, they can be referred to as *original expenses*. Having derived reasonable, acceptable, approved figures for each original expense, a summary by cost center is prepared. This set of cost center summaries shows how much money is to be spent by each cost center; this, then, is the budget on which active cost control is to be based, at the point of initial expenditure. Exhibit 62 shows such a summary.

BASES OF ALLOCATION

At this point in the evolution of the expense budget, all of the basic data for cost control has been prepared. Detailed cost summaries of original expense have been approved for every cost center.

As a tool for profit planning, however, the budget work has only begun.

All costs must be allocated to some profit center, because all costs have to be paid for by income from a revenue-producing profit center. It is to be hoped that no costs will be entirely unrelated to at least one profit center, even though the relation may be a tenuous one. That phrase was deliberately selected to put cost allocation in its most unfavorable light. Until the profit contribution idea illustrated in Exhibit 6 on page 51 is accepted for profit reporting, cost allocations, will continue to plague the controller.

EXHIBIT 62

ORIGINAL EXPENSE DIRECT TO BUDGET CENTER

Center _____ CONTROLLERS GENERAL _____ BUDGET CENTER SUMMARY Page _____

TERM EXPENSE	PAGE	BUDGET LAST	BUDGET THIS	DIRECT EXPENSE	PAGE	BUDGET LAST	BUDGET THIS
ALL SALARIES	1	6540	4647	DIRECT ASSIGNED WAGES	40		
RSX	2	122	38	POWER - ENERGY	41		
VACATION ACCRUED	3			COAL & COKE	42		
HOLIDAY PAY	4						
WORKMANS COMPENSATION	5	17	16				
F. O. A. B. & UNEMP. INS.	6	127	123				
GROUP INS. SALARY	7	122	108				
GROUP INS. HOURLY	8						
PENSIONS, SALARY	9	313	169				
PENSIONS, HOURLY	10						
DEPRECIATION	11	1100	1262				
FIRE AND OTHER INS.	12						
TAXES, STATE & PROPERTY	13						
OFFICE SUPPLIES & EXP.	14	803	820				
POWER DEMAND	15						
PERIOD ASSIGNED WAGES	16						
MAJOR OPER. SUPPLIES	17						
MINOR OPER. SUPPLIES	18						
TRANSFER TO CAPITAL	19						
SUB TOTAL		9144	7183	SUB - TOTAL			
MECHANICAL MAINTENANCE	60						
ELECTRICAL MAINTENANCE	61						
MECHANICAL CONSTRUCTION	62						
ELECTRICAL CONSTRUCTION	63						
INSTRUMENT	64						

Allocations, by definition, are unscientific and arbitrary decisions. To the extent possible, they must be made on the basis of direct use.

If a single plant has separate production, inspection, and shipping departments for responsibility accounting and cost control, with all departments servicing only the one mill, all costs are allocated to that mill as a profit center. This is clear cut.

Few other allocations are so easy to define. In the case of a multi-plant division with five profit centers and a consolidated central staff, there is an imposing list of allocation decisions to be made. This list would include some or all of the following:

General Administration	Selling Expense
Controller	Industrial Engineering
R & D	Personnel
Quality Control	Traffic & Shipping
Engineering	Production Control
Maintenance	Central Stores

Methods of allocation can be as diverse or as simple as you want them to be. Generally, however, the simpler the plan, the less exact—hence more misleading—are the results.

One technique is to divide the total "overhead" by total "direct labor" and to apply overhead in that fixed ratio to labor. This should be so patently foolish as to require no further condemnation.

Because the objective of cost allocation is greater accuracy and validity in machine-hour rates for costing and for better direction of market efforts, the basis for allocation must be selected so as to minimize the possibility of invalidity to a reasonably significant degree. The dollar value to be allocated is important here. With $10,000/year to be allocated, a 10 percent error means $1,000 versus a $100,000 allocation where only 1 percent is $1,000.

There is no *correct* basis for allocation. Each situation requires an individual test. *Acceptable* bases, however, should include at least the following:

a. Reported man-hours, by staff department, for each profit center (engineering, maintenance, industrial engineering, R & D, controller)
b. Number of employees (personnel, general administration)
c. Units of production handled (shipping, receiving)
d. Number of documents (orders, purchase requisitions, invoices) processed for each profit center (controller, purchasing, production control)
e. Area or cubage of building occupied (maintenance, property taxes, insurance)
f. Units of production generated by each profit center (general administration, selling expense, shipping)

g. Metered consumption (power)
h. Asset value (property taxes, insurance)
i. Value added (general administration, selling expense)
j. Total sales value (general administration, selling expense)

There is no implication that the above list is complete; it is intended to illustrate the scope of the problem, not to suggest specific solutions to a general problem.

Often the question is raised of allocations direct to profit centers versus successive allocations and reallocations among cost centers, ultimately reaching the profit centers. There may be little difference in the end result; if tested and found true, this would eliminate any need for further debate. To the extent that usage by profit center can be measured, this makes direct allocation the only sensible course.

For later analysis, actual distribution bases used each period must be consistent with budget; there is seldom time enough to carry actual costs each period through the succesive allocations such a technique would require. In general, there is little to recommend the time-consuming scheme over the more direct one.

Exhibit 63 shows a profit center with full costs allocated to it for the total budget expense of the center. At this point, the budget data is ready for use in machine-hour rate calculations and in profit forecasting.

MACHINE-HOUR RATES

Every unit of operating equipment is represented in the budget by a budget center. Groups of similar machines can be treated together in a single budget center. The activity schedule for each machine defines the number of operating hours for that machine. By dividing the total cost by the total scheduled operating hours, you get the machine hour rate to be used in product costing.

Assume that Plant A is a ten identical-machine plant scheduled to operate twenty-four hours a day, five days a week, with seven down holidays and a two week vacation shutdown, and with an average 5 percent downtime for repair and maintenance. The calculation of the $15.04/hr. machine rate is described in Exhibit 64.

RAW MATERIAL FORECAST

The marketing plan converted into detail product material costs and then summarized gives the total material cost by type of raw material and in total as an input to the final cost summary.

EXHIBIT 63

PLANT A BUDGET CENTER SUMMARY

Center_____ BUDGET CENTER SUMMARY				Page _____			

TERM EXPENSE	PAGE	BUDGET		DIRECT EXPENSE	PAGE	BUDGET	
		LAST	THIS			LAST	THIS
ALL SALARIES	1	1485	1520	DIRECT ASSIGNED WAGES	40	5792	5984
RSX	2	24		POWER - ENERGY	41		
VACATION ACCRUED	3	346	415	COAL & COKE	42		
HOLIDAY PAY	4	127	131				
WORKMANS COMPENSATION	5	28	23				
F. O. A. B. & UNEMP. INS.	6	206	193				
GROUP INS. SALARY	7	27	32				
GROUP INS. HOURLY	8	218	191				
PENSIONS, SALARY	9	99	127				
PENSIONS, HOURLY	10	112	117				
DEPRECIATION	11	2950	3131				
FIRE AND OTHER INS.	12	122	134				
TAXES, STATE & PROPERTY	13	1270	1333				
OFFICE SUPPLIES & EXP.	14						
POWER DEMAND	15						
PERIOD ASSIGNED WAGES	16						
MAJOR OPER. SUPPLIES	17	2900	2692				
MINOR OPER. SUPPLIES	18	350	428				
TRANSFER TO CAPITAL	19						
SUB TOTAL		10264	10467	SUB - TOTAL		5792	5984
MECHANICAL MAINTENANCE	60	1670	1841				
ELECTRICAL MAINTENANCE	61	507	525				
MECHANICAL CONSTRUCTION	62	158	196				
ELECTRICAL CONSTRUCTION	63						
INSTRUMENT	64	145	149				
PERSONNEL	66	2813	2974				
TRAFFIC	67						
PURCHASING	68						
CONTROLLER'S DEPT. GENERAL	69	198	189				
TABULATING	70	2758	2495				
ENGINEERING GENERAL	71	1730	1793				
POWER, STEAM & WATER	72	5299	5540	POWER, STEAM & WATER	96	9075	9710
LABORATORY, GENERAL	73						
	74						
PULP PREPARATION	75	6540	6586	PULP PREPARATION	109	3055	3339
PAPER MACHINE GENERAL	76	5610	6116				
	77						
	78						
	79						
	80						
	81						
	82						
	83						
DISTRIBUTED TOTAL		27428	28404	DISTRIBUTED TOTAL		12130	13049
GRAND TOTAL		37692	38871	GRAND TOTAL		17922	19033

EXHIBIT 64

CALCULATION OF MACHINE-HOUR RATE

1. *Operating Hours:*

   10 machines $\times$ 52 wks./yr. $\times$ 5 days/wk. $\times$ 24 hrs./day = 62,400 hrs./yr.

   less holidays 10 $\times$ 7 $\times$ 24   = (1,680) " "

   less vacation 10 $\times$ 10 $\times$ 24   = (2,400) " "

                                                              58,320 hrs./yr.

   58,320 hrs./yr $\times$ 95% running time   = 55,404 hrs./yr.

2. *Machine Hour Rate:*

$$\frac{(\$602,350 + \$230,920)}{55,404 \text{ hrs.}} = \$15.04/\text{hr.}$$

PROFIT FORECAST

The controller has completed his function as a cost consultant to operating and staff department heads with the completion of the expense budget. He is now ready to function as a professional manager in the preparation of the profit forecast.

From the marketing plan, he has extracted standard sales income and standard material cost for the forecast mix. The controller must now forecast profits based on that plan, tempered by history of actual performance versus plan.

If he feels certain historical precedents or economic forecasts were not adequately considered in the marketing plan, the controller must resolve these differences before he can proceed with the forecast.

The translation into the profit forecast should take the form, if not the format, of Exhibit 65.

1. Sales value. The original marketing plan has been revised upward by 5 percent to take into account the standard economic forecast (consensus forecast) for the year. Price is unchanged.
2. Material cost. Each product in the marketing plan was costed at standard.
3. Direct cost. Directly as shown in the budget.
4. Material and direct cost variances are forecast based on recent history. Last year, variances ran 6 percent of standard cost. Some improvement is expected this year, to 5.5 percent.
5. Term costs. Directly as shown in the budget.
6. Term variance. Last year, Plant A ran $85,000 over budget.

EXHIBIT 65

PROFIT FORECAST

1. Sales forecast (as adjusted)	
10,000,000 lbs. @ average	
selling price $15.00/cwt.	$1,500,000
2. Standard raw material cost	500,000
3. Standard direct cost	230,920
Standard Profit Contribution	$ 769,080
P.C. Ratio	51.3%
4. Material and direct cost variances (at 5.5% of standard cost)	40,000
5. Budgeted term costs	602,350
6. Term cost variance	70,000
Profit	$ 56,730

The profit thus forecast must be evaluated for reasonableness and for adequacy. Comparisons with previous years for

> Total Sales
> Price per Unit
> Material and Direct Cost per Unit
> P. C. Ratio ($ P.C. to $ Sales)
> Total Term Costs
> Variances
> Profit

are necessary to validate the current forecast. Once validated, the profit as forecast must be tested for adequacy.

Is this an acceptable profit for this operation?

It may well be inadequate! The forecast at this point includes the total inherent conservatism of every executive involved in the process to date. Top management should review the forecast and reject it as a profit plan if the profit is insufficient. Among tests for insufficiency would be:

a. Declining sales volume.
b. Declining unit price.
c. Costs increasing too fast—greater than known inflationary factors, or inadequate cost reduction effort.
d. Declining profit in absence of pronounced effect of any of the foregoing.

The feedback process may go back through the entire system through marketing and/or operations plans to correct for the deficiencies in income and cost.

The marketing plan must be amended to give individual salesmen a two-fold assignment:

1. Maintain the sales originally forecast, and
2. Increase sales in specific products by specific quantities.

The revised marketing plan in total should now deliver adequate total income as measured by profit contribution.

Operating units must now amend the cost reduction program sufficiently to reduce costs to a level which will result in attaining the necessary total profit, when taken in combination with the added profit contribution from sales. The normal cost reduction program should hold costs at a constant level, offsetting annual wage and salary increases with crew reductions and efficiency gains. This is, unfortunately, very difficult except for direct labor costs. Increasing demands for technical and professional talent plus added depreciation and taxes from heavy capital investment can seldom be directly offset in the expense budget. Therefore, costs regularly trend upward in spite of cost reduction programs. Simultaneouly, inefficiencies are tolerated because measures of performance are difficult to apply. When the profit forecast comes up too low and is rejected as a plan, then is the time to apply the "across-the-board cut" program, but with discretion.

Require plans of each department head which if implemented would reduce costs 10 percent; review each plan, implementing selectively, reducing inefficiencies but leaving alone departments *already* lean and efficient. Increase efforts to cut labor costs by automation. Concentrate particularly on material and direct cost variances. Hold as a last resort the flat-out 10 percent cut by every department without exception.

COST IMPROVEMENT PROGRAM

The summary of all cost reduction and variance improvement plans becomes the cost improvement program, to be reported on and followed up regularly for action. The plan is worthless until costs are actually reduced.

PROFIT PLAN

The focal point of the entire short range planning process is the profit plan.

This plan includes an assignment—not merely a goal—for every department, every plant, every division of the company.

Each assignment is clearly defined in words and in numbers in the profit plan. Each assignment is backed up in one or more elements of the subsidiary, contributory plan.

Each manager is expected to deliver on his assignment. Fulfillment of each and every assignment means fulfillment of the profit assignment, since profit is the end result of all the contributory activities.

Control reports should be published on each phase of the assignment so that each manager knows the extent to which he is better than or worse than the assignment rate. The trend format is the best format. In Exhibit 66 you can see that the marketing assignment calls for total annual sales of 10,000,000 pounds; for the first quarter, sales are running ahead of the assignment rate at 3,500,000 for

EXHIBIT 66

ASSIGNMENT CONTROL CHARTS

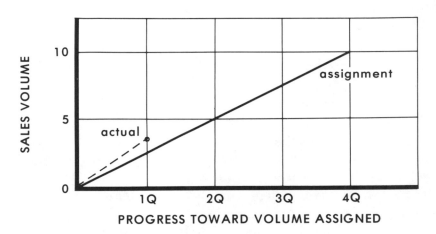

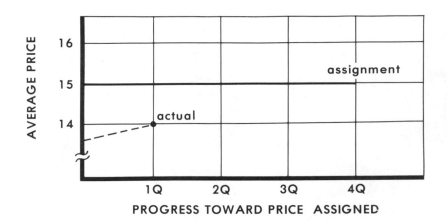

the quarter. Price, however, is expected to average $15.00 and is only at $14.00. Exhibit 67 gives the detail necessary to isolate the sources of these differences for corrective action on price as well as for holding action on volume. Similar charts should be used for each element of the assignment.

By using detailed profit plans and charts such as these, it will be apparent early in the year where trouble spots lie. Departments falling below assignment will be spotlighted so that corrective action can be taken early enough to assure meeting assignment by the end of the year.

EXHIBIT 67

ANALYSIS OF ORDERS VERSUS ASSIGNMENT

First Quarter

Salesman	Customer	Product	Volume		Price	
			Orders	Assignment	Orders	Assignment
J. Smith	ABC Company	Product A	60	45	21.00	21.00
		" B	52	50	14.00	15.00
		" D	370	350	10.45	10.50
		" E	28	—	18.50	—
	XYZ, Inc.	Product A	45	40	15.00	16.00
	Grand Total		3,500	2,500	14.00	15.00

11

Cost-Volume-Profit Analysis

It is in the area of C-V-P analysis that the controller is called on to exercise the consultative capacity defined earlier in Chapter 2.

The controller is in a unique position in that his assignments cut across *all* organization lines giving him free access to, a welcome in, and a depth of knowledge of all other functional and operating departments. This, coupled with his capability for analytical work, enables him to serve the very useful role of internal consultant to all general and operating management.

Analysis in the sense implied in this chapter is the application of the "Scientific Method" to the evaluation of economic problems. The Scientific Method refers to techniques in the observation and collection of facts together with their arrangement and analysis to make inferences of their true significance, including inferences, verification of inferences, and their application to final solutions. The analyst must be alert to maintain a careful scientific attitude in his analysis, remembering that the observer himself is often a variable, producing inconsistent observations.

Discussion of several typical types of financial analysis follows in this chapter. Specific examples will be used in each case in order better to illustrate the specific application of the general principles. Exhibit 68 summarizes several aspects of cost prediction modeling, the details of which are available in standard cost accounting textbooks

MEASURES OF PROFITABILITY

In general, direct costs and profit contribution should be used in economic analyses. You often need to establish the incremental effect of a specific action. Avoid like the plague any analysis which includes reallocation of term costs between old and new operations; no realistic inference of a single action can be made when allocations are allowed to become part of the analysis.

To measure the relative worth of alternative operations, use incremental profit contribution and P.C. ratio. It is not necessary to use any particular "text-

EXHIBIT 68

ASPECTS OF COST PREDICTION MODELING

Managers frequently must choose one of several competing or conflicting alternatives. Quantitative techniques are available to aid in selecting the cost minimizing or the profit maximizing alternative. Accountants must supply most of the data for such quantitative techniques.

A. *Cost Classifications:*

1. Cost/Volume
   Fixed
   Variable
   Semi-variable
   Semi-fixed

2. Controllable/Noncontrollable
3. Product
4. Incremental, Sunk, Opportunity

B. *Cost Estimating*

1. Engineering Analysis
2. Historical Cost Analysis
   Account Analysis
   High-Low (Exhibit 69)
   Visual Curve Fitting
   Statistical Curve Fitting
      Linear Regression (Exhibit 71)
   Relevant Range

3. Problems in Using Historical Data
   Homogeneity of Product
   Stationarity of Process
   Historical Data versus Capacity
   Causality
   Multiple Variable Dependence

4. Sensitivity to Error
   Usefulness for Predictions of Cost Behavior
      Example: EOQ Model

---

book" definition of incremental costs; this unnecessarily restricts your freedom to analyze the situation. Define incremental costs and then apply your definition. In the case of an entire new plant, all of the plant "overhead" is incremental, direct insofar as this analysis is concerned, including the plant manager, foremen, janitors, office staff, maintenance, plant depreciation, and the like. So as not to confuse the recipients of your analysis results, I strongly recommend this use of the term "incremental costs" rather than any other term.

Incremental costs are those costs to be incurred *solely* because of the project which is the subject of analysis. This definition gives you a useful word with inherent significance but unencumbered with previous definition. Profit contribution can become "incremental contribution" with equally gratifying results. Incremental contribution is:

Incremental Sales Value

Less Incremental Material Costs

Less Incremental Operating Expense

Incremental Contribution

The "ratio" is, of course, incremental contribution divided by incremental sales value. This ratio has no inherent significance. It is an abstract index with no dimensional tag; dimensional analysis of the derivation of the ratio shows that both numerator and denominator are labeled "$/Year" which cancel out in division. The index has significance only when used in comparison with other indexes *derived the same way*.

If several plans show about the same dollar profit but from different sales values, the better choice might be the one with the highest ratio. This indicates a greater portion of the sales dollar is available for profit with a greater margin for future cost increases or price reductions. Consider the following:

	Plant A		Plant B	
Incremental Sales	100 M	100%	150 M	100%
Incremental Material	50 M	50%	95 M	63%
Incremental Expense	25 M	25%	30 M	20%
Incremental Contribution	25 M	25%	25 M	17%

Even though operating expense is only $5M greater in Plant B, a much greater fraction of sales value is used up in material costs. Insofar as profit potential is concerned, Plant A is the better of the two. See what price changes and material cost increases will do:

a. Prices are reduced 10%. Plant A's contribution drops to $15M and Plant B's to $10M. The ratios are 15% and 7%.
b. Material prices go up 10%. Plant A's contribution goes to $20M (20%) while Plant B's is $15M (10%).

The same type comparisons of investment are necessary. Perhaps expenses and waste are lower solely because of specialized equipment worth considerably more.

	Plant A	Plant B
Investment	$ 75M	$ 75M
Return on Investment	33%	33%

In this case, equipment value is not contributing to the difference. Plant A remains a more desirable choice.

When differences in level of activity, operating-hours, or multiple and different processes are involved, absolute contribution dollars is the appropriate measure of worth—not of efficiency or relative performance, however.

When a choice is to be made between two alternative uses of the same equipment, the better choice is that one producing the higher contribution per hour in order to realize the maximum absolute dollar income from the time available.

	Product A	Product B
Sales Value	$25.00/cwt.	$20.00/cwt.
Material Cost	9.00/cwt.	6.00/cwt.
Direct Cost	3.00/cwt.	1.50/cwt.
Profit Contribution	$13.00/cwt.	$12.50/cwt.
Production Rate	1,000#/Hour	2,000#/Hour
Contribution/Hour	$130/Hour	$250/Hour

In this example, Product A has $.50/cwt. greater contribution. However, its production rate is only one-half that of Product B. For a given interval of time, a much greater gain will be realized by producing Product B.

ANALYSIS OF COST BEHAVIOR

Methods for the prediction of cost behavior must be developed and implemented within the firm by the controller. Two basic choices are available. In one, normative models of what cost behavior ought to be can be developed using engineered standard cost data. In the other, prediction models can be inferred from historical data, available within the accounting system. Since the recent past is the best predictor of the near-term future, there is considerable merit in such an approach to the problem.

Total costs are composed of fixed costs and variable costs. The fixed costs are associated with capacities or available services and support activities. Variable costs in total are directly proportional to activity.

Costs must be broken down into their fixed and variable segments. Once this is done, then one can devise a formula expressing the amount of fixed costs and the rate at which variable costs change in total with changes in production volume.

Normative or standard costs are discussed in another chapter. Historical cost analysis will be described here.

The Historical Approach

The historical approach deals with past cost data. Assume that data on production and factory expenses (as shown in Exhibit 69) are available.

EXHIBIT 69

HIGH-LOW METHOD

PERIOD	PRODUCTION (000)	TOTAL COST (000)
1	11.0	1,390
2	9.0 (low)	1,200
3	14.0	1,725
4	12.0	1,530
5	10.0	1,090
6	15.0 (high)	1,780

The High-Low Method. Analysis of the tabulation will reveal that for every 1000 unit increase in production there is a corresponding $96,000 increase in costs. One way to derive this figure is to segregate the fixed and variable elements by calculating the relationship between the cost figures, for the high and low production values. That is, the variable rate (b) is determined by dividing the dollar change in mixed costs by the change in volume; in our example,

$$b = \frac{TC_H - TC_L}{X_H - X_L} = \frac{\$1,776,000 - \$1,200,000}{15,000 \quad - \quad 9,000}$$

$$= \frac{\$576,000}{6,000} = \$96/\text{unit}$$

The fixed overhead component (a) of mixed costs is equal to the total mixed costs at a given volume less the variable component at that volume. For our example, fixed costs at 15,000 hours, "a," can be calculated as follows:

$$a = TC_H - TVC_H = \$1,776,000 - \$96 \, (15,000)$$

$$= \$1,776,000 - 1,440,000 = \$336,000$$

From the graph of Exhibit 69, an "a" of $360,000 could be inferred, confirming the $336,000 above.

Scattergram Method. An alternative to the High-Low technique is the Scattergram, depicted in Exhibit 70. This technique uses all the available data and is not subject to undue influence from a single point, as is the High-Low method. All values are plotted and a line of best fit is visually plotted. From the diagram, fixed costs are inferred to be $60,000 and variable costs $127/unit.

Ideally, there should be as many points above the line as below the line. Another way of stating this is that the total vertical distance to the line from the points above the line should be equal to the total vertical distance from the points below the line to the line. The Scattergram method is an attempt to find such a line.

Regression Analysis. A technique to find the exact line of best fit is the method of Least Squares, a form of regression analysis, in which a straight line is fitted to the data according to the formula:

$$y = a + bx$$

where y is total cost, a is fixed cost, b is the unit variable cost, and x is total production. The Least Squares method fits a line to the data in a way that minimizes the total squared vertical deviation from the line, as shown in Exhibit 71. The resulting formula is:

$$TC = \$92,000 + 115x$$

EXHIBIT 70

SCATTERGRAM

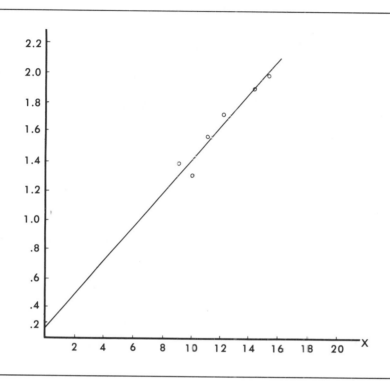

which compares favorably with the two actual extreme points:

x	TC (actual)	TC (predicted)
9,000	$1,200,000	$1,127,000
15,000	$1,776,000	$1,817,000

Summary

Cost prediction models from the three techniques, then, can be compared as follows:

High-Low TC = $336,000 + $96x
Scattergram: TC = $60,000 + $127x
Regression: TC = $92,000 + $115x

Because the technique is precise, the regression method is the "best," based on the full set of data. For more details, consult any current cost accounting textbook.

EXHIBIT 71

LEAST SQUARES CALCULATION

Period	(X) Production (000)	(Y) Costs (000)	X^2	XY
1	11.0	1.390	121	15.29
2	9.0	1.200	81	10.80
3	14.0	1.725	196	24.15
4	12.0	1.530	144	18.36
5	10.0	1.090	100	10.90
6	15.0	1.780	225	26.70
Total n = 6	71.0	8.715	867	106.20

The values of a and b in the formula for a straight line ($y = a + bx$) can be found by solving the simultaneous equations:

$$na + b \Sigma x = \Sigma y$$
$$a \Sigma x + b \Sigma x^2 = \Sigma xy$$

$$6a + b(71) = 8.715$$
$$a(71) + b(867) = 106.20$$

$$a = \$ \ 92{,}000$$
$$b = \$115/\text{unit}$$

Check: $TC = a + bx$

$$TC_g = \$92{,}000 + \$115(9{,}000) = \$1{,}127{,}000$$
$$TC_{15} = \$92{,}000 + \$115(15{,}000) = \$1{,}817{,}000$$

BREAKEVEN ANALYSIS

The Breakeven Chart displays in one chart the linear approximations of the economists total cost and total revenue curves. The linear estimates of the total cost and revenue curves illustrate a firm's commitment to a particular combination of fixed and variable inputs. This combination is to be used, let's say, in the production of 120,000 units of output which would have a selling price of $180 per unit. The lines on the chart do not, of course, represent the actual absolute behavior of total costs and total revenues over the range of outputs from shut-down to absolute capacity. They do, however, reflect the cost and revenue changes to be expected on the average, given management's decision to produce within some relevant range. The relevant range, in this instance, is defined above and below the 120,000 unit output level in which we are interested.

At this output, an expected profit of about $10,400,000 is indicated in Exhibit 72. Further, in the same Exhibit, a breakeven point of approximately $7,000,000 of revenue, or 39,000 units of output is indicated, reflecting the commitment to a given relevant range of output by the firm with selling prices and cost inputs consistent with that predetermined range. The linear estimates used in the breakdown chart are intended to be accurate only within this relevant range. In order to examine the effects of large changes in output, one would have to construct entirely new charts, which would then reflect totally different input-output commitments for the newly defined relevant range.

EXHIBIT 72

BREAKEVEN ANALYSIS

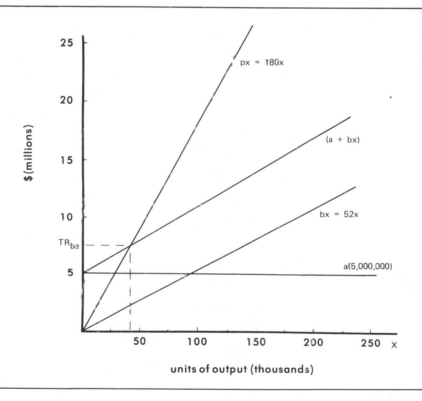

Cost-Volume-Profit Analysis is based on the basic profit equation as follows:

Profit (P) = px − bx − a

where p = selling price/unit
      x = number of units of output
      b = variable cost per unit
      a = total fixed costs

Obviously, the firm will break even when total revenue equals total cost:

$$P = px - bx - a$$
$$\emptyset = px - bx - a$$
$$px = bx + a$$
$$TR = TC$$

The breakeven point in units of output can be calculated as follows:

$$\emptyset = px - bx - a$$
$$px - bx = a$$
$$x = \frac{a}{(p - b)}$$

This simply says that the breakeven output is the number of units calculated by dividing fixed costs by the difference between the unit selling price and the unit variable costs. This difference (p − b) is called the profit contribution.

    The breakeven point in dollars of sales can be determined by multiplying both sides of the above formula by the unit selling price. If then the right-hand side of the equation is simplified by dividing the numerator and denominator by price, it can be shown that the breakeven point in total dollar sales is equal to the fixed costs divided by the profit contribution ratio which is (p − b)/p. To illustrate:

Assume p = $180/unit
      b = $52/unit
      a = $5,000,000
      P = $180 x − $52 x − $5,000,000

$$X_{be} = \frac{a}{(p-b)} = \frac{\$5,000,000}{(\$180 - \$52)} = 39,063 \text{ units}$$

$$TR_{be} = px_{be} = \$180\,(39,063) = \$7,031,000$$

$$TR_{be} = \frac{a}{(p-b)/p} = \frac{a}{\%P.C.} = \frac{5,000,000}{71.1\%} = \$7,031,000$$

Sensitivity Analysis

    Breakeven charts can be used to evaluate proposed changes in the operating characteristics of a firm. For example, if management is contemplating a change that will alter the magnitude of the fixed or variable costs, the impact of these (and other) changes may be evaluated using the breakeven model as shown in Exhibit 73 below.

EXHIBIT 73

SENSITIVITY ANALYSIS

USING THE BREAKEVEN MODEL

1. Initially, a = 5,000,000
   b = \$52
   p = \$180
   P = \$180x − \$52x − \$5,000,000
   x_{be} = 39,063 units
   TR_{be} = \$7,031,000

2. If management wishes to implement a new advertising program costing \$1,500,000 which with a price cut of \$5 will increase sales from 120,000 units to 135,000 units, the change in profit will be:

   P_{120} = \$180 (120,000) − \$52 (120,000) − \$5,000,000 = \$10,360,000

   P_{135} = \$175 (135,000) − \$52 (135,000) − (\$5,000,000 + \$1,500,000) = \$10,105,000

3. An alternative to the above is a change in quality which will allow a price reduction of \$20.00 and a cost reduction of \$9.00 per unit but will require a fixed cost increase of \$1,250,000. This change will increase volume to 140,000.

   P_{140} = (\$180 − 20) (140,000) − (\$52 − 9) (140,000) − (\$5,000,000 + \$1,250,000)
   = \$160 (140,000) − \$43 (140,000) − \$6,250,000 = \$10,130,000

4. Management's ultimate decision will depend on whether the alternatives are in response to competitive pressures and on the confidence it has in the premises in each case. Expected value analysis could be a useful next step in such a situation.

RATIO ANALYSIS

Comparison by ratio analysis is a valuable financial analysis tool. Major differences in ratio data are areas which should be investigated in detail. Ratio analysis merely points out differences without direct indication of the significance of the differences.

Particularly when comparing operating management in non-homogenous markets, care must be taken to find the causes of significant differences.

Exhibit 74 shows an array of control statistics of potential value to the reader. Definitions are clearly implied in the line titles.

CAPACITY STUDIES

At some point in the growth cycle of a product the question, "Can

EXHIBIT 74

RATIO ANALYSIS

PARTICULARS		PLANT A	PLANT B
INCOME RATIOS			
NET INCOME BT ÷ TOTAL ASSETS	%	10.5	11.8
SAME PERIOD YEAR AGO	%	7.9	8.4
AVERAGE 12 PAST PERIODS	%	10.5	11.8
NET INCOME BT ÷ C & ID SALES*	%	13.3	8.4
SAME PERIOD YEAR AGO	%	10.5	6.9
AVERAGE 12 PAST PERIODS	%	13.3	8.4
NET INCOME BT ÷ CUSTOMER SALES	%	15.2	8.4
NET INCOME AT ÷ NET WORTH (STOCKHOLDERS' EQUITY)	%	9.1	16.7
NET INCOME AT ÷ GROSS INVESTED CAPITAL USED	%	3.8	6.9
AZ NET INCOME AT ÷ TOTAL ASSETS	%	5.7	11.4
NET INCOME AT ÷ C & ID SALES	%	6.4	4.9
NET INCOME AT ÷ CUSTOMER SALES	%	7.3	6.2
CASH FLOW ÷ STOCKHOLDERS' EQUITY	%	20.9	25.7
CASH FLOW ÷ C & ID SALES*	%	14.7	7.5
DUPONT TYPE APPRAISAL			
INVESTMENT TURNOVER (C & ID SALES* ÷ TOTAL GROSS ASSETS) (A)		0.6	1.3
% EARNINGS ON SALES (NET INCOME BT ÷ C & ID SALES) (B)	%	13.3	10.1
% RETURN ON INVESTMENT (A) X (B)	%	8.0	13.1
INVENTORIES, REPLACEMENT VALUE			
RAW MATERIALS	M$	1 140	1 517
OPERATING DAYS ON HAND	DAYS	23	32
WORK IN PROCESS & FINISHED GOODS	M$	2 935	791
ABOVE ÷ C & ID* SALES	%	10.6	22.2
TOTAL INVENTORIES	M$	4 107	1 034
ABOVE ÷ C & ID* SALES	%	14.9	29.0

additional equipment be justified?" is raised. The controller must supply the economic answer to this question, based on the best information he can obtain from all interested parties:

a. Marketing must provide a sales projection for the life of the product or the new equipment, whichever is shorter.
b. Engineering must provide its best estimate of the costs of acquisition and installation.
c. Manufacturing must provide the premises upon which a cost projection for the life in (a) can be based.

As in any study of new facilities, premises accepted are the controlling factor in justification analysis. Generally, the "new sales" premise is the dominant single premise in the entire study.

For this reason, great care must be taken to document the prediction of new business to directly result from the new facility. It should be documented as to item, customer, price, and volume.

This documentation will, then, permit a better evaluation of incremental material costs, generally the major item of incremental costs. The research and manufacturing departments should specify the particular bill of materials for each item in the sales projection, from which the controller can calculate total material costs.

To illustrate the significance of such premises, the following example of a need for incremental production capacity is given:

A plant is operating seven days a week producing 60,000#/week of product. A new product breakthrough indicates total average demand will be 125,000#/week within two years, with no significant later growth. What new capacity should be installed?

Obviously, 65,000#/week additional capacity is needed for sales as projected. Should this be the maximum installed? The minimum? Should this be a seven day operation or something less?

This is a business with seasonal peaks in demand. Plans for the future should be based on having capacity available for satisfying peak demand. This conclusion results in the premise: operations should be less than seven days as a standard operation.

Because material costs are 80 percent of selling price, operating expenses are critical to profits. For this reason, a preliminary premise is that overtime pay should be avoided by operating a standard five day week. (This is subject to change based on the difference in investment required to produce the needed volume in five days versus six days.)

The five day operation premise establishes the need for a production schedule of 125,000#/week at the rate of 25,000#/day. The existing facility produces 60,000# in seven days or 8,600#/day. Therefore, the new facility must produce 16,400#/day or 82,000#/week.

Old Facility	$8,600 \times 5 =$	43,000#/Week
New Facility	$16,400 \times 5 =$	82,000#/Week
		125,000#/Week

Having arrived at this point, a re-examination of the sales projection is necessary. Is the 125,000#/week projection valid? Is it verified by other evidence? Is this an economically feasible increment of capacity insofar as capital cost is concerned; would 25 percent more or less make a significant difference in capital cost? Is current technology such that total operating costs would be low enough to justify a new facility with a 125,000#/week capacity, permitting the old facility to be held in reserve for future growth? What are the competitive forces in this market? Have they been accurately reflected in the immediate and long term projections? What are the implications of the plateau after two years? Are prices expected to remain at present levels? Would a lower price in two years result in additional volume?

Acceptable answers to these questions should precede further economic evaluation.

PRODUCT PROFITABILITY ANALYSIS

In addition to regular "actual cost" studies of product profitability, occasional comprehensive special project analyses should be undertaken by the controller. This becomes particularly valuable when products cross division lines prior to sale to the ultimate customer.

This study should be designed to cover a period of time long enough to include the range of product mix variety and volume. In this way, the product in total is examined rather than a single item or a customer's selection. The value of the product line is thus established. Typical of the questions the controller should find the answers to are the following:

a. Why is the price range so wide? Is there a logical relationship between prices?
b. Why are special terms applied to some products but not to others?
c. Where in the spectrum of unit profits is the volume concentrated?
d. What prevents upgrading the low profit portion of the line? What would be the net loss from raising prices to be in line, with some loss of volume?
e. Why is the cost range so wide?
f. Are variances unusually high in a particular segment of the line?
g. Where in the spectrum of unit costs is the volume concentrated?

Interdivision operations require special handling. Accounting systems may be different. Definitions may differ, so that direct cost rates are not directly comparable. One division may use process cost accounting while the second uses job-shop accounting. Extreme care, then, is necessary to insure that like quantities are merged and that yield losses in the second operation are properly reflected in the unit costs of the first operation. Exhibit 75 is an example that illustrates the handling of interdivision cost data. Note that only 92 percent of the product sold from Division A leaves Division B as a sale to the customer; therefore, per unit customer sale, the cost data for Division A is divided by 92 percent for the consolidated costs. Further, the cost elements are consolidated for sensible cost analysis in addition to the overall profitability determination.

EXHIBIT 75

COMPARISON INTERDIVISION PRODUCT PROFITABILITY

As Reported	Division A	Division B	
Transfer Price	$25.35		
Customer Price		$64.00	
Discount	.25	.60	
Net Price	$25.10	$63.40	
Freight Cost	—	4.24	
Net Income	$25.10	$59.16	
Material Cost (Incremental)	7.25	33.53	
Gross Margin	$17.85	$25.63	
Direct Cost	3.90	1.43	
Profit Contribution	$13.95	$24.20	
Term Cost	7.32	5.91	
Profit	$ 6.63	$18.29	
Yield	—	92.0 %	

As Required for Consolidation	From Division A	From Division B	Consolidated
Price	—	$64.00	$64.00
Discount	—	.60	.60
Freight Cost	—	4.24	4.24
Material Cost—Division A	(7.25 ÷ 92%)	—	7.90
" " —Added	—	6.23	6.23
Direct Cost—Division A	(3.90 ÷ 92%)	—	4.25
" " —Added	—	1.43	1.43
Profit Contribution	—	—	$39.35
Term Cost—Division A	(7.32 ÷ 92%)	—	7.95
" " —Added	—	5.91	5.91
Profit, Overall			$25.49
Check: Profit—Division A	(6.63 ÷ 92%)		$ 7.20
" —Division B			18.29
Profit, Overall			$25.49

NEW PRODUCT ANALYSIS

Often a research department will develop a major modification of an existing product line. Cost comparisons with the existing line are necessary to a determination of whether to market the new item. The following pertinent questions must be answered in this analysis:

a. Why should a modification be marketed? Will volume be lost to competition if we do not? Will our volume be increased if we do?
b. What is the value of the modification? Can prices be increased? What does it do for the customer for which he would be willing to pay a higher price?
c. How do costs compare? Is the modification more or less expensive? Is it enough cheaper that a price reduction can be made? Will volume be increased if the price is reduced?

Exhibit 76 illustrates a cost comparison of a new development versus an existing product. Extreme care must be taken not to bias a comparison of this sort in favor of the new development. This is an easy trap to fall into. All of the problems of the old item are known. The tendency will be to use actual cost data for the comparison. However, you will have estimates, only, for the new item. These estimates will generally be optimistic and must be evaluated prior to their use in calculations by comparing them with standards and variances of the existing item.

In Exhibit 76, the new product has a higher material cost hence a lower profit contribution than the old product. Presumably, there must be something in this higher cost which will give the customer greater value in the product. Will he pay more than just enough to offset the added material costs?

While material costs are higher, direct costs are lower for the new product because of the higher production rate. In fact, the new product gives an improved P.C./hour because the higher production rate more than offsets the reduced P.C. per unit of production. If valid, this means that the new product would warrant a better use of machine time in spite of the lower P.C. per unit. This data should be analyzed to determine whether the reported higher production rate is the result of unjustified optimism or is well founded and based on known reasons for an improved rate of production.

OBSOLETE EQUIPMENT

As old equipment grows less competitive there is often pressure to shut it down because of its antique condition. Two points must be made about this type situation:

EXHIBIT 76

COMPARISON NEW PRODUCT VERSUS OLD PRODUCT

	New	Old
Average Selling Price/Cwt.	$47.80	$47.80
Freight and Discount	2.82	2.82
Purchased Material	24.34	24.34
Material Added	9.10	8.13
Direct Cost	2.60	3.02
Profit Contribution/Cwt.	$ 8.94	$ 9.49
Term Cost	5.10	5.93
Profit/Cwt.	$ 3.84	$ 3.56
Production/Hour	675#/Hour	585#/Hour
P.C./Hour	$61.00/Hour	$55.00/Hour

a. As long as the equipment is producing a product, there is a profit contribution from the equipment that cannot be dismissed lightly. Profits will be affected dramatically if the equipment is simply shut down and the volume is not made up on some other piece of equipment. Exhibit 77 illustrates this situation.

b. It is often very difficult to justify new capital investment that merely replaces old with new. Unless direct labor unit costs are very high, the out-of-pocket savings will not yield an adequate return on the new investment.

Exhibit 77 demonstrates, too, the small out-of pocket savings often available with which to justify new investment. In this case, total gross savings are only $930,000/year if the equipment is completely shut down and scrapped. If it were replaced with a new piece of equipment at a cost of $10,000,000 in new investment, labor and depreciation charges alone would be close to $750,000 leaving a maximum net savings of $180,000, a 1.8 percent return on the $10,000,000 investment.

Another spectre of vulnerability on old equipment can also be disputed by the data in Exhibit 77. It is often said that new, faster, equipment will "force" older pieces out of business on price competion. The fact is that in many cases price competition has relatively little to do with costs of specific pieces of equipment. In Exhibit 77 assume that price competition has severely cut into the price of products of the old machine to the extent of a 15 percent price cut. Sales value drops by $750,000 to $4,250,000. Sales value of the total plant drops to $92,250,000. If it is decided to give up the business and shut down the old machine, profits fall to $13,430,000 as shown. If, on the other hand, the price cut is met and the business is retained the figures are as follows:

Sales Value	$92,250,000
Material Cost	46,500,000
Direct Costs	4,650,000
Profit Contribution	$41,100,000
Term Costs	26,850,000
Profit	$14,250,000

Profit has dropped only by the $750,000 price cut. As long as the price cut was *less than* $1,570,000, the company would be better off to meet the price than to give up the business.

EXHIBIT 77

PROFIT CONTRIBUTION VERSUS OBSOLETE EQUIPMENT

Assume an operation consisting of ten production units all running a full seven days a week. One machine is 70 years old and is very slow in comparison with other machines in the plant and in the industry in general. Because of its age, the machine is a prime candidate for shutdown. The controller is asked for the effect on profits of such a shutdown.

	Total Plant	Old Machine (Specific Costs)	Revised Plant
Sales Value	$93,000,000	$5,000,000	$88,000,000
Material Cost	46,500,000	2,500,000	44,000,000
Direct Costs	4,650,000	250,000	4,400,000
Profit Contribution	$41,850,000	$2,250,000	$39,600,000
Term Costs	26,850,000	680,000	26,170,000
Profit	$15,000,000	$1,570,000	$13,430,000

This is a vivid demonstration of the overall worth of profit contribution as a measure of value. It clearly shows that lost volume has a great leverage on total profits.

There are practical limits to this line of reasoning. If someone is out to buy business by price-cutting, he can get it one place or another. If you meet the cut in one area, and keep the business, he will crop up somewhere else and repeat the effort. You may, after successive countermoves, end up with all your volume at a severely reduced price. You will not have broken the market; your competitor did. But broken it is, just the same. It may well have been better to give up the first increment of volume so as to hold prices firm on all the rest.

Further, you may want to take the initiative by building new capacity sufficient to replace your old equipment plus allowing for a sizeable new volume. New volume can often justify new equipment. By shutting down obsolete equipment and making the production on new equipment, you may have a breakeven operation with careful planning. An aggressive sales effort to get new volume to produce in the remaining increment of capacity from competitors or from new market areas can result in an attractive overall new investment.

This points out that price competition never "forces" a piece of equipment out of business. Instead, it requires a management decision on the strategy to be used in facing such competition. When the decision is to give up the business, it is because that course is the best choice of several alternatives, not because that course is forced on management.

DATA FOR LABOR NEGOTIATIONS

In any labor contract negotiations, the company negotiators need to know the cost of union demands and company proposals. The controller should supply this data to the negotiating team.

Costs should be expressed in total dollar cost per year for an evaluation of the impact on profits. Costs should also be expressed in "cents per hour" because this is the parlance for expressing the value of the settlement package to the union membership.

While each item on the list must be treated according to the specific facts applicable to the individual company situation, several typical examples will serve to illustrate the methods to be used in these problem areas.

a. **Across-the-board increase.** This will be either $.xx/hour or a x% increase. First establish the total "hours paid" for the budget year. Apply $.01/hour to this number of hours to get dollars per year. This gives the annual cost of a $.01/hour increase. Compare this with the total wages budget for a 1% increase:

1. Hours worked 1,250,000
2. $/year @ $.01/hour $12,500/year
3. Budgeted wages $2,500,000
4. $.01/hour as % of wages 0.5%

5. 1% increase $25,000/year
6. 1% increase .... $ .02/hour
7. Average wage $2.00/hour

All subsequent costs can be converted to equivalent cents/hour or per cent of wages by comparison with lines (2) and (5).

b. **Four weeks vacation after 25 years.** From a listing of employees by date of hire, find out how many people would become eligible for the extra week's vacation next year. Assuming 40 hours' pay at $2.00/hour, each week costs $80.00/person. If 200 people are affected by the shift from 30 years to 25 years, this is a cost of:

$$200 \times \$80 = \$16,000/\text{year}$$
$$(\$.01) \times (16,000 \div 12,500) = \$.0128/\text{hour}$$
$$(1\%) \quad \times (16,000 \div 25,000) = 0.64\%$$

c. **Triple time for all Sundays.** Assuming the entire work force of 500 people are on a four-shift, seven-day schedule, every Sunday during the year will call for triple-time pay. Present contracts call for double time. Each employee works three Sundays out of four.

$$3 \times \$2.00/\text{hr.} \times 8 \text{ hrs./Sun./empl.} \times \tfrac{3}{4} \times 500 \text{ empl.} \times 52 \text{ Sun./yr.} = \$936,000/\text{yr.}$$
$$2 \times \$2.00/\text{hr.} \times 8 \text{ hrs./Sun./empl.} \times \tfrac{3}{4} \times 500 \text{ empl.} \times 52 \text{ Sun./yr.} = \$624,000/\text{yr.}$$
$$\text{Increase} \quad \$312,000/\text{yr.}$$
$$\$.01 \times (312,000 \div 12,500) = \$.249/\text{hr.}$$
$$1\% \times (312,000 \div 25,000) = 12.5\%$$

d. **One additional holiday.** Assuming eight hours pay per employee per holiday, the cost of one holiday for a 500 man work force is:

$$\$2.00/\text{hr.} \times 8 \text{ hrs./empl.} \times 500 \text{ empl.} = \$8,000/\text{yr.}$$
$$\$.0064/\text{hr.}$$
$$0.32\%$$

OPERATIONS RESEARCH

All of the tools of the operations research practitioners are, in fact, devices to facilitate cost-volume-profit analysis. Optimizing techniques are used to establish the best choice from a variety of choices. Heuristic techniques are used to establish logical rules for economic decision making based on the way decisions are actually made in the real life situation. Simulation techniques are used to test the economic (and other) effects of various operating decisions, to rule out undesirable selections without ever disrupting the status quo of current operations. All of these techniques are within the scope of the controller's charter.

Application of these schemes does require special technical knowledge. Experienced men are required to apply them to practical problems. They can be hired or trained, however, as specialists working for the controller just as accountants, economists, industrial engineers, systems men, and programmers are technical specialists under the controller. There is no real reason for separating operations research as a separate department as long as the controller has the breadth and depth to fully utilize the tools and the talents of this highly trained technical staff.

Output reports from operations research studies take uncertainty into account, specifically, in the mathematical manipulations. A good report will include in the set of alternatives placed before management predictions concerning the best solution, the worst solution, and the most probable solution to be expected from a particular course of action.

No attempt will be made to explain any of the mathematical techniques here. Bookshelves abound with texts, case histories, and bibliographies on the subject from all of the major publishers. Operations Research Committees have been formed in many industry associations. Short and long college courses are available in specific areas. The American Management Association offers courses and seminars in operations research. The Operations Research Society of America boasts thousands of members in the United States; there are similar organizations in many other countries. There is a tremendous variety of sources of expert technical knowledge.

General areas of applicability can be listed, for emphasis on the breadth and value of these techniques:

a. Operations research techniques allow mathematical treatment of increasingly complex business problems, including process control, product distribution, materials blending, and resource utilization.
b. Heuristic decision rules can be programmed to take over routine decision making, leaving managerial time free for creative problem solving.
c. Systematic analysis can bring order out of seeming chaos, structuring the previously unstructured. This alone may be sufficient to generate substantial improvements.

If you and your management are unfamiliar with operations research, your best attitude to assume as you get started in it (and you'd better! Your competitors are!) is as follows:

Operations research may be a little bit complicated for us and our management to follow. A lot of it may not be practical, yet. But there is a great potential for improving our return on investment. That's reason enough for using it where we can. When we can begin to realize its full potential, the gain will be quite substantial.

MANAGING INVENTORY COSTS

Inventory control models are designed to minimize total cost of inventory, the sum of the cost of acquiring and the cost of holding inventory.

EXHIBIT 78

UNIFORM CONSUMPTION WITH INSTANT

REPLACEMENT OF INVENTORY

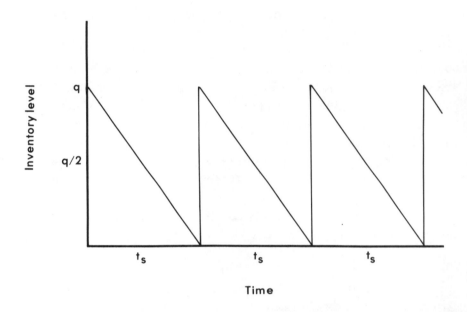

If a firm has decided that some quantity of an item must be available for sale during some future period, the two inventory cost-related decisions to be made are: (1) How many units to acquire at a time, and (2) When the specific orders should be placed. The firm could purchase the entire quantity, D, at one time and draw down inventory as needed. Alternatively, the firm could buy units so that they arrive just as needed, with no inventory ever on hand. Neither action will be optimal. Two basic categories of cost will influence optimal inventory decisions: the cost of acquiring inventory and the cost of holding inventory. (Stock-out costs may be a third category of concern if customers will not wait for back-orders to be shipped.) The general Economic Order Quantity (EOQ) model is designed to give an optimal set of decisions based on minimizing these inventory costs.

Suppose that a firm decides to order "q" units at a time, with each order timed to arrive just as the previous order is depleted at time "t_s." Under this policy, no stock-outs will occur. Assuming a constant rate of usage of D over the time period, the purchase-usage pattern will be as shown in Exhibit 78. Average inventory will equal q/2.

The total annual cost of inventory policy will be the sum of the costs of acquisitions plus total holding costs. The acquisition costs will include the following:

- costs of determining the quantity to acquire in each order,
- costs of processing the orders,
- costs of inspecting the shipments and placing them into inventory, and
- the cost of processing the payments for the purchases.

These costs are not easy to determine. It is difficult to determine these incremental costs of processing individual purchase orders. An accurate analysis of such costs can be made, within limits, using multiple regression analysis techniques.

One can represent annual acquisition cost as $C_p(\frac{D}{q})$. In this formula, C_p denotes the constant cost of placing one order; D/q is the total number of orders of size "q" placed during the period of time.

Inventory holding costs will include the following:

- costs of money tied up in inventory (interest),
- costs of storage,
- costs of obsolescence, and
- costs of insurance and property taxes

Annual inventory holding cost is $C_s(\frac{q}{2})$ where C_s is the average holding cost per unit and $q/2$ is the average inventory (assuming a uniform rate of usage.) Holding costs are usually specified as a certain amount per dollar of inventory investment since many of these costs vary as a function of inventory value. Taxes, insurance, storage costs, and interest costs can be estimated with a reasonable degree of accuracy; obsolescence is more difficult to estimate.

With the cost functions specified, one can now determine the optimal order quantity which will minimize total annual inventory costs. The total annual inventory cost will equal the sum of the acquisition and holding cost:

$$TC = C_s \left(\frac{q}{2}\right) + C_p \left(\frac{D}{q}\right)$$

The minimum value for this cost function can be found by differentiating with respect to "q" and setting the derivative equal to zero:

$$q^* = \sqrt{\frac{2C_p D}{C_s}}$$

where q^* is the Economic Order Quantity for optimal total costs. Substituting values, total cost can be found as follows:

$$TC^* = \sqrt{2C_p D C_s}$$

To illustrate, assume the following situation:

$$D = 7200/\text{year}$$
$$C_p = \$23.47$$
$$C_s = \$ 5.00$$

$$q^* = \sqrt{\frac{2C_p D}{C_s}} = \sqrt{\frac{2(23.47)\ 7200}{5}} = 260$$

$$TC^* = \sqrt{2C_p DC_s} = \sqrt{2(23.47)\ (7200)5} = \$1300$$

The above description is a grossly simplified presentation of what can be an extremely complex quantitative approach to optimizing inventory costs. The purpose here is not to give a full exposition of inventory management techniques through quantitative methods. The purpose is, instead, to illustrate the accounting issues that are involved regardless of the quantitative model selected and its complexity.

Accounting Issues

The accounting issues of primary relevance to the controller are those of cost predictions. The EOQ model requires a prediction of the incremental costs of processing an order and of holding inventory; the controller will be expected to provide a basis for making such cost predictions. Of concern to the controller is the degree to which accurate measurement of these costs can be obtained at reasonable costs; also of concern is the degree of accuracy that is worthwhile. The answers to both of these concerns depend on the sensitivity of the EOQ model to measurement errors.

In the above example, the estimate of C_p is \$23.47 and of C_s, \$5 per unit. Absolute accuracy can be shown not to be essential in measuring these costs. Suppose the storage cost per unit is actually \$7.50 per unit, a 50 percent error. Using the $q^* = 260$ units as previously determined, a firm would incur an actual incremental total cost as follows:

$$TC = C_s \left(\frac{q}{2}\right) + C_p \left(\frac{D}{q}\right)$$
$$= \$7.50 \left(\frac{260}{2}\right) + \$23.47 \left(\frac{7200}{260}\right)$$
$$= \$1625$$

Had the true value of C_s been known, the EOQ and TC^* would have been:

$$q^* = \sqrt{\frac{2C_pD}{C_s}} = \sqrt{\frac{2(23.47)7200}{7.50}} = 212$$

$$TC^* = \sqrt{2C_pDC_s} = \sqrt{2(23.47)(7200)7.50} = \$212$$
$$= \$1592$$

Thus, it can be seen that a 50 percent error in estimating the holding cost per unit results in an insignificant $33(2.0 percent) excess cost *per year*. This apparent insensitivity to cost errors is generally characteristic of this EOQ model.

To further demonstrate this insensitivity, suppose the correct value of acquiring inventory, C_p, is $17.60, a 25 percent error. Again using the original EOQ of 260 units, actual total costs would be:

$$TC = C_s \left(\frac{q}{2}\right) + C_p \left(\frac{D}{q}\right)$$
$$= \$5.00 \left(\frac{260}{2}\right) + \$17.60 \left(\frac{7200}{260}\right)$$
$$= \$1137$$

Had the true value of C_p been known, the EOQ and TC^* would have been:

$$q^* = \sqrt{\frac{2(17.60)7200}{5.00}} = 225$$

$$TC^* = \sqrt{2(17.60)(7200)5} = \$1125$$

In this case, a 25 percent error has caused an insignificant $12 (1 percent) error in total costs. The controller, in order to provide acceptable data for the EOQ management system, must make initial estimates of these cost parameters. Then, the controller should also provide a range of values above and below his initial estimates within which he expects the true value probably will fall. These extreme values should be calculated along with the initial estimate. The range of potential impact on costs could then be derived; given this information, the controller could determine whether the impact on inventory costs is sufficiently great to justify additional expenditure resources in order to reduce the dollar impact on total inventory cost.

LINEAR PROGRAMMING

Linear programming is a useful method for allocating scarce resources to more than one product, an extension of cost-volume-profit analysis. Computational techniques for optimal resource allocations are sometimes quite complex. Linear programming (LP) offers a methodology of relatively simple computational requirements for such allocations in multi-product firms.

Firms do not maintain production facilities sufficient to produce unlimited quanitities of all their products. Therefore, common facilities are constraints on the output of firms. Whenever the unit variable cost and unit contribution margin of each product are constant, the resource allocation is a linear programming problem. Generally, it is accepted that a single-product firm should continue to expand output so long as incremental revenues exceed incremental costs. For a multi-product firm, however, the expansion of output of one product causes an opportunity cost, that being the lost contribution margin of not being able to produce some alternative product.

Consider the case in which a firm produces products Y and Z. Product Y offers a contribution margin of $6 per unit; Product Z offers a contribution of $4 per unit. If the firm has the capacity of 1000 production hours and if production of 1 unit of Y requires 4 hours of production capacity, and the production of 1 unit of Z requires 2 hours of production capacity, then the appropriate question is "What is the optimum combination of products which will maximize contribution margin?" Since this problem involves linear functions, one can quickly note that product Z generates $2 in contribution per hour of capacity utilized whereas product Y generates only $1.50 of contribution per hour of capacity utilized. The solution, obviously, is to use all of the capacity in the production of product Z, that is to produce 500 units of Z; contribution margin will be $2,000. To test this conclusion, if one unit of Y is produced, only 498 units of Z can be produced; total contribution margin will be $1998.

The above problem can be stated in linear programming terms. The 1000 production hours of capacity is a constraint; whatever output of Y and Z is generated, the firm cannot consume more than the 1000 hours of production capacity. Given the above production requirements, the firm can produce either 250 units of Y or 500 units of Z, or any combination of Y and Z, such that $4y + 2z$ is equal to or less than 1000, where y and z are quantities of Y and Z respectively. The objective of the firm continues to be that of maximizing the total contribution generated.

Algebraically this problem may be stated as follows:

Maximize CM = $6y + $4z
such that: $4y + 2z \leq 1000$
$y, z \geq 0$

In the graphical solution of Exhibit 79, there is an area of feasible production defined by the triangle formed by the points 0, 0; 250, 0; 0, 500. A solid line drawn between the 250, 0 point and the 0, 500 point defines the maximum production possibilities. Any point on that line represents a combination of production of Y and Z which fully utilizes the available 1000 hours of capacity.

EXHIBIT 79

LINEAR PROGRAMMING GRAPHICAL SOLUTION

STEP 1

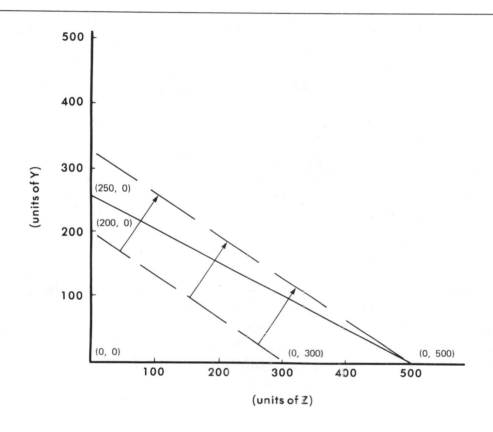

1. Draw constraint line:
    $$4y + 2z - 1000$$
    set $y = 0$; $2z = 1000$; $z = 500$ (0, 500)
    set $z = 0$; $4y = 1000$; $y = 250$ (250, 0)

2. Draw equal CM line:
    $$CM = \$6y + \$4z;$$
    assume $CM = \$1200$;
    set $y = 0$; $\$4z = \$1200$; $z = 300$ (0, 300)
    set $z = 0$; $\$6y = \$1200$; $y = 200$ (200, 0)

The dashed line (from 0, 200 to 300, 0) in the Exhibit represents a line of total contribution margin equal to $1200; for instance, the production of 200 units of Y at $6 per unit generates $1200 contribution, while the production of 300 units of Z at $4 per unit generates $1200 of contribution margin. The optimal solution to this problem can be found graphically by moving that equal contribution margin line out parallel from the $1200 line until the line being moved passes through the most extreme point of the previously defined feasible region. As a generalization, it can be said that the solution to any linear programming problem will occur at an extreme point of the defined feasible region. In this specific example, when you move the parallel line out to its most extreme intersection with the feasible region we find that this occurs at the 500, 0 point indicating that the optimal solution is the production of 500 units of Z and 0 units of Y; total contribution margin is $2,000.

The analysis becomes considerably more complicated when more than one constraint is introduced into the problem. For instance, assume that these products must pass through another production department in sequence; this second department has the constraint 2.5y plus 4z ≤ 1000 hours. The graphical solution would have to be changed as shown in Exhibit 80 to introduce the new constraint line. A new feasible region is now defined as that area between the origin and the constraint lines nearest the origin. In this Exhibit, the feasible region is shown by the shaded area as bounded by the constraint lines. If we take our original $1200 contribution line and move it up to an extreme point in this newly defined feasible region, we find the optimal solution occuring at the point where approximately 180 units of Y and 140 units of Z are produced.

It is not expected that the average controller's responsibilities will include producing linear programming solutions to resource allocation problems. These activities will generally be delegated to quantitative methods specialists. However, it will remain the controller's responsibility, generally, to produce estimates of unit costs, contribution margin, and often resource requirements for products for which such analyses are to be made. In producing this information, the controller realizes that his figures are not absolute, that there is some calculation error involved in generating all of the required data. A crucial question for the controller is the consideration of the extent to which a management decision may be affected by his estimating errors. One way in which the controller can evaluate the extent to which an LP decision is sensitive to estimation errors is to perform a sensitivity analysis on the model as designed by the specialist. The results of such an analysis will guide the controller in determining the extent to which more resources need to be allocated, in his department, to making better estimates.

Consider how the above problem might vary if an error in the estimate of the contribution margin of product Y were made. The contribution margin estimates might be in error because of mistakes in either the revenue or variable costs calculations. Regardless of the source, the effect of the contribution margin error

EXHIBIT 80

LINEAR PROGRAMMING GRAPHICAL SOLUTION

STEP 2

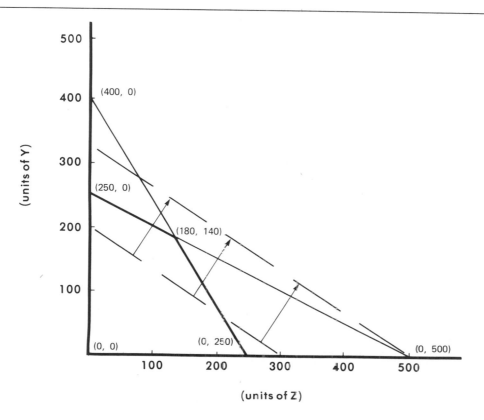

(units of Y)

(units of Z)

3. Draw second constraint line:

    $2.5y + 4z \leq 1000$

    set y = 0; 4z = 1000; z = 250 (0, 250)

    set z = 0; 2.5y = 1000; y = 400 (400, 0)

would be to change the slope of the equal contribution line. For instance, if the contribution margin of product Y is overstated by $1 per unit, then the equal contribution margin line would have a slope of 5y to 4z (1.25) instead of 6y to 4z (1.5). In Exhibit 81, this new contribution line is shown. In this particular case, this new line does not change the optimal solution which remains at Y = 180 and Z = 140, but of course, the contribution margin at this new optimal solution is now only $1460 instead of the $1640.

In point of fact, the optimal solution in terms of quantities of Y and Z will not change until the slope of the equal contribution line becomes that of one of the

EXHIBIT 81

LINEAR PROGRAMMING GRAPHICAL SOLUTION

STEP 3

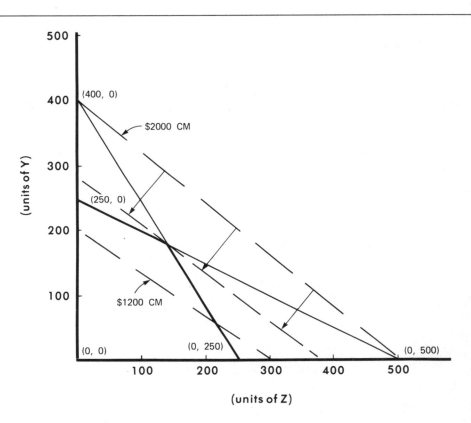

4. Calculate new equal CM line:

    CM = $5y + $4z

        assume CM = $2000

          set y = 0; $4z = $2000; z = 500 (0, 500)

          set z = 0; $5y = $2000; y = 400 (400, 0)

5. Move $2000 CM line in to most extreme point of feasible region: (180, 140)

constraint lines. That will happen when the slope becomes greater than 1.6 or less than 0.5.

    The effect of other estimating errors that might be made by the controller can be evaluated in a similar manner. For instance, errors in the coefficients of production can be evaluated by changing the constraint lines to reflect the different amounts of Y and Z which can be produced assuming different coefficient of production.

It is generally assumed through sensitivity analysis of this sort, that errors can be tolerated so long as the optimal solution does not change, within the magnitude of errors that can reasonably be expected to occur. If, however, a small error in an estimate does cause a shift in the optimal solution, some action must be taken by the contoller to generate better estimates. One possibility is that greater resources might be invested by the controller in his estimating techniques. A different possibility is that greater control might be exercised over the price and cost elements in order to eliminate some of the causes of the estimation error. Either of these techniques will result in added costs for the controller who must balance these costs against the magnitude of the decision error that might otherwise take place.

12

Capital Appropriations

If markets provide the food and nourishment from the outside world necessary to sustain the system, capital planning is the cardiovascular system that provides for the regeneration of the worn-out cells and the simultaneous growth of new and greater system capacity. There, unfortunately, the analogy stops. While the human body grows according to a well-structured, orderly, repetitive scheme, industrial systems respond to no inherent scheme and follow no pattern at all unless management provides one and works to follow it.

Capital planning is a response to management's need to:

1. Maintain the plant in a reasonable condition and to continue in business. Examples are:
   a. Normal maintenance type of capital expenditure such as a new roof, replaced bearings, etc.
   b. Items required by law or regulation for improved safety or for environmental control.
2. Improve the profitability of the operation. Examples are:
   a. Items that contain no element of replacement, such as new equipment necessary to increase volume or to go into an entirely new field of business.
   b. Items that contain some minor element of replacement, but which are being recommended because they primarily will provide an increase in profitability, generally cost reduction.
3. Provide for industrial and personnel relations improvements desirable for morale and recreation. Examples are:
   a. Items necessary to maintain good personnel relations, e.g., parking lots, cafeterias.
   b. Items necessary to maintain good community relations, e.g., picnic sites, odor reduction.

This response must be timely and must also be within the scope of the company's available funds. Since funds are limited to retained earnings and borrowed money plus occasional issues of stock, a careful plan for the optimum use of these funds is mandatory. A capital rationing plan is required.

CAPITAL FORECAST

Management must insist upon a well-thought-out capital investment plan from operating management, integrated with the plans of the marketing organization. The only way to achieve this goal is to require annual capital forecasts, or budgets, detailing the needs of the current year plus three to five years ahead; three years should be adequate in most cases.

The capital budget should be prepared by each department head who anticipates that his department will need capital money within the next three years. The forecast should be prepared according to a fixed format (see Exhibit 82) so that there will be a consistency in the data to facilitate subsequent review and approval. Cost data should be as realistic as possible. The controller should provide return on investment information to the department head for inclusion in the forecast for cost reduction and new product items. Division management, including the controller, should sit as a review committee to consider each departmental forecast before forwarding the consolidated division forecast for corporate level review, considering the following:

a. Is enough investment forecast for ordinary replacement? Is depreciation being reinvested? If not, should it be?
b. Do departmental forecasts tie in together where major changes in one department will surely affect the next in line?
c. Is sufficient service capacity (heat, steam, electricity) forecast to meet the requirements of operations?
d. Are all known items included in the written forecast? Check recent improvement program reports for investments in cost reduction items. Check the marketing plan for new capacity items. Check this year's items in last year's budget. Check last year's budget for items not accomplished.
e. Are costs reasonable for items named, based on experience and judgment?
f. Is the total forecast too high or not high enough? Are funds likely to be available? If departmental forecasts are "wish lists" should they now be trimmed?

The final forecasts should be received by the corporate review group in time to review, modify, reject, and ultimately approve all division forecasts early enough to permit inclusion of pertinent data in the expense budget and profit plan for the coming year. A timetable adequate for this might be as follows, assuming a calendar year operation:

EXHIBIT 82

CAPITAL FORECAST FORMAT

PRELIMINARY FORECAST 19 ___ CAPITAL EXPENDITURES DEPARTMENT: _____		Date _____ Page _____ of _____
Particulars	**Estimated Cost**	**Justification**
Replacement		
1. Work saver	$ 10,000	
2. Repair Roofs	20,000	
3. Stream Improvement	260,000	
4. Reserve	10,000	For Unforeseen Situations
Total	$300,000	
Improvement		
5. New Clamp Truck	$ 21,000	Crew Reduction One Man
2. Front End Loader	34,500	Eliminate Outside Contract
Total	$ 55,500	
Other		
7. Renovate Reception Room	$ 7,500	
8. Pave Parking Lot	9,500	
9. Build Picnic Pavilions	5,000	
Total	$ 22,000	
GRAND TOTAL	$377,500	

a. Begin work at departmental level on September 15th.

b. Complete departmental forecasts on September 30th.

c. Complete division review by October 10th.

d. Prepare forecast for corporate review as required, presenting in proper format and number of copies by October 15th.

e. Complete corporate review by November 15th. Give divisions approved capital budget.

This completion date should allow for companion expense work and man-power planning in the expense budget normally due to be completed between December 1st and 15th.

EXPENDITURE APPROVALS AND FOLLOW-UP

Approved budgets should not be considered to imply approval to spend money without subsequent action. Budgets are indications of capital planning, of management's approval of the direction implied in that planning, of the money needed for the current year for financial planning. Budgets, when approved, indicate management's commitment to provide the budgeted money *when department heads provide detailed justification.*

A formal scheme of forwarding that justification and requesting approval is necessary. This scheme should include:

a. Forms for use by department heads.
b. Routing to all approval authorities. Dollar limits should be set so as to prevent top management from having to waste time on small-dollar items. These levels are very much specific to each company; no general guides are appropriate.
c. Economic justifications and return on investment analysis by the controller prior to final approval. Department heads should supply the justification. The controller should have the authority to require "completed staff work" of the department heads before stating the premises upon which he calculates the return on investment.
d. Notification of final approval.
e. Collection of all cost data relating to purchase and installation.
f. Close out of the project. Addition of the item to the asset listing and to the depreciation schedule.
g. Post-completion audit of savings on improvement items.

A useful format for appropriation requests is shown in Exhibit 83. All pertinent information is included on one sheet of paper: description, capital cost, expense cost, justification, return on investment, and approvals. Supporting documents may be attached. Examples of information approval that authorities might want to see are engineering cost estimating sheets, quotes from suppliers, and premises for the return on investment calculation. When additional capacity and greater sales are part of the economic justification, a complete Marketing Plan must be prepared.

MARKETING PLAN

The Marketing Plan is a complete documentation of the present and future position in the marketplace. In outline form, it should include the following:

1. A history of the marketplace, including the growth trend of the past five years and the projection for the next five—ten years. Include reasons for the rate of growth, product characteristics that will tend to change the rate of growth, competitive factors, and new or declining use areas. Sufficient

EXHIBIT 83

FORM FOR APPROPRIATION REQUEST

APPROPRIATION REQUEST		DATE	DIVISION
		MILL	A R NO.

PROJECT (SHORT DESCRIPTION OF WHAT IS REQUESTED)	PLANT ORDER NO.	PROJ. LOCATION(BLDG.NO.)
	DEPARTMENT	CHECK ONE
	DESIRED COMPLETION DATE	☐ REPLACEMENT ☐ IMPROVEMENT ☐ OTHER

SUMMARY OF FUNDS REQUIRED: (IN EVEN $100'S) First cost of new equipment delivered, installation cost including labor, materials, overhead, and start up cost, cost of auxiliary equipment, cost of building changes or modifications.

COMPONENTS	EXPENSE	PURCHASE COST	INSTALL. COST	TOTAL

SAVINGS OR OTHER BENEFITS EXPECTED: (ATTACH DETAIL TO SUPPORT FIGURES)

COMMENTS:

IF REPLACEMENT FILL IN THIS SECTION	TO BE COMPLETED BY CONTROLLER'S DEPT.	REQUISITIONS TO BE ORIGINATED BY:
DISPOSITION OF EXISTING PROPERTY ☐ SCRAP ☐ TRADE IN ☐ REBUILD ☐ SELL	☐ EXPENSE ☐ CAPITALIZE ☐ BUDGET PAGE ___	
ORIGINAL COST / NET BOOK VALUE / SALES OR TRADE-IN VALUE	☐ RENT ☐ PURCHASE / ITEM ___	A R PREPARED BY:
DESCRIPTION(SHOW BRASS TAG NOS.) / YEAR ACQUIRED	R O I. ___ %	

APPROVALS - Signature indicates approval. If you disapprove indicate in comments.

SIGNATURE	DATE	SIGNATURE	DATE
SUPERINTENDENT		DIVISION GENERAL MANAGER	
MANAGER		CAPITAL EXPENDITURES COMMITTEE	
CHIEF ENGINEER			
DIVISION CONTROLLER			

narrative should accompany the statistics so that no matter how uninformed the approval authorities up the line, they can read enough in the Marketing Plan to comprehend the market picture.

2. A detailed history of the product acceptance in the market and reasons for its future projections. Include actual sales each year for five years. Show percent of market for those years. Forecast sales for the next five years and show share of market. Give the reasons which justify that market position.

3. Name the major customers, present and anticipated. Give the reasons for sales to each, justifying indicated increases in volume.

ASSET ACCOUNTING

The duties of the plant accountant concerning the collection and posting of cost data relating to a project and the eventual closing out of the project must be clearly defined. Several benefits accrue from a formal system maintained in a current condition:

a. It is known that actual costs are closely watched and are charged against the correct project. This discourages over-buying for subsequent use elsewhere.

b. Valid actual costs serve as a measure of the accuracy of those responsible for initial estimates upon which approvals are based. Persistent over or under closeouts should be fed back to the estimators to improve the accuracy of their estimates.

c. Having an independent responsibility for accumulation of actual costs reinforces the validity of the actual cost of each project, reducing the opportunity to charge costs to other projects or to expense if costs exceed the approved appropriation.

The duties of the plant accountant would include the following, in subdivided or combined steps depending on the volume of transactions to be processed:

1. Receives appropriation request from originator.

2. Logs request.

3. Forwards appropriation request to chief engineer and division controller.

4. Receives pencil copy returned by chief engineer and division controller with comments.

   a. If the item has been classified as an expense item, returns it to the originator with proper expense account number.

   b. Processes capital items that are approved or disapproved according to basic procedure.

   c. With respect to items marked "hold," returns a photocopy to the originator with that notation written on it. Files original and all work papers (including R.O.I. calculations) in a pending file.

5. Assigns plant order number on capital items.
6. Types appropriation request in required number of copies.
7. Forwards copies of appropriation request and previous comments for approval:
   a. Appropriation request $1,000 or less: to the individual in whose area the item originated.
   b. Appropriation request over $1,000: higher authority.
8. Files one copy in pending file.
9. Receives final approval or disapproval of appropriation request.
10. Distributes copies of approved appropriation request—capital.
11. Destroys remaining copies, including the one from the pending file.
12. Prepares posting sheets for each approved appropriation request.
13. Records on the posting sheets all expenditures for material and labor from:
    a. Vendors' Invoices.
    b. Stores' Withdrawal Slips.
    c. Maintenance Department's Time Sheets.
14. Follows up actively to determine the correctness of all charges to the plant order.
15. Upon receipt of final charges, prepares plant ledger sheet using plant order posing sheets, engineering estimate sheets, plant orders, purchase orders, invoices, etc.
16. Analyzes the posting sheets and segregates the cost of each identifiable unit of equipment into required categories.
17. Records each unit of equipment on a separate plant ledger sheet. Assigns an asset number to each item. Describes each as completely as possible, including a manufacturer's name, model number, serial number, size, capacity, and a reference to the plant order number. Numbers costing sheets consecutively by cost center. If existing equipment is being replaced, the existing and new plant ledger sheets will be appropriately cross-referenced.
18. Determines the estimated useful life to be assigned on each plant ledger sheet. This will be determined by engineering estimate and good accounting practice.
19. Upon completion of the entire project described in the appropriation request, closes the plant order.

Additional work necessary to the success of the project should be charged to the project even though not covered by the original appropriation request. If the cost exceeds the original by more than, say 10 percent, a supplemental appropriation request should be entered.

ECONOMIC JUSTIFICATION

Proposed expenditures for profit improvement typically are the high dollar expenditures. Careful analysis is necessary in this area to insure that the funds available are put to the best possible use. A profitability analysis should be made on all of these proposals to:

a. Insure that each approved request meets at least a minimum yield. Any proposal below a predetermined figure is rejected.
b. Permit selection of the most profitable combination of investments when there are more requests than the available funds can satisfy.

There are, basically, three different ways to consider the economic justification of proposed expenditures. Each differs significantly from the others in measurement, complexity, and merit as a comparative tool.

Years' Payback. Years' payback is simply the number of years' accumulation of net savings required to "pay back" the investment. The chief value of this tool is to measure the liquidity of the investment. It does not measure the economic worth of the investment because it does not include the full economic life of the project. Clearly, an investment with a 3-year payback and a 6-year life is better than one with a 3-year payback and only a 3-year life. In the latter, there is no return *on* investment, merely a return *of* investment. This technique can be used to identify the very obviously good projects with paybacks of less than a year, and to screen out the very obviously poor projects with paybacks so long as to merit no further consideration. It is a useful device for companies with a very short supply of funds when quick return of investment is vital. Payback ignores the time value of money.

Return on Investment. Return on investment calculations compare annual savings with investment, with the index of comparison expressed in percentage values. There are several variations of this calculation, each resulting in different numbers. In principle, this technique is superior to years payback because it evaluates the entire economic life of the project. It results in numbers which are then directly usable to compare the relative worth of several projects, all competing for part of a limited supply of funds. Further, return on investment requires considering depreciation as an expense in the calculation of incremental profit. R.O.I. does not consider the time value of money which can be an important factor in two similar projects. Consider the case of two equal investments, the first of which generates peak income the first year and gradually drops down to zero in ten years while the second starts slowly, peaks in five years, and then declines; both average the same net savings per year. The first is the better choice because it generates money sooner, which can be reinvested sooner. This will not be visible in the comparative return on investment calculations.

a. Simple R.O.I. is calculated as follows:

Average Annual Savings
Less Average Annual Incremental Costs
Less Average Depreciation

= Net Savings

$$\text{R.O.I.} = (\text{Net Savings} \times 50\% \text{ Tax}) \div (\text{Original Investment})$$

b. Average rate of return is calculated as follows:

$$\text{R.O.I.} = (\text{Net Savings} \times 50\% \text{ Tax}) \div \left(\begin{array}{c} \text{Original} \\ \text{Investment} \end{array} \div 2 \right)$$

Both can be calculated on savings before tax, for additional variations. The simple rate of return is recommended over the average rate of return; it is the more severe test of an investment's worth.

Discounted Cash Flow. This technique adds two valuable additional considerations: the time value of money and the concept of cash flow.

This method combines all of the good points of both of the above techniques. Its major disadvantages are that it is more difficult to calculate, and it is considerably more difficult for the average manager to fully comprehend in his infrequent contacts with the calculation.

Illustration of Techniques. To show the difference in calculation and resulting index, two simplified problems will be carried through each technique and summarized in Exhibit 86.

Problem 1. A $100,000 investment with a five-year project life produces a uniform $35,000/year net savings before depreciation.

Problem 2. A $100,000 investment with a five-year life produces net savings before depreciation as follows:

Year 1	$40,000
Year 2	45,000
Year 3	40,000
Year 4	30,000
Year 5	20,000
Average	$35,000

Years' Payback. Calculate the number of years required for cash flow to return the original investment.

1. $100,000 \div \$35,000 = 2.85$ years.
2. Year 1 1.00 year $ 40,000
   Year 2 1.00 "   45,000
                                                                   _____
                                                                       $ 85,000
   Year 3   .38 " $15,000 \div 40,000 = 0.38$ 15,000
   _____   _____
   2.38 years $100,000

Simple Rate of Return

  1. R.O.I. before tax:

$$\frac{35,000-20,000}{100,000} = 15\%$$

  R.O.I. after tax:

$$\frac{(35,000+20,000)\ 50\%}{100,000} = 7.5\%$$

  2. R.O.I. before tax:

$$\frac{35,000-20,000}{100,000} = 15\%$$

  R.O.I. after tax:

$$\frac{(35,000-20,000)\ 50\%}{100,000} = 7.5\%$$

Average Rate of Return

  1. R.O.I. before tax:

$$\frac{35,000-20,000}{(100,000 \div 2)} = 30\%$$

  R.O.I. after tax:

$$\frac{(35,000-20,000)\ 50\%}{(100,000 \div 2)} = 15\%$$

  2. R.O.I. before tax:

$$\frac{(35,000-20,000)}{(100,000 \div 2)} = 30\%$$

  R.O.I. after tax:

$$\frac{(35,000-20,000)\ 50\%}{(100,000 \div 2)} = 15\%$$

Discounted Cash Flow. Use any standard discount table for present value factors. This calculation is considerably more complex than any of those given. See exhibits 84 and 85 for the calculations of Problems 1 and 2.

EXHIBIT 84

INTERNAL RATE OF RETURN—PROBLEM 1

2	3	4	5	6	7	8	9	10	11
PERIOD	YEARLY OPERATING ADVANTAGE	DEPRE-CIATION	NET INCOME BEFORE TAX 3-4	NET INCOME AFTER TAX 5 X 50%	TRIAL No. 1 0% INTEREST RATE CASH FLOW RECEIPTS 6 + 4	TRIAL No. 2 15% INTEREST RATE		TRIAL No. 3 25% INTEREST RATE	
						FAC-TOR	PRESENT VALUE 7 x 8	FAC-TOR	PRESENT VALUE 7 x 10
1st	35,000	20,000	15,000	7,500	27,500	.929	25,500	.885	24,400
2nd	35,000	20,000	15,000	7,500	27,500	.799	22,000	.689	18,800
3rd	35,000	20,000	15,000	7,500	27,500	.688	18,800	.537	14,700
4th	35,000	20,000	15,000	7,500	27,500	.592	16,200	.418	11,500
5th	35,000	20,000	15,000	7,500	27 500	.510	14,000	.326	8,800
				(B) TOTALS	137,500		96,500		78,200

INSTRUCTIONS:

Plot each trial on the graph. Draw a curve connecting these points. The point at which the curve intersects the unity ratio line may be read on the interest rate scale.

This is the internal rate of return the project will generate.

(A) TOTAL EXPENDITURES	100,000	100,000	100,000
(B) TOTAL RECEIPTS (transfer from (B) above	137,500	96,500	78,200
RATIO B/A PV INDEX	1.375	.965	.782
EXCESS PRESENT VALUE	37,500	(3,500)	(21,800)

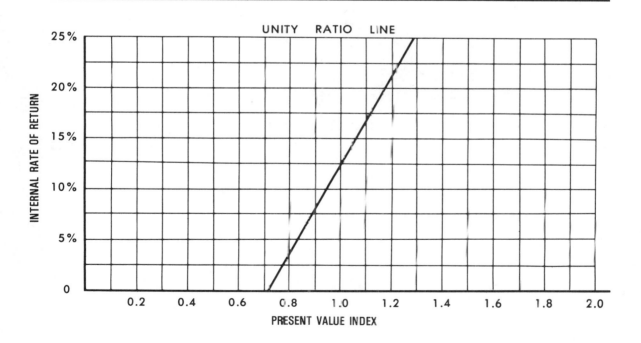

EXHIBIT 85

INTERNAL RATE OF RETURN—PROBLEM 2

2	3	4	5	6	7	8	9	10	11
PERIOD	YEARLY OPERATING ADVANTAGE	DEPRE-CIATION	NET INCOME BEFORE TAX 3 – 4	NET INCOME AFTER TAX 5 x 50%	TRIAL No. 1 0% INTEREST RATE CASH FLOW RECEIPTS 6 + 4	TRIAL No. 2 15% INTEREST RATE		TRIAL No. 3 25% INTEREST RATE	
						FAC-TOR	PRESENT VALUE 7 x 8	FAC-TOR	PRESENT VALUE 7 x 10
1st	40,000	20,000	20,000	10,000	30,000	.929	27,900	.885	26,500
2nd	45,000	20,000	25,000	12,500	32,500	.799	26,000	.689	22,400
3rd	40,000	20,000	20,000	10,000	30,000	.688	20,600	.537	16,100
4th	30,000	20,000	10,000	5,000	25,000	.592	14,800	.418	10,400
5th	20,000	20,000			20,000	.510	10,200	.326	6,500
(B) TOTALS					137,500		99,500		81,900

INSTRUCTIONS:

Plot each trial on the graph. Draw a curve connecting these points. The point at which the curve intersects the unity ratio line may be read on the interest rate scale.

This is the internal rate of return the project will generate.

		Trial 1	Trial 2	Trial 3
(A)	TOTAL EXPENDITURES	100,000	100,000	100,000
(B)	TOTAL RECEIPTS (transfer from (B) above)	137,500	99,500	81,900
	RATIO B/A PV INDEX	1.375	.995	.819
	EXCESS PRESENT VALUE	37,500	(500)	(18,100)

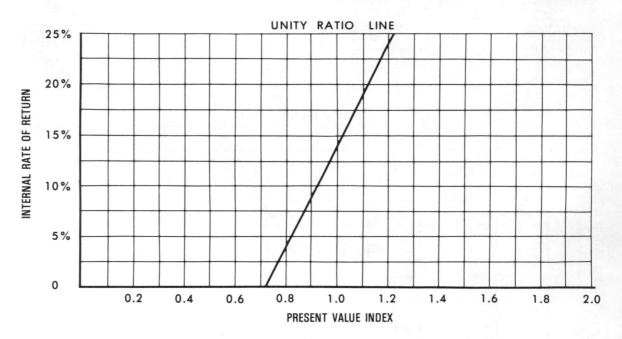

UNITY RATIO LINE

INTERNAL RATE OF RETURN — PRESENT VALUE INDEX

Summary. Each return on investment calculation results in numbers different in significance and content. Which is the correct rate of return? Which should be used in real, not academic, investment decisions?

All of them are correct. Since there is no one correct definition, any calculation which is performed according to a specific set of rules and definitions cannot be faulted on correctness.

That, however, does not say that all definitions are equally desirable and useful. As shown earlier, there are important shortcomings in the years' payback and the return on investment calculations. Only the discounted cash flow technique adequately treats the variables of net savings, time, depreciation, taxes, and economic life.

In the example problems, as summarized in Exhibit 86, the discounted cash flow technique stands alone in pointing to Problem 2 as the better choice in the absolute sense and in the comparative sense. Years' payback does indicate that #2 is better than #1 due to the shorter payback. The other two come out the same because no recognition is given to the value of the higher payoff in the early years. In Exhibit 87, the comparative aspects are further illustrated.

EXHIBIT 86

SUMMARY R.O.I. CALCULATIONS

	Years Payback	Simple Rate of Return	Average Rate of Return	Discounted Cash Flow	PV Index @ 15%	Excess PV @ 15%
Before Tax:						
Problem 1	2.85	15%	30%	—	—	—
Problem 2	2.38	15%	30%	—	—	—
After Tax:						
Problem 1	—	7.5%	15%	13.0%	.965	(3500)
Problem 2	—	7.5%	15%	14.5%	.995	(500)

EVALUATION OF PROPOSED EXPENDITURES

While the mathematical technique used in the evaluation of proposed expenditures is important, a topic of far greater importance is the completeness and validity of the premises that generate data for use in the analysis. Invalid premises cannot be improved on by any technique. The controller is generally not involved in the request for an expenditure as the requesting party. He is always involved, however, in the economic evaluation of the request. Although the controller may not be competent to state specific premises, he is responsible for *getting* the premises from those who are competent.

EXHIBIT 87

CAPITAL PROJECT EVALUATION

I. Compound Interest:

    PV = Present Value

    R = Interest Rate

    FV = Future Value

$FV = PV (1.00 + R)$ for 1 year

$FV = PV (1.00 + R)^2$ for 2 years

$\therefore FV = PV (1.00 + R)^n$ for n years

II. Present Value:

$$PV = \frac{FV}{(1.00 + R)^n}; \quad FV = \frac{1}{(1.00 + R)^n}$$

Example:

$$FV = \quad \$20,000 \quad (1.00 + .06)^3 \quad = \quad 23,820$$

$$PV = \quad \$23,820 \quad \left(\frac{1}{(1.00 + .06)^3}\right) = \$20,000$$

For 6% column and 3 periods, the PV factor is 0.840. This value is calculated as follows:

$$\frac{1}{(1.00 + .06)^3} \quad = 0.840$$

III. Excess Present Value Criterion:

    A.   Investment: $50,000

         Income (Cash In-Flow): $20,000/year

            EPV = PV (Cash In-Flow) − PV (Investment)

                = $20,000 (2.673) − $50,000

                = $53,460 − $50,000 = $3,460

    B.   Investment: $40,000

         Cash In-Flow: $16,100/year for 3 years

        EPV = $16,100(2.673) − $40,000

           = $43,000 − $40,000 = $3,000

Alternative A is preferred.

IV. Present Value Index:

PVI = PV(Cash Inflows) ÷ PV(Investment)

    A.   PVI = $53,460 ÷ $50,000 = 1.069

EXHIBIT 87

CAPITAL PROJECT EVALUATION
continued

B. $\quad PVI = \$43,000 \div \$40,000 = 1.075$
Alternative B is preferred.

V. Internal Rate of Return:

$IRR =$ Interest (Discount) Rate at which: PV(Cash Inflow) = PV(Investment)

$$FV(\text{Cash Inflow}) \left(\frac{1}{(1.00 + R)^n} \right) = PV(\text{Investment})$$

$$\frac{1}{(1.00 + R)^n} = \frac{PV(\text{Investment})}{FV(\text{Cash Inflow})}$$

A. $\quad \dfrac{1}{(1.00 + R)^3} = \$50,000 \div \$20,000 = 2.500$

$\quad R = 9.8\%$

B. $\quad \dfrac{1}{(1.00 + R)^3} = \$40,000 \div \$16,100 = 2.484$

$\quad R = 10\%$

Alternative B is preferred.

VI. Years' Payback:
Years' Payback = Number of Years' of Cash Inflow Required to Recover Investment
A. $\$50,000 \div \$20,000/\text{year} = 2.50$ years
B. $\$40,000 \div \$16,100/\text{year} = 2.48$ years
Alternative B is preferred

VII. Accounting Rate of Return:
ARR is based on a "profit" calculated similarly to an Income Statement "profit."

$$ARR = \frac{\text{Profit}}{\text{Initial Investment}} \quad \text{or} \quad \frac{\text{Profit}}{\text{Average Investment}}$$

A. $\quad ARR = \dfrac{\$20,000 - (50,000 \div 3)}{\$50,000/2} = \dfrac{\$3,333}{\$25,000} = 13.4\%$

B. $\quad ARR = \dfrac{\$16,100 - (40,000 \div 3)}{\$40,000/2} = \dfrac{\$2,767}{\$20,000} = 13.8\%$ $\quad$ Alternative B is preferred

A two-step procedure should be followed. First, all premises should be stated, documented, and recorded. Often, research into production and sales records is necessary to this procedure. Engineering equipment configurations and cost estimates are needed. Marketing forecasts of sales volume and prices are necessary. Manufacturing estimates of material costs, yield losses, and production rates are required. In all of this, the controller's role is that of demanding full deliberation and acceptable documentation. When all premises are furnished, a consolidated statement of the premises should be written by the controller and approved by the requesting parties. Only then should the second step, the discounted cash flow calculation, be initiated.

As a guide to the full statement of all pertinent premises, a checklist such as that shown in Exhibit 88 is useful.

POST-COMPLETION AUDIT

For all profit improvement expenditures above a minimum dollar figure peculiar to the circumstances of each company, a post-completion audit of expenditures versus profit improvement should be made.

The purpose of this is to verify that promised gains are actually realized. This also serves to give approving authorities confidence in the requests coming to them for approval. It serves, too, to hold down initial enthusiasm to realistic levels and to spur operating and sales management to full performance upon installation. In all cases, the knowledge that post-completion audits will be made generates an incentive not so easily obtainable from any other source.

In format, the audit is simply an item-by-item review of the approved premises to measure actual accomplishment. This data with the actual investment is cranked through the discounted cash flow technique and the resulting values are compared to the initial claims.

This audit should be made one year after the appropriation is closed out and the asset entered on the books. Copies of the audit report should be sent to everyone on the initial approval list.

REPORTS

Relatively few reports are needed in the area of capital budgeting and expenditure programs. The forecast and budget are, themselves, both primary documents and control reports.

As appropriations are approved, the page and line item should be so annotated in the budget book of the plant accountant. From this, he can prepare a monthly report showing a capsule summary of the budget status. Exhibit 89 shows the information useful in such a report. The primary purpose of this report is to spur department heads to a consistent level of appropriations during the year to prevent undue haste to "spend what's budgeted" at the end of the budget year.

EXHIBIT 88

DATA SHEET FOR R.O.I. CALCULATIONS

TO	FROM	DATE

Please calculate an *ROI* on the investment and savings as detailed below.
(Note: It is the Requestor's responsibility to provide complete investment and savings data. Staff departments should be used, as required, to get the best data possible.)

INVESTMENT

1. APPROPRIATION TO BE REQUESTED $ _____

2. ADDITIONAL FACILITIES WHICH WILL ALSO BE REQUIRED:

	CHECK ONE		
	YES	NO	AMOUNT
a) LAND	____	____	____
b) OFFICE BUILDING	____	____	____
c) STORAGE BUILDING	____	____	____
d) OTHER	____	____	____
e) RELOCATION OR DISMANTLING	____	____	____
f) WORKING CAPITAL	____	____	____

PRICE, VOLUME AND INCREMENTAL

		CHECK ONE	
	INCREASE	DECREASE	NO CHANGE
1. SALES VOLUME	____	____	____
2. SALES PRICE /UNIT	____	____	____
3. RAW MATERIAL COST/UNIT	____	____	____
4. FUEL	____	____	____
5. POWER	____	____	____
6. LABOR	____	____	____
7. SALARIES	____	____	____
8. MACHINE SPEED	____	____	____
9. MACHINE DOWNTIME	____	____	____
10. MAINTENANCE COST	____	____	____
11. INSURANCE	____	____	____
12. TAXES	____	____	____
13. OTHER	____	____	____

Describe below any additional investment checked "Yes" and all margin and cost changes checked "increase" or decrease. (Continue on plain paper.)

ITEM	DESCRIPTION AND AMOUNT	ESTIMATED BY

EXHIBIT 89

CAPITAL BUDGET STATUS

Date: 1 August 19__

Plant	Current Budget	Appropriations Approved	Pending Approval	Unappropriated Balance
PLANT A	500,000	250,000	50,000	200,000
B	500,000	190,000	10,000	300,000
C	500,000	175,000	100,000	225,000
D	500,000	210,000	25,000	265,000
E	500,000	305,000	—	195,000
Total	2,500,000	1,130,000	185,000	1,185,000

A useful information report can be prepared to show the current balance not yet expended on each approved appropriation. This report lists each open appropriation, shows the initial appropriation, expenditures last year, balance unexpended, adjustments this year, expenditures this year, and balance unexpended. Exhibit 90 displays a sample format.

EXHIBIT 90

STATUS OF APPROVED PROJECTS

Item	Prior Year			This Year		
	Appropriated	Expended	Balance	Adjustment or Appropriation	Expended	Balance
Lathe	250 M	50 M	200 M	—	200 M	—
Press	200 M	100 M	100 M	—	50 M	50 M
Stream Improvement	300 M	250 M	50 M	100 M	50 M	100 M
Boiler	600 M	100 M	500 M	—	250 M	250 M
Turbine	—	—	—	400 M	200 M	200 M
Warehouse	—	—	—	500 M	300 M	200 M
Other	—	—	—	1,250 M	1,000 M	250 M
Total	1,350 M	500 M	850 M	2,250 M	2,050 M	1,050 M

For cash control purposes, the controller will want a quarterly forecast of capital expenditures anticipated against approved appropriations. This missing ingredient cannot be forecast from history or budget as can cash requirements for payroll and accounts payable. A four-quarter forecast revised quarterly is a useful format. Some detail of major expenditures plus a catchall "other" category is needed for interpretation of the significance of the total for each quarter. A sample report is shown in Exhibit 91. Column 1 shows the total to be accounted for. Columns 2-5 show some detail and the expenditure total for each quarter. The balance to be carried over into some future quarter is shown in Column 6.

EXHIBIT 91

CAPITAL EXPENDITURE FORECAST

	To be Expended	\multicolumn{4}{c}{Expenditures Forecast}	Carry-Over
		1st Q.	2nd Q.	3rd Q.	4th Q.	
Prior Year's Appro-priation Not Yet Spent	1,000 M					
This Year's Budget	2,500 M					
Lathe		250 M				
Press			200 M			
Stream Improvement		100 M		100 M	100 M	
Boiler			100 M	200 M	300 M	
Turbine					400 M	
Warehouse				500 M		
Other		150 M	200 M	200 M	200 M	500 M
Total	3,500 M	500 M	500 M	1,000 M	1,000 M	500 M
Cumulative Total			1,000 M	2,000 M	3,000 M	3,500 M

Part Four

COMPUTERIZED ACCOUNTING

INFORMATION SYSTEMS

13

Planning for Manual
Data Capture Systems

Systems planning is an area of vital importance to the accountant. Clerical and electronic systems execute the procedures used in carrying out his assigned functions. Therefore, the controller must provide the definitions that will then be translated into clerical and electronic systems by the systems specialists and computer programmers.

A first mistake inexperienced controllers make is to presume that all manual effort must be automated.

Nothing could be farther from the truth. In fact, many instances are known to the author of automated systems being scrapped in favor of manual systems. The sales order set previously described is one such case.

Manual systems provide immediate flexibility plus the application of the clerk's judgment to every item processed. Automated systems, on the contrary, are completely rigid and inflexible and, of course, no judgment is applied by any machine.

Where the volume of transactions is low, where the system or the organization is changing, where alertness to variations from the standard scheme is necessary, manual systems must be kept and improved by the application of the techniques described here. The controller must make the decision as to the direction in which to go in a specific application area. He must be careful to automate only when the system has been prepared for automation. He must insist on manual schemes unless and until automation can be shown to be justified.

DEFINITION OF JOBS

The accountant must provide the definition of the job to be accomplished. Generally, this means defining the content and format of output reports and files. It can also include the timing of reports, control totals and cutoff dates, audit trail, and documentation. With this information, the systems analyst can plan the input reporting and processing steps necessary to give the accountant his data in the most economical manner feasible.

259

CLERICAL STUDY TECHNIQUES

Among the techniques used in systems studies are several relating to workload analysis. Given the output requirements of an operating system, the analyst's job is to restructure the things being done to achieve a cost reduction while maintaining or improving the functional value of the system. To do this, he must find out exactly who is doing what.

Task lists can be prepared by every person, listing the things they do to perform their assigned routines. These listings should be prepared over several days, with additional entries to the lists made as activities come up; no one can do an adequate listing in five minutes, from memory. The lists are then discussed with the supervisor to be sure they are complete and, simultaneously, that duties listed are truly so assigned.

Time logs can be prepared by each person, using the format shown in Exhibit 13 of Chapter 3. This is effective both to establish time requirements as well as to validate task lists. Many minor duties are uncovered this way. A complete work cycle must be included. For a payroll department, this would be enough time to include the hourly payroll and the salary payroll preparation. For general accounting, it would include a complete closing cycle from close of one period to close of the next.

Work sampling can be used to establish gross categories of work plus pinning down accurately the extent, if any, of idle time, excess personal time, and other categories of time-wasting activities. This can be a very useful device, particularly if new systems result in complaints of too little time to get the work done. For the first two to three days of work sampling, the non-productive time will be nil. After this interval, all the accumulated backlog of odd jobs will have been cleaned up. If make-work doesn't show up and if non-productive time remains low, there probably is a legitimate cause for further study. If there was no legitimate complaint in the first place, the people will have worked themselves out of a smoke screen and the time situation can be seen in its true perspective.

Work sampling is done on the basis of statistical, random sampling. Observations are made at random, unpredictable times all during the day. A record is made of the activity of an individual the instant he is observed, not a few seconds later after he has become aware of your presence and has started doing something different. All the observations for, say, two weeks are summarized. The observations in each category on the study sheet are then totaled and expressed as a percentage of the grand total number of observations. This establishes the portion of time actually devoted to that activity by the individual studied. Statistical tables are used to establish the statistical validity of the percentage, based on the total number of observations taken. A summary of a typical work sampling study is shown in Exhibit 92. A graph for the derivation of the validity figures is shown in Exhibit 93; this shows that for a study with 4,000 total observations, an activity recorded at 15% occurrence is really 15% plus/minus 7.5% of 15%, or 15% ± 1.1%.

EXHIBIT 92

WORK SAMPLING SUMMARY

Department: Accounts Payable   Observations: 4,000
Date: January 1—February 1, 19___

Activity	Percentage of Time on Activity	Minutes per Day on Activity
Matching Vouchers	35% ± 1.2%	168 ± 6
Filing in Desk	10% ± 1.0%	48 ± 5
Filing in Accounts Payable File	15% ± 1.1%	72 ± 5
Other Desk Work	25% ± 1.6%	120 ± 8
With Supervisor	2% ± 0.4%	10 ± 2
Personal	5% ± 0.7%	24 ± 3
Idle	5% ± 0.7%	24 ± 3
Out of Area	3% ± 0.5%	14 ± 2
Total	100%	480

CLERICAL IMPROVEMENT TECHNIQUES

Improvements in clerical systems fall into one of four categories:

1. Elimination of needless activity.
2. Combination of activities so that one effort produces two results.
3. Redesign of forms or work flow for greater efficiency.
4. Automation of repetitive, high volume tasks.

1. The first is difficult only in the getting of unanimous opinion that needless activity is going on. Not many supervisors are happy to admit that their people are doing needless work. Instances of duplication, however, may be found. In such cases, one person can be taken off the task without argument.

2. Combinations of activities based on time logs and work sampling can produce significant results. Much clerical cost goes into mailing, delivering, and

EXHIBIT 93

SAMPLE SIZE

Based on 95% Certainty

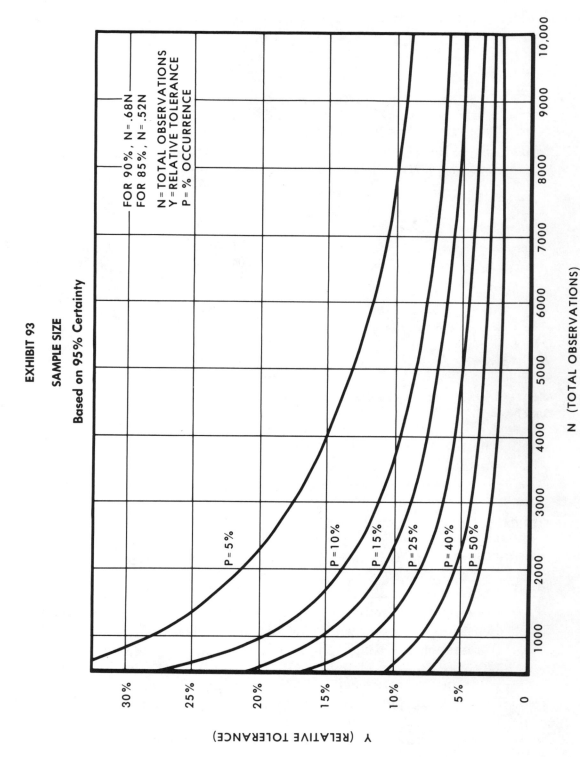

FOR 90%, N = .68N
FOR 85%, N = .52N

N = TOTAL OBSERVATIONS
Y = RELATIVE TOLERANCE
P = % OCCURRENCE

P = 5%
P = 10%
P = 15%
P = 25%
P = 40%
P = 50%

N (TOTAL OBSERVATIONS)

Y (RELATIVE TOLERANCE)

receiving documents. Reducing that activity by giving more of the work to a single person rather than several can simultaneously improve the efficiency with which the work is performed.

Similarly, it is often found that two people process the same data for two different reports. With judicious rearrangement of data, one person can often get both reports in a single pass of the data for very little more time than was previously spent in each pass. This kind of combination often crosses departmental lines. There is no room for narrow provincialism in systems design and improvement.

3. Forms redesign can frequently result in one-time writing with repetitive data captured for subsequent operations. This eliminates the need to spend clerical time rewriting and retyping data previously recorded. Exhibits 94 and 95 illustrate this idea. The sales order is typed in a carbon set with an acknowledgement copy and a four-part weight list with interleaved carbons. The typist types in all the required data:

a. The top copy is a ditto master. From this copy, all internally routed copies of the order are produced.
b. The second copy is the customer acknowledgement.
c. The balance of the set is the weight list set with all indicative information already filled in. Pencil carbon is interleaved in the set so that the weight lists can be filled in as the production comes over the finishing scale.

The benefits in clerical time-saving in preheaded weight lists that are prepared right on the production floor are obvious.

A similar example of the elimination of repetitive writing is shown in Exhibits 96 and 97. Formerly, the entire manufacturing order was typed for "greater clarity in later use." Detailed studies showed that handwritten information was completely adequate and that up to one-third of the information was constant from order to order. The following was done:

a. An original master sheet is prepared. Constant data are typed on the front. From this original, a supply of second generation masters are prepared.
b. Information specific to the order at hand is *written* on a second generation master. Copies of this sheet are made for internal distribution, as required.

4. Repetitive operations should be automated through the use of computers. Prime examples of good candidates for automation are:

Inventory Costing	Hourly Payroll Calculations
Sales Costing	Accounts Payable Distribution
Production Costing	Labor Distribution
Efficiency Calculations	

EXHIBIT 94

SALES ORDER/WEIGHT LIST

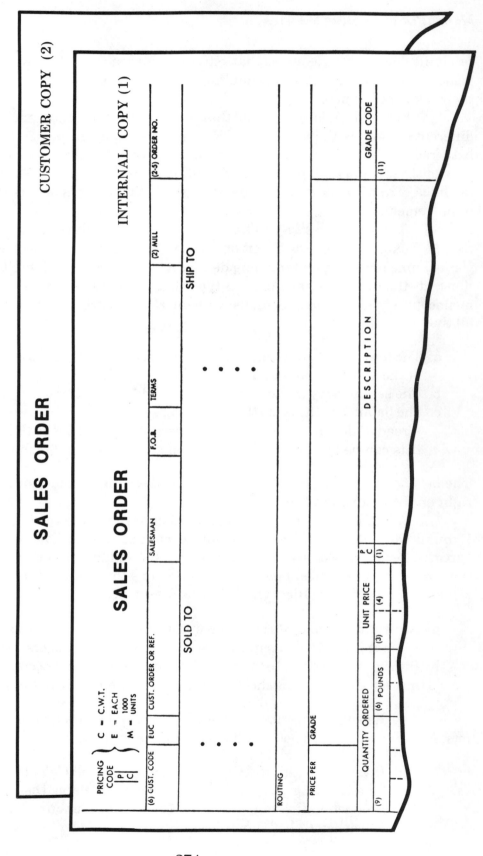

EXHIBIT 95

WEIGHT LIST

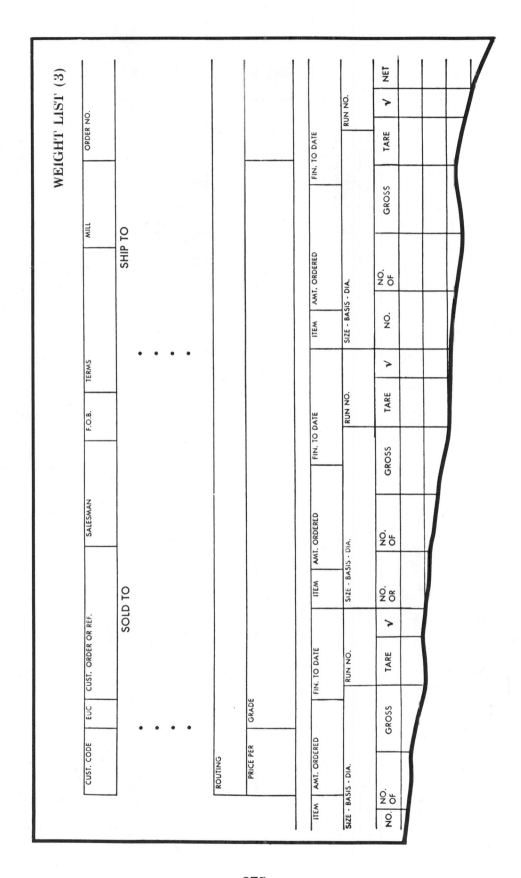

WEIGHT LIST (3)

EXHIBIT 96

PAPER MACHINE PRODUCTION ORDER

RUN	GRADE				BS. WT. 24x36-			/500 DATE		

| CODE | | | | COLOR STD. | | | | | | |

PAPER MACHINE SPECS.							PLASTIC SPECS.			
	MIN.	STD.	MAX.		MIN.	STD.	MAX.	RETENTION MIN.		MAX.
BS. WT.									1 ST PRESS	STARCH PRESS
MULLEN										
TEAR										
G. PROOF										
QUALITY										
RL. MST.										
DAMP MST.										

ORDER NO.	CUSTOMER	END USE	CORES

EXHIBIT 97

PAPER MACHINE PRODUCTION ORDER

COPY

COPIES - AS REQUIRED

COPY

RUN	GRADE				BS. WT. 24x36- 25 /500 DATE					
	CODE					COLOR STD. 40 AG				

PAPER MACHINE SPECS.				SUPER CAL. SPECS.				PLASTIC SPECS.		
	MIN.	STD.	MAX.		MIN.	STD.	MAX.	RETENTION MIN. 3	MAX. 5	
									1 ST PRESS	STARCH PRESS
BS. WT.	23.7	25	26.3	BS. WT.	23.7	25	26.3			
MULLEN	16	19		MULLEN	16	19		GLYCERINE		
TEAR	36			TEAR	16/18	18/20		UREA	40	
G. PROOF				G. PROOF	50			KOK		
QUALITY	TT CHECK			TRANS.	20	20-27		NITRATE		
RL. MST.				CAL. MST.	7		9	STARCH		
DAMP MST.				NIPS		11		NOPCO		
				BRITENESS				FLOWRATOR		
				OPACITY				BAUME		

ORDER NO.	CUSTOMER	END USE	CORES
PM2279	NEWARK		39 CORES

3000#

39" rolls

117" deckle - 30" dia

above cut on end of PM
use roll tickets - do not stencil
(INTERMEDIATE)

14

The Controller's Role in Planning for Computerized Accounting Information Systems

Initially the majority of data processing and computer installations were organizationally the responsibility of the controller. Such equipment was sold as business data handling apparatus. Who had more data to handle than the controller? It was a natural consequence to find the controller vigorously installing equipment with which he could do a better and less expensive job.

With the technological state of advancement now attained by computer manufacturers, it is reasonable and feasible for the controller to begin to plan to integrate his assorted accounting applications into an integrated Accounting Information System. He should initiate the move. He stands to reduce his costs the most and to improve control information the most by guiding his company to consider and use the full resources and facilities now available.

The controller may not remain in charge of the computer when the A.I.S. momentum builds up. Many other departments will want to use and benefit from the new equipment. Duties will shift across organization lines. More reliance will be placed on the computer system. Organization structure will be directly affected. This will serve to bring the manager of the Accounting Information System closer to a direct reporting relationship to the chief executive officer simply because of the power and influence this manager can exert on the entire organization.

COST REDUCTION

The purpose of most of the activities that come under the heading of systems planning is to be able to accomplish existing functions at a lower cost. A very large share of administrative costs are clustered in accounting clerical groups. The accountant can make a significant contribution to profit improvement by working to reduce the total cost of the accounting function through systems improvements.

279

In order to carry out this purpose, change is inevitable. Often accountants resist change because the current method is familiar; it works; all the bugs have been worked out; the right answers come out with a minimum of trouble. Change means unfamiliar methods, new problems to be solved, people to be retrained, and wrong numbers during the shakedown period. The accountant, however, must reorient his thinking to an attitude of expediting change, for his field is changing more rapidly than any other because of computers.

COMPUTERIZED INFORMATION SYSTEMS

Data processing has rapidly progressed from the individual punched card application stage toward integrated management information systems. Because the controller recognized the need for faster, more accurate data handling, EDP equipment has been widely used for applications in the accounting and control areas. The controller has found himself with the knowledge and the equipment, hence has been assigned the responsibility to plan and install, for the organization, an Accounting Information System which integrates order handling, production reporting, cost control, inventory, billing, and accounting systems.

Basic applications areas generally found in computer systems will include the following list, the actual routine program package for a division of a major manufacturer:

Order Entry

Customer and inter-division orders booked, listed by customer, by grade.

Inventory Action Information

a. Mill finished inventory: perpetual inventory, updated daily. Report inventory by customer by grade and by salesman by customer by grade, weekly.
b. Stock inventory, weekly report by stock item. Forecasts next six weeks' production requirements by exponential smoothing.
c. Base paper, daily perpetual inventory report.
d. Class 3 daily perpetual inventory report.

Accounts Receivable

All accounts receivable:

a. Daily application of billings and cash receipts to receivables records.
b. Weekly reports on aged trial balance and protection listings.
c. Reports on a 3-week cycle are dunning statements, other customer statements, and overdues by customer.

    d. As required, customer code number books are printed for corporate-wide distribution.

Sales Analysis and Forecasts; Marketing Analysis

Invoices keypunched for analysis and reports:

a. Generate accounts receivables cards from sales detail cards.
b. Calculate standard cost of sales.
c. Report weekly and period shipments by profit center by item, customer, and inter-division.
d. Period sales by destination (state, county).
e. For forecasts and market analysis, quarterly report, as follows:

    1. Sales by grade by customer
    2. Sales by customer by grade
    3. Salesman's forecast work sheets (by salesman by customer by grade)
    4. Forecast by customer by grade
    5. Forecast by grade
    6. End use by grade
    7. Destination by product
    8. Product by destination

Raw Material

a. Weekly pulp consumption, by grade of pulp.
b. Period raw material receipts—consumption—inventory "work sheets" for mill offices.
c. Period packing and shipping inventory and consumption.
d. Period Coating chemical consumption.
e. Period Coating and Wax Plant base paper consumption.
f. Period calculation of purchase price variance and reserve, by item by mill.
g. Quarterly calculation of reprice reserve.
h. Quarterly print for distribution standard furnish lists.

Accounts Payable

Punched cards are by-product of bookkeeping machine posting to:

a. Distribute expenses by account.
b. Report purchases by vendor.
c. Reconcile drafts.
d. Quarterly report expenses by salesman.
e. Annually summarize expense by account for expense budget.
f. Distribute central management accounts payable.

Payroll

Salary, hourly, pension payrolls:

a. Calculate earnings, taxes; write drafts.
b. Prepare tax reports and W-2's.
c. Report payroll statistics.
d. Distribute costs by account.
e. List vacation eligibility by employee for Personnel Department.
f. Alphabetic listing of employees, quarterly, for Personnel Department.
g. Annual vacation accrual calculation.
h. Standard work force costs and vacation eligibility for Expense Budget.

Variance and Production Reports

a. Period in-process and finished inventory reports, valued at standard cost.
b. Weekly Production, valued at standard cost.
c. Weekly period reject reports by defect, by grade by defect, by run number.
d. Weekly winder waste by grade by run number.
e. Winder operator productivity (% of standard) by foreman by employee, by employee by day.
f. Quarterly profit contribution by customer, by grade.
g. Summaries of grade cost data for standards reviews.
h. Standard cost calculations and Product Book printing.

Other Reports

a. Laboratory project costs by division, by profit center.
b. Paper machine schedule print out.
c. Tower machine schedule print out.
d. Wax Plant prime machine schedule print out.
e. Print mailing labels from master name and address files, for employee mailings, Merchant weekly stock lists.
f. Depreciation and asset accounting.
g. Budget preparation data.

In addition to routinely scheduled reports of the type listed, many requests for special, one-time data processing reports capitalize on data and programs already captured for additional uses. A representative list of requests processed in a typical year by the same division were as follows:

For Division

1. Machine production data for Mill Task Force.

2. Special reports on age, length of service, and hours worked/paid, for contract negotiations.
3. Analysis of rejects for process development study.
4. Critical path schedule reports.
5. Listings of cost standards for I.E. comprehensive review.
6. Analysis of sales, to compare with contest goals.
7. Special reports on machine efficiency for analysis of high efficiency variances.
8. Regression analysis calculations of production data for Engineering for drive design.

For Corporate

1. For Market Research, prospect lists on 3×5 cards for each salesman from Dun and Bradstreet SIC punched card files.
2. Special depreciation calculations and reports in connection with change in depreciation policy.
3. Proxy count for annual stockholders' meeting.
4. Central Mangement accounts payable review of accounts.

AIS PLANNING

Beyond the simple applications listed above, an integrated Accounting Information System is an absolute requirement for the management and control of the firm of the future. The potential of present equipment and systems to produce strategic and tactical information that will improve decision making will be utilized by competitors; the controller's obligation is to persuade his management to keep pace with competition. The objective is profit improvement, not cost reduction.

The basic purpose for developing information systems is to aid in coordinating strategy for profit improvement; it is not the mechanization of bookkeeping systems or the reduction in clerical employees. The expectation of great and immediate clerical cost reductions and the inevitable failure to achieve that objective has discredited information systems. It should be recognized from the beginning that it may be impossible to assign a specific dollar value to that information generated that is not specifically cost-reduction oriented.

An Accounting Information System study is, in many of its phases, similar to the engineering and development of a new product. All of the activities involved in engineering a product—preparing detailed instructions, scheduling manpower and machines, ordering materials, and selling the system to the management people for whom it is designed—are activities that are actually an integral part of an overall AIS study.

Manufacturers of hard goods spend thousands of dollars on research and development for a prototype prior to tooling up to manufacture a production model. This is exactly what is necessary for a sound information system. The data and information required by all departments of a business must be carefully inventoried and analyzed for their contribution in achieving stated objectives. Simultaneously, there must be a willingness to experiment in the development of the ultimate system. Just as each new product experiment may not be successful, each experiment in developing information systems will not be successful.

The most important aspect of top management's relationship to the information system study is "attitude." The attitude toward information systems in general and the assigned task force in particular must be reflected, both consciously and unconsciously, down the line throughout the organization. There is absolutely no substitute for the personal endorsement and public support of top management for a study of this sort. Top management's endorsement of the AIS Study must be communicated to all management before detailed studies are begun. There should remain no doubts as to the intent of the AIS team assigned to visit all locations and collect data for future planning. Because of its impact on the organization, a letter from the president assigning the team and defining the scope and general plan to be followed is a most effective tool to ensure full cooperation down the line. The letter might follow that shown in Exhibit 98.

EXHIBIT 98

LETTER FROM PRESIDENT

July 23, 19__

TO: Division Managers

                                                    CC: Messrs: Chairman of the Board
                                                                  Exec. Vice President
FROM: President   Controller
                                                                  Treasurer
                                                                  Dir. Personnel

SUBJECT: ACCOUNTING INFORMATION SYSTEMS

The Accounting Information Systems Review Committee met today to discuss the Corporate program for further development of Accounting Information Systems.

Mr. J. V. Bennett was instructed to proceed with a thorough, company-wide analysis of our information requirements for management and control. This study is to include subsidiaries and affiliated companies.

The studies are to lead to the development of Accounting Information Systems that begin with basic, factual information from each operation, supplemented with such derived information (interpreta-

EXHIBIT 98

LETTER FROM PRESIDENT (Cont.)

---

tive or analytical) as is required by the managers accountable for the operations or groups of operations in question. Information collected and developed at each level of operation is to be able to yield, in consolidation, the information required at the next level, culminating finally in the Corporate consolidated statements of Sales, Earnings, Financial Position, etc. All needed information is to develop from this systematic flow without need for setting up separate "cells" of information collectors or interpreters around and about the Company.

Specifically, within the above instructions, the objective is to design and implement a system furnishing corporate and division management with improved data collection and information reporting that will:

1. Provide better information for planning for profitability and for future growth.
2. Provide better and faster information for operating control and implementation of control decisions, hence profit improvement.
3. Provide profit improvement which justifies the investment in the system.

The scope of the program shall include the entire corporation, including subsidiaries and affiliated companies.

In accomplishing the objectives, the program will include:

Phase	Comment
I—Preliminary Survey	Initial outline of content and sequence of the work to be done.
II—Definition of System's Requirements	Analysis of management needs, to define output information requirements.
III—Design of System	Including input data and equipment selection.
IV—Installation and Implementation	

Divisional General Managers and their Controllers are requested to give Mr. Bennett's program complete and prompt cooperation.

SURVEY TEAM

The AIS Survey Team must have a nucleus of people with computer systems design experience assigned as analysts. The top man must be an able administrator, planner, organizer; it is less important that he have specific computer knowledge. Beyond this, two techniques are possible:

a. Enough people can be assigned to the team on a full-time basis to do the detailed work, or
b. Analysts can be assigned on a part-time basis from each department at each location.

Experience has shown (b) to be undesirable except as a last resort. The pressures of the regular job load interfere with progress. Absenteeism further adds to regular job pressures. Details not documented remain with the analysts and are lost to the team for subsequent consideration.

The need for the thorough analysis of the true needs of management cannot be stressed too heavily. Until confronted with the task of being quite specific in reply to specific questions, managers are unable to put in words their genuine control information requirements. A carefully designed program (Exhibit 99) to document existing system functions and future managerial requirements must be prepared for the survey team to follow.

The area to be surveyed is the mainstream of the business: the order/ production/shipment cycle. Businesses exist to receive orders from customers, produce the product in the requested quantities in accordance with customer specifications, ship on the required dates, and charge what the customer can afford to pay while earning a profit for the owners. Therefore, the mainstream of the Accounting Information System is concerned with:

Mainstream of Business:		*Order/Shipment Cycle*
Receipt of Order	:	Order Entry, Backlog Status, Comparisons with Forecast, Allocation to Plants.
Scheduling	:	Machine Backlog, Optimizing Schedules, Schedule Revisions, Schedule Reports.
Production		Backlog Status, Order Tracking, Order Status, Actual Costs, Variance and Efficiency Reports, Finished Production.
Inventory Control	:	Inventory Status and Trends, Aged Inventory Reports, Stock Inventory Level/Customer Service.
Shipment	:	Routing, Pooling, Release, Billing, Accounts Receivable, Sales Analysis, Marketing Planning, Sales Forecasts.

EXHIBIT 99

SYSTEMS ANALYSIS AND DESIGN PROGRAM

I. Identification of Need:
   A. New requirement
   B. Change in circumstances
   C. Present system does not satisfy management's requirements

II. Management Authorization

III. Data Collection
   A. Interviews
   B. Analysis of present system
   C. Checklists
   D. Analysis of documents
   E. Flowcharting

IV. Identify Alternative Solutions

V. Management Approval to Proceed
   A. Alternatives costed and benefits identified
   B. Management selection of alternative

VI. Detailed Design and Programming
   A. Project timetable
   B. Checkpoints
   C. Test data

VII. Management Acceptance of New Systems
   A. Demonstration
   B. Approval to install
   C. Equipment selection
     1. Requests for proposals
     2. Evaluations
     3. Vendor selection
     4. Contracts
     5. Installation
   D. Implementation
     1. Training
     2. Parallel Operations
     3. Cease operation of old system

SYSTEM DESIGN

System Design techniques to accomplish the desired tasks have to be correlated with cost of accomplishment and with value received. Computer manufacturer's systems engineers can be of significant value at this point in the program. Consecutive steps in this procedure require consideration of the following:

I. Design of systems to fulfill requirements:

a. Identify all major sub-systems.

b. Tentatively identify costs and value (Exhibit 100). Prime factors to be considered in the selection of the system to be recommended should include the following:

1. *Degree of Improvement Obtained (amount, timing)*

    (a) Cost reduction
    (b) Other profit improvement
    (c) Customer service

2. *Installation/Design Requirements (time, cost)*
    (a) Complexity of new system and program logic
    (b) Geography
        Communications
        Travel
    (c) Present staff experience
    (d) Priority for subsequent installations

3. *Political/Psychological*

    (a) Organizational realignment
    (b) Attitude and sophistication of operating and management personnel
    (c) Level of management affected

c. Select major payoff areas for further detailed design. Factors to be quantified in selecting the major payoff areas include the following:

1. *Order Entry.* Present high clerical costs. Improved cost, service through reduced delays. Faster input to scheduling. Bill of materials generation. Specs standardized, widely available.

2. *Scheduling of Production Facilities.* Scheduling changes. Increase production. Improved cost of service. Right facilities for orders. Stored forms; lower costs.

3. *Control of All Inventories.* Optimized. Higher inventory for better service and more efficient production. Reduced inventory in other

cases. Better information for sales direction. Lower clerical costs. Special reports.

4. *Control of Production Facilities.* Implementation of schedule. Performance measurement; actual costs vs. estimate. Reduced clerical "cost accounting."

5. *Improved Sales and Market Analysis.* Prospect analyses. Product profitability. Industry comparisons. Reduced clerical costs.

6. *Traffic/Shipping/Billing.* Pooling. Freight rates. Faster billing. Under- and overruns. Faster input to receivables.

  d. Proceed with sub-system design.

II. Identify equipment and personnel costs of sub-systems. Get quotes from vendors. Identify, specifically, and validate value to be received.

III. Select the best system, including a phased installation plan leading to the overall system.

IV. Present recommendations to management for approval.

Simultaneous with the survey work described above, an education program to acquaint management with the complexities and potential of computers should be begun for the following reasons:

1. Management must understand the implications of AIS work of competitors.
2. AIS requirements will affect conventional functional organizational lines.
3. Standardization of report content and timing will inhibit individual freedom of action in areas such as codes and report definition.
4. The total cost of systems planning, design, programming, and installation will be high. Equipment rental rates are substantial. Management must be sufficiently informed to exercise independent judgment on recommendations.

It is inevitable that greater use will be made of computers. Computers are coming because of the increasing speed with which managerial decisions must be made. In today's world, the allowable time to make a decision and to make it right is abbreviated. The capability of making such decisions in time will become a matter of survival for a company.

EXHIBIT 100

COST/BENEFIT CHECKLIST

I. Costs

    A. *Facilities:*
        1. Independent power supply
        2. Building and building modifications
        3. Air conditioning
        4. Raised flooring
        5. Fire protection
        6. Security

    B. *Hardware:*
    Determine all equipment needed. Get prices for buying, renting and leasing to find which would be most economical.

    C. *Software:*
    Compilers, applications packages, communications systems, etc.

    D. *Personnel:*
        1. Operations staff—keypunch, computer operator, etc.
        2. Systems staff
        3. Programming
        4. Manager, control function
        5. Recruiting, fringe benefits, training

    E. *Operations:*
        1. Power
        2. Maintenance, if not included in hardware lease
        3. Supplies (cards, printed forms), reels of tape, disk packs
        4. Security system

    F. *Programming and Conversion:*
        1. Training, old people or new ones hired in.
        2. Systems analysis and design to meet user's needs.
        3. Changing or recompilation of programs, documents, and files (file organization differences, from manual to computer.)
        4. Testing system (rent or borrow like system) and debugging
        5. Consultant fees

    G. *Overhead:*
        1. Variables—indirect expenses
        2. Direct expenses such as insurance and property taxes

EXHIBIT 100

COST/BENEFIT CHECKLIST (Cont.)

H. *Opportunity Cost:*
1. Income lost from money put into computer

I. *Intangibles:*
1. Layoffs (morale)
2. Community relations
3. Management time

II. Benefits

A. *Cost Reduction:*
1. Clerical
2. Inventory (elimination, lower levels)
3. Better track of receivables increases working capital
4. Production models (mfg. cost variances—labor and material inefficiencies)

B. *More Timely Information:*
Gives users faster, more timely information for decision making

C. *Greater Accuracy:*
1. Correct materials and amounts delivered to customers
2. Delete human error in calculations

D. *Better Service:*
1. Process orders faster
2. Fewer stockouts
3. Fewer lost orders caused by poor service

E. *Management:*
Relieve management of routine duties so they may spend time on more creative things

---

15

Internal Controls in a
Computerized Accounting System

There are several basic reasons why controls are vital in data processing systems: There is a growing reliance by management on computer generated reports; the accuracy and reliability of reports is a function of the controls that are exercised over the data input and the processing of the data processing system; an increasing amount of resources is being allocated to computer operations; good control is required to insure that the resources are effectively used; the potential for control problems is greater in computer systems than in manual systems because of the greater reliance on predetermined program steps and the absence of human judgment in the processing operations.

ACCOUNTING CONTROLS

In the broad sense, controls include accounting controls and administrative controls. Accounting controls include the plan of organization and those procedures that are concerned with safeguarding the accuracy and reliability of financial records. Consequently, accounting control in data processing systems must be designed to provide assurance that transactions are executed in accordance with management's specifications, that transactions are properly recorded to permit the preparation of financial statements in accordance with accounting principles, that access to assets is permitted only in accordance with authorization, and that the recorded accountability for assets is compared with the existing assets at reasonable intervals and appropriate action is taken with respect to any differences.

PREVENTIVE AND FEEDBACK CONTROLS

Controls in data processing operations are of two kinds—preventive controls and feedback controls. Preventive controls are designed to eliminate the possibility of an error from occurring or to find errors in input information and have them corrected before the processing operation begins. Feedback controls, on the other hand, are designed to identify control problems occurring during processing operations, to communicate the fact of those problems to the appropriate management personnel, and to arrange for corrections in the system to be made and the result of those corrections to be monitored and reported to management.

Preventive controls in the operation of data processing systems include the prevention of errors in processing caused by input data, by operators, by program problems, by embezzlement and by fraud. A separate category of preventive controls relate to physical security aspects including the prevention of damage to equipment caused by deliberate sabotage by fire, by flood, by theft, and the like.

Separation of functions results in organizational-dependence-related preventive controls. The data processing structure which provides this preventive control includes the separation of programming from systems analysis, the separation of the systems analysis and programming from computer operation, the separation of data input from computer processing, the institution of a separate tape library for the physical maintenance and custody of tape files, and finally, a data control function. Separation of analysis and programming is done to prevent analysts and programmers from designing programs specifically to manipulate data to accomplish fraud. The tape library separation makes it impossible for unauthorized access to data files. The separation of operation from programming prevents operators from modifying programs and then running the programs to accomplish fraudulent ends.

The separation of the analysis and programming function requires the use of some kind of formal authorization for program changes. A written description of any changes and justification for those changes should be submitted in writing from the person requesting the change to the data processing manager. The data processing manager must authorize program changes before they are made by analysts and programmers. Test results from program changes should be approved by the analysts, by the programmer, and by the user who requested the changes in the first place.

To accomplish separation of the operations functions from all other functions requires a printout of all of the daily computer operations as a console log. The console log should be reviewed on a regular basis for evidence of any irregularities in computer operation and in program modification. Every instance of a manual intervention by the operator with the program should be investigated. Every instance of program modification should be checked against valid authorizations for modification.

PHYSICAL SECURITY

Physical protection includes a limitation on access to the computer room and to data terminals. Access should be available to authorized personnel, only; visitors and unauthorized company personnel should not be routinely permitted in the computer room. The use of computer rooms open for public relations purposes or the installation of computers at street level behind store windows (which used to be done on a routine basis) has been recognized to be a dangerously expensive proposition. Computers should be installed in very secure locations with limited access, to prevent deliberate sabotage or accidental damage in the case of general riot or natural disaster.

There must be specific provisions made for the protection of files and for the protection of operational programs from physical loss or destruction or accidental damage. The tape library, from which tapes and disks may be taken only for authorized operational purposes, is a necessary element of this kind of control. The file storage location should be protected against such things as dust, heat, humidity, or any other adverse conditions that might affect the physical stability of the files themselves. As a protection against accidental writing-over onto tape files, tape rings and file labels are necessary devices. A tape file protection ring is a device which, when inserted on a reel of magnetic tape, permits writing on the tape; when the file protect ring is removed the tape may not be written on because of certain physical and mechanical aspects of the tape drive; the data on the reel of tape is thus protected. It is the responsibility of the tape librarian to insert a file protection ring when writing is to be allowed on that tape. File labels, on the other hand, are both internal and external to the reel of magnetic tape itself. An external label is generally a gummed paper label attached to the outside of the tape reel identifying the content of the reel. An internal file label is a magnetic record written on the tape itself which identifies the contents of the file and the programs which are to be run in association with that file.

In addition to the controls against physical loss or destruction, the control system must provide for the reconstruction of files in case there is some accidental loss in spite of all the controls. One such protection is to insure that duplicate magnetic tapes of programs and files are physically stored in a location separate from the computer facility and tape library. One file reconstruction procedure commonly used with magnetic tape files is a grandfather/father/son concept. Under this plan, the three most recent master files are all retained, with the son file being the most current. Along with these three generations of files, the data necessary to create each next generation is retained. If, for instance, the son file is accidentally destroyed, then the father file can be used in combination with the transaction data necessary to create the son file to recreate that file.

Of great significance in the protection against major losses due to some uncontrollable natural disaster or major system malfunction is the provision for backup facilities. Some other data processing location needs to be identified which has a physical equipment configuration similar to that being employed, to which recourse can be taken for emergency processing time in the event of disaster. Such arrangements can often be made on a mutual basis with another facility which is most like yours, each being the backup system for the other.

In some cases, hardware failures in system components can be isolated as they occur, enabling the remainder of the entire hardware system to continue in operation although in a less efficient and less effective manner. This operation can continue in this lower level of efficiency until the malfunctioning component can be repaired or replaced. This kind of system modification is often referred to as "graceful degradation" in that, as the system degrades in efficiency, it is accomplished in a controlled manner and not allowed to collapse in an instant.

SOURCE DATA CONTROL

Management's authorization of transactions is the starting point for establishing accounting control of transactions. In a manual operation, the control process can be described as a people-oriented system because there are people at each step of the process who have assigned responsibilities for personally implementing control techniques to safeguard the accuracy and reliability of data and to perform the prescribed operational steps. Each person in the sequence provides a judgmental check on the work previously performed. However, when data processing systems are introduced to replace people, those human judgments can no longer take place. The only checking that can be done is that which is prescribed in the computer programs.

The source data control phase consists of procedures and control techniques related to the collection and recording of transaction data on appropriate forms for subsequent processing and the authorization of the data to be processed.

All of the conventional design considerations for source documents for any accounting system are appropriate to the design of source documents for data processing systems. Such specially designed forms promote the accuracy of the initial recording of the data and their control to insure that the documents are not lost in processing. Sequential numbering of the input transaction form, with full accountability at the point of origin of the document for the correct recording and the transmission of the form, is a traditionally established control technique. Some visual pre-audit of the source documents by the originating personnel is appropriate to detect invalid codes, unreasonable amounts, missing data, and the like. Data that has been properly recorded must nevertheless be properly authorized for further processing. Authorization includes such things as approval of time cards, approval of credit terms, approval of new prices, approval of new customers, and so forth. These input documents should have some visible evidence of authorization; when authorization is required, the internal control group should insure that authorization is indicated on the documents as received at data processing.

A point to keep in mind in designing source data controls is that there may be some data errors which are acceptable if they do not cause an interruption in the processing. For instance, a misspelled description of an item is not a major problem. In deciding whether to accept such errors, one should compare the cost of correcting the error to the consequences of accepting it.

A very important control technique at this point, is the grouping of transaction documents. This grouping or batching of documents typically relates more to sequential processing systems in which transactions have to be arranged in the same order as the master file. However, batching of input documents may also apply to disk systems where it is desirable to batch input for control purposes. Control totals must be developed on selected important fields of data and each input document, to insure that all of the documents have been transmitted properly from the source to the data processing center. Controls might be developed on the number of records in each batch or can be based on some quantitative field such as invoice amount or hours worked. Such control serves as a check on the completeness of the transaction being processed and insures that all transactions have been received in the data processing center.

Batch totals are essential to computerized batch processing. Batch totals are accumulated manually from the source documents by the department originating the input to data processing. The original totals are provided to data processing along with the source documents themselves. The original totals are compared to computer-generated data at appropriate processing steps. Any discrepancy observed is an indication that there has been a loss of records or that an error has occurred in the data transcription or the data processing steps. Forms of control totals used on batches include hash totals, valid data totals, and counts of records. A hash total is a numeric sum of numbers which have no meaning when added, for instance, employee numbers on time cards. A data total would be the total of the actual hours worked as recorded on those time cards. A document count would be a physical count of the number of time cards included in the batch of input documents being provided to data processing.

DATA CONVERSION CONTROLS

Data conversion is the process of converting data from the original source documents into a machine-readable form such as punch cards or magnetic tapes. The data conversion process is typically a manual operation. Controls are needed to insure that data conversion has been completely and properly performed. Data conversion control techniques include key verification of punched data by verifying significant fields and by sampling on a statistical basis to verify that the punching process has a minimum acceptable error level. Control techniques also include the creation of source documents as the byproduct of the recording operation itself by the use of devices coupled with some recording device for an automatic output of a punched card or punched paper tape or a magnetic cassette tape.

In the data encoding operation, a control is made over the accuracy of the input data by key verification of the encoded data. In this process an operator, separate from the original encoding operator, reencodes all of the source documents into the encoded form as provided by the first encoding operation. However, instead of actually encoding the data the second time, the machine compares the keyed-in data with the original recorded data and indicates differences when they are observed by the machine.

Another source data control over such important things as customer numbers is that known as check digit control. In check digit control, all authorized identification numbers contain an additional digit beyond the identification number itself. This digit is called the check digit; it results from a numerical algorithm being applied to the valid identification digits in the number. There are many routines used for generating check digits. All check digit verifications result in a comparison of the encoded check digit as provided on the source document versus a computer processing calculation of a check digit from the identification number; the computer compares that calculated check digit with the keyed-in check digit. With increasingly complex check digit mathematical algorithms, the accuracy rate of this system has increased significantly.

A turnaround document is often used as a means of reducing the data input workload and as a means of improving the reliability of the data. If data can be encoded in the document by the computer and simply returned to the computer for subsequent processing, that data not only does not have to be re-keyed, saving labor, but it also is not subject to encoding errors.

COMPUTER VALIDATION CONTROLS

Once data is received in machine-readable form in the computer room, it must be validated for processing. This is the last point in the input sequence where errors can be detected before they will affect files and other processing steps.

A very important set of controls are those that are used in the processing steps themselves to control data accuracy. These controls are performed by computer programs and occur as data is processed in the system. The editing capabilities of the computer are used to validate the input data. This editing involves the ability to inspect and then to accept or reject transactions according to the validity and reasonableness of quantities, values, codes and other data contained in the input records. The editing ability of the computer can be used to detect errors in input preparation that have not been detected by other control techniques described previously. This editing ability of the computer is performed by writing specific programs which are designed to perform certain program checks. The list of program checks is extensive. Validity tests are used to insure that the transactions contain valid transaction codes and valid characters and are of a valid field size. Completeness checks are made to insure that the input has the prescribed number of characters in all data fields. A check may be used to insure that all characters in the field are either numeric or alphabetic, as appropriate. Logical checks are used in transactions where various portions of fields bear logical relationships to one another. Computer programs can check these logical relationships to reject combinations that are erroneous even though the individual values are acceptable. Limit tests are used to test fields to see whether certain predetermined limits have been exceeded. In most cases, reasonable limits can be established for terms, prices, and volume conditions associated with the business transaction. Control totals are used with each batch of input data. Control totals are prepared manually prior to processing and then are incorporated as input to the computer processing phase. The computer is programmed to accumulate the control totals internally in the same way that the control totals were accumulated externally. The computer then compares its generated control total with the presupplied batch total. A message confirming the comparison should be printed, whether an error was disclosed or not, to insure that the control function has been performed. Sequence checks determine whether the batch of input data is in the proper numerical or alphabetical sequence. If the data is being processed sequentially against the numerical file, then the data must be in the same numerical sequence as the file itself or errors will occur. A field check is a check on the characters keyed in the field to insure that they are of the same type which the field is intended to contain. For instance, a field check on a numeric field is used to indicate an error if the field contains either blanks or alphabetic characters. Check digit verification is performed as an input validation routine.

The point in the processing flow at which it is most desirable to exercise computer editing must be determined. The general answer to this is that the error should be detected as soon as possible to avoid unnecessary computer processing. Some controls depend on access to master files and must be timed to coincide with the processing step in which that file is available. On the other hand, there are input validation tests that may be performed independently of any master files. These tests should be performed in a separate input edit run at the very beginning of computer processing. These input validation tests are normally included in programs that perform data conversion operations, such as reading cards to transfer them to tape; the edit routines can be accomplished while the tape is being generated.

DATA CONTROL FUNCTION

A separate data control function should be set up to monitor the flow of input and output between the source of the data, input preparation, computer processing, and report distribution. This data control function should be responsible for reviewing source documents for proper form and controls for input, for maintaining logs of all data input into the process, for establishing control totals on batches of input data, and for checking those controls at the output stage. Data control should follow up on all errors identified at the editing and computer validation processing steps, to insure that errors are corrected and resubmitted to the process.

The data control group is assigned the basic responsibility of assuring that processing steps are performed accurately and that data are not lost during the processing operations. Internal control responsibilities include the scheduling of computer input and output to make sure that input is received on source documents on the appropriate timetables and the following up to insure that missing data is received. Input control totals are logged for later use to balance with totals produced by computer processing steps. Errors rejected in computer input routines must be controlled by data control to insure that all errors are ultimately corrected by the appropriate originating departments and that the corrections are re-entered into the system. This monitoring of error frequency is necessary to initiate corrective action in the areas where the errors originate. Output reports must be distributed according to the timetable for those reports. Prior to that distribution, the final output must be checked against the control totals with corrective action taken in the event that the totals do not balance.

Once input errors have been detected, there must be established some specific control procedures to insure that such detected errors are corrected and that the corrected transactions are re-entered into the system. Such procedures should include having the control group enter all data rejected in an error log. As corrected transactions are returned to the control group for further processing, these errors should be checked off as being re-entered. The control group should, at routine intervals, follow up on open items to investigate why they have not been re-entered into the system. As the control group returns rejected input data to the source department, some information explaining the reason for the rejection should be given to the originator. The source department, of course, must have some specifically established procedures for the handling of errors that are returned for correction by the control group. Finally, as the corrected transactions are accepted for reprocessing by the control group, these transactions must be run through the same error detection and input validation processes as any original transactions.

16

Auditing
Computerized Accounting Systems

The integrity of financial records is assured to the auditor through his review and evaluation of the internal control system, providing assurance to the auditor that errors and irregularities in the system are discovered and corrected. The auditor's review of the data processing system and its controls assists in determining whether additional auditing procedures are required to form an opinion on the financial statements. In determining that a company's data processing system and controls provide reliable and accurate financial information, the auditor must evaluate the system in sufficient detail to provide reasonable assurances that the following are done:

a. That input data are correctly recorded and transcribed at the source departments.
b. That all authorized transactions are processed into the computer system without additions and without omissions.
c. That all the processing steps performed are desirable, proper, and correct.
d. That output is distributed to individuals on a timely basis after appropriate output controls are exercised.

AUDITOR'S CONCERNS

The auditor evaluates the elements of the internal control system which has been designed to provide reliable and accurate records, to safeguard assets, and to promote operational efficiencies in the conduct of company activities. The auditor is concerned with three primary areas of internal accounting control: organization control, documentation, and operating practices and processing controls. The review of the data processing system is designed to help the auditor evaluate the organizational controls and operating practices within the data processing system and to determine the extent to which a more detailed review should be made of specific processing applications in which the auditor is interested. The principal sources of data for making the review are organization charts, documentation standards, and interviews with data processing personnel.

AUDIT QUESTIONNAIRES

There are data processing control questionnaires that are useful for obtaining information on specific controls. In Exhibit 101 is one such questionnaire. As the structure of the questionnaire suggests, the review of the organization of the data processing department begins by obtaining and reviewing an organization chart.

EXHIBIT 101

EDP AUDIT CHECKLIST

A. ORGANIZATION OF THE EDP GROUP

1. Prepare or obtain an organization chart of the EDP group, showing lines of authority, position title, names of incumbents, and the number of people in each organizational unit.

2. Examine job descriptions or otherwise determine the duties and reponsibilities of EDP personnel.

	CHECK WHICH	
	YES	NO
3. Is the EDP group organizationally accountable to the controller or some other person who is independent of the operating or custodial departments being served?	——	——
4. Are the employees in the EDP group separated from all duties relating to the initiation of transactions and of master file changes?	——	——
5. Are incoming media (source documents, cards, or paper tape) accounted for by persons who have no duties relating to programming or the operation of the computer?	——	——
6. Do control clerks reconcile the record counts, dollar totals, and other control records prepared by the computer?	——	——
7. Is the responsibility for issuing and storing magnetic tapes assigned to a tape librarian, either as a full-time or part-time duty?	——	——
8. Are the machine operators:		
a. Separated from all duties relating to the investigation of data errors?	——	——
b. Not authorized to obtain program listings, block diagrams, and other documents which describe the machine's procedures?	——	——

EXHIBIT 101

EDP AUDIT CHECKLIST (Cont.)

	CHECK WHICH	
	YES	NO

    c. Not authorized to make changes in data or programs except as prescribed in written "halt lists"? ____ ____

9. Are the programmers:
    a. Organizationally independent within the framework of the EDP group? ____ ____
    b. Limited in their duties to the development and documentation of computer applications and programs? ____ ____

B. CONTROLS BY INITIATING DEPARTMENTS

1. Prepare or obtain a list of machine applications that relate to the processing of accounting information.

2. For each application, identify the components of the audit trail, such as:
    a. Source documents for the respective types of input transactions and master file changes, and
    b. Transaction registers, ledger print-outs, master file change notices, error listings, and printed documents and reports representing the output.

3. Review procedures in the initiating department relating to:
    a. The control of input data transmitted to the EDP group.
    b. The checking of output data received from the EDP group.

4. Determine the scope of any review of the internal control aspects of the EDP applications by the internal auditing department.

5. Are source documents required for every transaction and master file change? ____ ____

6. Are source documents retained for a reasonable period of time in a sequence that facilitates identification with related output records and documents? ____ ____

7. Are the following kinds of output prepared by the EDP group and furnished to the initiating departments:
    a. Notices or registers showing changes in master file data? ____ ____
    b. Error listings showing transactions rejected by the computer and other records requiring investigation? ____ ____
    c. Transaction registers or other listings showing the individual transactions processed by the computer? ____ ____

8. When general ledgers or subsidiary ledgers are maintained on computer media, does the output of the processing provide:
    a. A complete historical record of activity in the accounts? ____ ____

EXHIBIT 101

EDP AUDIT CHECKLIST (Cont.)

	CHECK WHICH	
	YES	*NO*

    b. A periodic trial balance of the accounts? — —

    c. A means of tracing all postings in the ledger accounts to supporting transaction registers? — —

9. Do the records provide the opportunity to trace any transaction back to the original source or forward to a final total? — —

10. Do the procedures provide that each type of transaction and master file change shall originate outside the EDP group? — —

11. Are master file changes authorized in writing by initiating department? — —

12. Do the initiating departments establish independent control over data submitted for processing, through use of batch totals, document counts, or otherwise? — —

13. Are output reports and documents reviewed outside the EDP group to ascertain that established requirements are met, through comparison with predetermined totals or other tests of correctness or reasonableness? — —

14. Is there an effective means of assuring that data errors reported by the EDP group are investigated, corrected and resubmitted for processing? — —

15. Are master file changes, as reported by the EDP group, reviewed by the initiating department? — —

16. Where there is a separate internal auditor or internal auditing department, does such auditor or department periodically review the arrangement of duties and responsibilities in the EDP group and the controls by initiating departments over processing by the EDP group? — —

C. COMPUTER CONTROLS—OPERATIONS

1. For the application(s) selected for review, obtain copies of the following:
   a. General flow chart, showing source documents, master files, major processing functions, and output reports and documents.
   b. List of computer runs comprising the application(s).
   c. Run descriptions of the major programs.

2. For the selected application(s), inspect the following:
   a. Block diagrams of the individual computer runs.
   b. Record layouts of the various types of transactions, master files, and output records.
   c. Halt lists and set-up sheets for the console operator.

3. Are the flow charts of the application(s):

EXHIBIT 101

EDP AUDIT CHECKLIST (Cont.)

	CHECK WHICH	
	YES	NO
a. Up-to-date, depicting procedures currently in effect?	___	___
b. Complete, depicting the sequence of operations from the receipt of source documents, through various peripheral machine operations and computer runs to the preparation of final reports and documents?	___	___
c. Supported with run descriptions, job instructions, or other explanatory material?	___	___

4. Are the block diagrams of individual computer runs:
   a. Up-to-date? ___ ___
   b. Separated into: (1) general block diagrams showing the inter-relationship of subroutines; and (2) detailed block diagrams showing the flow of data within the subroutines? ___ ___

5. Do the record layouts reflect the current format of every record? ___ ___

6. Do the halt instructions prescribe the procedure to be followed by the console operator for each type of programmed stop? ___ ___

7. Do the set-up sheets provide complete instructions to the machine operators? ___ ___

8. Are program changes noted in a manner which preserves an accurate chronological record of the system? ___ ___

D. COMPUTER CONTROLS—PROCESSING

1. For the application(s) under review, identify the various programmed checks through discussion with EDP employees and reference to related block diagrams and record layouts.

2. Verify the existence and use of the programmed controls by inspecting:
   a. Manual control registers kept by control clerks or other persons within the data processing department.
   b. Console typewriter sheets.
   c. Error listing prepared by the EDP equipment.

3. Are card-punching or other keystroke operations verified? ___ ___

4. Where batch control records are furnished by the initiating departments, are the detail records accumulated and proved for control by the computer at an early stage in the processing? ___ ___

5. Where batch control records are not furnished by the initiating departments, are control records (cash totals, record counts, etc.) developed to

EXHIBIT 101

EDP AUDIT CHECKLIST (Cont.)

	CHECK WHICH	
	YES	NO

control subsequent processing by EDP control clerks prior to computer processing? ___ ___

6. Are the computer operations controlled by printing the control information on the console typewriter with run-to-run proofs being performed manually? ___ ___

7. Are master files controlled by carrying a control record in the file and proving the individual master records to the control each time the file is updated? ___ ___

8. Are record counts and control totals developed by the computer to control subsequent off-line processing? ___ ___

9. Is the sequence of records checked by the computer at the first opportunity and subsequently at appropriate points in the processing? ___ ___

10. Are the following types of input editing checks included in the programs where it appears advisable?
    a. Coding checks? ___ ___
    b. Validity checks? ___ ___
    c. Check digits? ___ ___
    d. Limit checks? ___ ___
    e. Reasonableness checks? ___ ___

11. Are the following types of processing checks included in the programs where it appears advisable?
    a. Limit checks? ___ ___
    b. Crossfooting checks? ___ ___
    c. Sign checks? ___ ___

E. SECURITY CONTROLS

1. Inspect the following records and review the policies underlying their preparation and use:
    a. Console typewriter sheets.
    b. Machine time records.

2. Review the procedures for safeguarding magnetic tape records, including:
    a. Tape retention policies.
    b. Tape labeling methods (internal and external).
    c. Tape library procedures.

EXHIBIT 101

EDP AUDIT CHECKLIST (Cont.)

	CHECK WHICH	
	YES	NO

3. Does the equipment provide for automatic display on the typewriter sheets of interventions by the console operator? ____ ____

4. Are the applications rotated from operator to operator through shift scheduling, rotation of job duties, or otherwise? ____ ____

5. Are production runs, program tests, and all other uses of the computer required to be clocked in on machine time records? ____ ____

6. Are data tapes protected from inadvertant erasure by:
   a. Designating an expiration date or other retention basis for each tape that is written? ____ ____
   b. Recording the retention basis on the exterior label? ____ ____
   c. Recording the retention basis on the interior label? ____ ____
   d. Reserving a supply of tapes for scientific programs, testing programs, nonrecurring programs, and other uses that do not require formal retention control? ____ ____

7. Are programs tapes protected from inadvertent or deliberate alteration or destruction by:
   a. Keeping the tapes in locked facilities during non-working periods? ____ ____
   b. Safeguarding supporting program cards, block diagrams, test data, and program listings? ____ ____
   c. Requiring written approval of new programs and changes to existing programs—by the head of the systems development group and by the head of the department being served? ____ ____

8. Are the reels of magnetic tape accounted for by keeping a written record of tapes issued and returned? ____ ____

9. Do the internal tape labels assure detection of an attempt to read an outdated master file or an out-of sequence reel? ____ ____

10. Are the tape retention policies sufficient to assure a means of reconstructing master files? ____ ____

11. Where random-access storage is involved, have appropriate measures been provided for reconstructing the records in the event the file is inadvertently destroyed? ____ ____

12. Where outlying stations are connected on-line to the computer, have appropriate measures been provided to guard against unauthorized access to the files? ____ ____

There should be a separation of functional responsibilities between systems designers, programmers, and computer operators. These functions should be staffed with competent personnel.

Access to the computer room should be limited to only authorized personel. Systems analysts, programmers, and users should be denied access to the computer room. These restrictions enhance operational efficiency by minimizing interruptions to schedules. By prohibiting access to the computer and thereby preventing access to the data files, systems analysts and programmers are prevented from fraudulently tampering with any of the information contained in the files.

Operating procedures of concern include the planning of future applications, the development of documentation standards, the development of control procedures as they apply to input and output, the testing of new programs and the testing of program changes, the physical security of the files for protection from hazards of fire, theft, and inadvertent destruction, and the provision of adequate backup as protection against the loss in processing equipment, software, and data files.

Pertinent to the auditor's investigation is a review of the new applications planned to be installed in the system in the near future. He will be interested in the specification and the priority assignment of the development of future applications and in equipment and personnel resources to be committed to the implementation of the new applications. The auditor should review existing applications in planning the current audit and should pay particular attention to planned applications to determine what processes the company uses in the planning and the control systems efforts.

TESTING

The auditor's review of program testing procedures should be sufficient to provide information about the effectiveness of testing of existing programs. The client's tests provide a useful starting point for the auditor in preparing test data for his own personal testing of programs.

In evaluating the accuracy of the system, the auditor will test around and through the computer using specialized audit programs. His other concerns are listed in Exhibit 102.

The authorization of changes in existing programs is a vital control point in computerized systems. Program changes should be made only in conformity with procedures that are designed to prevent the manipulation of programs for unauthorized purposes. The auditor's review should insure that such procedures are a routine part of the program change authorization system. The auditor is concerned with changes to programs which are involved in the processing of accounting and financial transactions or file data. Any changes to any of those

EXHIBIT 102

AUDITING OF COMPUTER SYSTEMS

Auditing around or through the computer

    A. Test Decks
    B. Specialized Software

Evaluation of Controls

    A. Organizational/Personnel
    B. Operating Procedures
    C. Documentation
    D. Input Controls
    E. Programmed Controls
    F. Output Controls

---

application areas during the period under examination will probably result in a detailed audit of the system by the auditor.

Basic to the security of any accounting system is the protection of the files in the system. The client's practices for protection of his data processing files are of major importance. If interruptions in processing are allowed to occur and reconstruction activities have to take place because of those interruptions, the client's systems will be of suspicious quality. Inadequate file protection procedures may cause problems for the auditor because the audit trail may be incomplete. Inadequate file retention schedules may result in the unavailability of detailed data for audit purposes. Without a specific knowledge of the file retention cycle of the client, the auditor may find himself planning to use files that are no longer in existence. The auditor should specify in writing in advance of the audit examination the files which must be maintained for audit purposes.

AUDIT CONCLUSIONS

Included in the auditor's work papers should be a general description of the system in narrative form supported by systems flow charts and the completed audit questionnaire. Conclusions from this preliminary review should be relevant to the significance of the data processing system to the audit, the significance of specific applications within the system to the audit with detailed reference to those applications which are to be analyzed in detail, and identified weaknesses in the internal control system and the significance to the audit of those weaknesses.

A thorough review and a detailed evaluation of all controls in the data processing system are required when the system in general or certain applications specifically are revealed to be deficient or otherwise to have significance to the audit.

Index